Helen E. Romanowsky

PROGRAMMING EMBEDDED SYSTEMS WITH ADA

PROGRAMMING EMBEDDED SYSTEMS WITH ADA

VALERIE A. DOWNES
and
STEPHEN J. GOLDSACK

Both of Imperial College, London

Prentice/Hall International

ENGLEWOOD CLIFFS, NEW JERSEY LONDON NEW DELHI
SINGAPORE SYDNEY TOKYO TORONTO WELLINGTON

Library of Congress Cataloging in Publication Data
Downes, Valerie A., 1944—
Programming embedded systems with Ada.

Bibliography: p.
Includes index.
1. Ada (Computer program language) I. Goldsack,
Stephen J., 1926— . II. Title.
QA76.73.A35D68 001.64'24 81-23458
ISBN 0-13-730010-7 AACR2

British Library Cataloguing in Publication Data
Downes, Valerie A.
Programming embedded systems with Ada.
1. Ada (Computer program language)
I. Title II. Goldsack, Stephen J.
001.64'24 QA76.73.A35

ISBN 0-13-730010-7

ISBN 0-13-730010-7

PRENTICE-HALL INTERNATIONAL, INC., *London*
PRENTICE-HALL OF AUSTRALIA PTY. LTD., *Sydney*
PRENTICE-HALL CANADA, INC., *Toronto*
PRENTICE-HALL OF INDIA PRIVATE LIMITED, *New Delhi*
PRENTICE-HALL OF JAPAN, INC., *Tokyo*
PRENTICE-HALL OF SOUTHEAST ASIA PTE., LTD., *Singapore*
PRENTICE-HALL, INC., *Englewood Cliffs, New Jersey*
WHITEHALL BOOKS LIMITED, *Wellington, New Zealand*

10 9 8 7 6 5 4 3 2 1

Printed in the United States of America

CONTENTS

PREFACE

The programming language Ada* has been developed by the United States Department of Defense (DoD) as part of a program aimed at reducing the high cost of software for embedded computer systems. The domain of embedded systems covers those application areas where the software interacts directly with electromechanical devices other than the hardware components of a computer system. Such systems require different programming techniques from those of traditional data processing, particularly with respect to real-time constraints, interactions with hardware, error recovery and concurrent processing.

Ada has been designed particularly for use in the implementation of embedded software and contains features aimed at facilitating the construction of reliable programs in this field. However, it is also a powerful general purpose high level language which will find many uses outside its main application domain. Not only is Ada expected to overtake FORTRAN by the 1990s [1] but it also has the potential for extension into the Data Processing stronghold of COBOL [2].

The authors' aim in this book is to present the language through a case study of an embedded system. In this way the rationale for each language feature is explained, wherever possible, in terms of the intended application area. Concepts and features are introduced by example rather than by rigorous syntactic or semantic definitions. This approach is considered suitable for experienced software engineers, systems designers and systems programmers, who wish to gain familiarity with the new language. It should also prove suitable for senior undergraduates and graduate students.

The book starts with an introduction to the circumstances that led the DoD to initiate the program from which Ada has evolved. The genesis of the language is described, starting with the formation of the High Order Language Working Group (HOLWG) in 1975 and concluding with the publication of the Language Reference Manual [3] in 1980. Ada has been designed as a vehicle for applying the concepts of software engineering to the construction of real-time software systems. The difficulties in creating such systems are described in chapter 1 and followed in chapter 2 by a 'state-of-the-art' discussion of these problems. The special problems of embedded systems come under consideration in chapter 3.

The remaining chapters describe (mainly via a case study) Ada solutions to the problems of software-building for large scale embedded systems. The case study itself is based on an existing system used in a hospital to monitor cardiac surgery patients. An Ada representation is developed for the software of this system. The purpose of this exercise is to provide an understanding of both the system's structure and the way in which it could have been implemented using Ada.

Although this book is primarily concerned with the facilities provided by the language, it would be undesirable to tackle so large a case study without giving some formalism to the specification of the problem. Chapter 4 contains an informal statement of the problem, followed by a more formal one using the method of CORE (COntrolled REquirement specification) [4]. This is a product of Systems Designers Ltd, of Camberley, England, and was designed and developed by Geoff Mullery.

* Ada is a registered trade mark of the US Department of Defense.

Between the description of the case study problem and its proposed solution (in chapter 16) are chapters explaining in detail those features of Ada essential to an understanding of its use. To test their comprehension of the text, readers may like to try the exercises at the end of each of these chapters. The appendix contains solutions to a representative sample of these exercises.

Chapter 5 presents a general overview of the modules that may be used to construct Ada programs, showing how such modules allow top-down development and the inclusion of independently compiled software components. These construction techniques are essential to the Ada philosophy when tackling programming problems in the large. Chapters 6 to 14 cover in detail separate aspects of the language.

In chapters 15 and 16 all the Ada features are brought together in a design for an Ada program for the patient monitoring system, which is followed through to the full annotated program listing. Whilst wishing to demonstrate that the code of the case study is accurate Ada, the authors were confronted with the present lack of Ada implementations. In the absence of production-quality Ada compilers it is not possible to test fully any Ada program in its target environment. However, New York University's Courant Institute has a training compiler, known as Ada/Ed, developed for VAX/VMS under a US Army contract, and the full code of the case study has been processed by this compiler for syntactic and semantic checking. We are grateful to SCICON Consultancy International Ltd, London, for providing access to their VAX and the Ada/Ed compiler.

The authors have been very conscious of the fact that Ada is, as yet, an untried language of considerable complexity. The nature of the systems for which Ada is intended as the implementation language is such that human life will often depend on the reliability of the software and on its ability to respond within a critical time. Because of this the introduction of an Ada system will have to be accompanied by a rigorous procedure for testing and monitoring. Chapter 15 suggests the steps that would have to be followed before the case study program could be converted into a live system, and it is here that many of the problems raised about the secure use of Ada [5] are addressed.

We are indebted to Geoff Mullery for the time that he has taken in checking that our use of CORE is consistent with its philosophy. We are also grateful to SDL for allowing us to use CORE in this book.

The authors wish to acknowledge the invaluable contribution made to this book by Dr David Preston of the Westminster Hospital, London, by providing us with descriptions of their Cardiac Patient Monitoring System, used as the basis of the case study. We also wish to thank Professor C A R Hoare for his helpful criticisms and advice during the development of this book; Chris Tily for painstakingly reading through the final draft, and Henry Hirschberg without whose good-natured goading this book would never have been finished.

Finally, it must again be stressed that the use of the language Ada is currently in an experimental phase and that many checks and safeguards will have to be incorporated into the development of Ada software before it can be used in a live application.

July, 1982

VALERIE A DOWNES
STEPHEN J GOLDSACK

References

[1] 'The Ada Language and Environment', Peter Wegner; *ACM SIGSOFT, Software Engineering Notes,* Vol. 5, No. 2, April 1980.
[2] 'Commercial Applications Software in Ada: A Reality', Ralph E Crafts; *Ada Letters*, Vol. 1, No. 4, 1982.
[3] *Reference Manual for the Ada Programming Language*, Jean Ichbiah *et al*; United States Department of Defense, July 1980.
[4] *CORE Seminar Manual*; Systems Designers Ltd, 1981.
[5] 'The Emperor's Old Clothes', C A R Hoare, 1980 Turing Award Lecture, *CACM*, Vol. 24, No. 2, February 1981.

PROGRAMMING EMBEDDED SYSTEMS WITH ADA

CHAPTER 1

INTRODUCTION - THE GENESIS OF ADA

1.1 The Background to the Ada Language Development

In the last few years there has been a growing awareness of the escalating cost of software as a proportion of the total cost of computer applications. As computer hardware costs have fallen with the introduction of new technologies software costs have mounted. Figure 1.1, taken from data supplied by the US Electronic Industries Association [1.1], shows the predicted rapid increase in the software costs for the Department of Defense's expenditure on embedded computer systems. The level of costs anticipated is clearly unacceptable. The situation is aggravated by the techniques currently employed in software production where there is insufficient application of rigorous engineering disciplines.

As early as 1974 the US Department of Defense (DoD) became concerned about the high cost of software production and maintenance. An analysis of where money was being spent [1.2] showed that some 56% of the DoD's expenditure on software was for the development of software embedded within weapons and control systems. These costs are increasing, as functions previously performed by special purpose hardware are being transferred to embedded software controlling microprocessors. Table 1.1 shows the breakdown of DoD expenditure on software for 1978.

Table 1.1

Breakdown of DoD software costs ($3,000 million in 1973):

56%	Embedded computer systems
19%	Data processing
5%	Scientific
20%	Other and indirect costs

Experience in scientific and commercial computing had shown that software costs can be reduced by technical improvements in the methods of implementation. A high level programming language can provide a vehicle for such improvements and also aids portability of software and personnel. The established use of FORTRAN and COBOL in these application areas, although these languages are now somewhat outdated, provides some basis for the implementation of standards and the transfer of expertise.

Figure 1.1
Predicted DoD Expenditure on Hardware and Software for Embedded Computer Systems
(in US$Billions, if present trends continue)

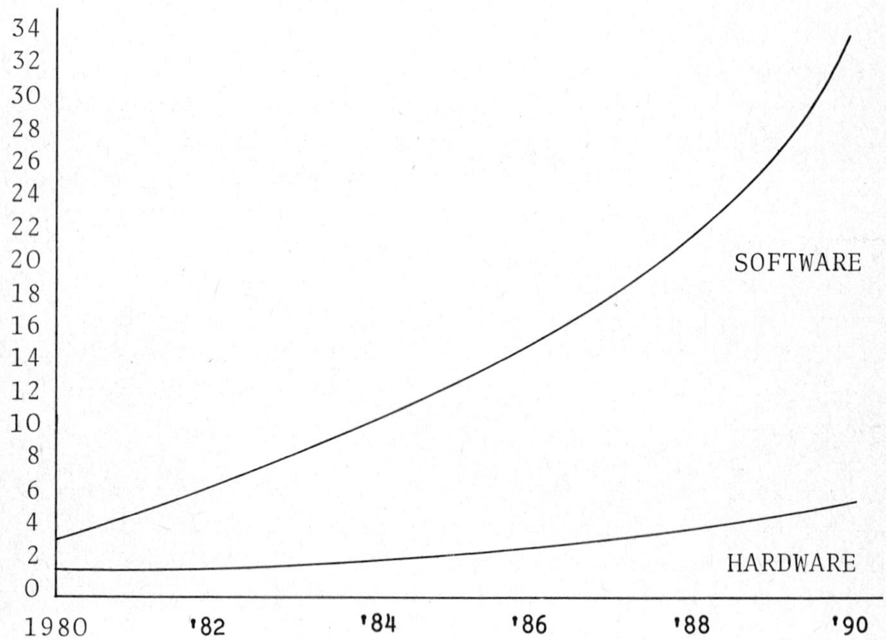

However, programming for embedded systems was in 1974, and still is, carried out in a variety of languages most of which are low level. In 1975 the DoD, through the Defense Advanced Research Projects Agency (DARPA), set out to investigate the requirements for high level languages suitable for introducing modern design techniques into the programming of embedded systems.

The High Order Language Working Group (HOLWG) was set up in January 1975 with the objective:

> "To produce a minimal number of common, modern High Order Computer Languages for the DoD embedded computer systems applications and to assure a unified, well supported, widely available, and powerful programming support environment for these languages."

Thus, from the start, the HOLWG project was seen as the development not of just a language but of a total environment of software support tools for all levels of systems implementation and management. This environment is now known as the Ada Programming Support Environment (APSE).

Before considering language requirements, it is first necessary to understand what is meant by 'embedded computer systems'. They are different from automatic data processing systems primarily because of how they are developed, acquired, and operated as part of an electromechanical system such as a ship, aircraft, missile, spacecraft, processing plant, or rapid transit system. Thus, an embedded computer system is physically incorporated into a larger system whose primary function is not data processing and which cannot be designed, implemented or operated without considering its computer components. An embedded computer must be capable of responding to input data by producing control signals within critical real time limits.

The HOLWG work has been conducted in three phases; firstly language definition and evaluation, secondly language design, and finally language and environment implementation. At the time of writing (1982) phases one and two have been completed and phase three is well underway.

1.2 Language Definition and Evaluation

The HOLWG considered that languages were required to provide facilities for applying the concepts of software engineering which are aimed at controlling the complexity of large scale software. Concepts, such as modularity, abstraction, careful control of module interfaces, and information hiding, have proved their value in languages developed for research purposes. However, the application area of embedded systems also imposed requirements for concurrent processes, interactions with hardware signals, and efficiency of run-time code. A discussion of these requirements is given in chapters 2 and 3.

The HOLWG developed statements of language requirements through the iterative production of the consultative documents STRAWMAN (April 1975), WOODENMAN (August 1976), and TINMAN (January 1977). Numerous existing languages, including CMS-2, JOVIAL, SPL/1, TACPOL, CORAL 66, LIS, LTR, PEARL, RTL/2, ECULID, MORAL, ECL, COBOL, FORTRAN, PASCAL, PL/1 and ALGOL 68 were evaluated against the TINMAN and all failed to meet the requirements. Only PL/1, Algol 68, and Pascal were seen as possible starting points from which a language could be developed to meet the requirements. However, it was concluded that a single language would be able to meet all the requirements.

Following this evaluation a new requirements document, IRONMAN, was produced (January 1977, revised July 1977) and this was considered to be the starting point for the development of a single high level language suitable for adoption as a DoD standard for embedded applications.

1.3 Language Design

The DoD, through DARPA, issued an invitation to tender for the design of a language to the IRONMAN specifications, starting from either Pascal, PL/1 or Algol 68 as a basis. Of the tenders received four were accepted which all offered Pascal as their starting point. These four were funded for a six months design study and the competing contractors were given colour coded names for their languages of red, green, blue and yellow.

At the end of these initial studies a review of the work of the four contractors was held which resulted in the production of a further, and final, requirements document, STEELMAN (June 1978). Two of the designs, Red and Green, were considered worthy of funding to completion based on STEELMAN.

A final evaluation of the two complete language designs in April 1979 chose Green, the language developed by a design team led by Jean Ichbiah of CII

Honeywell-Bull and including many contributors whose names are given in the forward to the language reference manual [1.3].

It was at this time that the new language was named Ada. This was in honour of Countess Augusta Ada Lovelace (1815 - 1852), daughter of Lord Byron, a gifted Mathematician who is considered to have been the world's first computer programmer in her work for Charles Babbage's analytical engine.

Between April 1979 and July 1980 the preliminary proposals for the language Ada underwent an extensive test and evaluation phase. The design of Ada and a rationale supporting this design were published by SIGPLAN [1.4]. Numerous potential end-users of the language were invited to code applications in the language and reported on the problems that they encountered.

This evaluation exercise was assisted by the use of a test translator, made available at MIT with ARPANET access, which could be used to checkout most of the syntax and semantics of programs in preliminary Ada. Many problems encountered during this phase were submitted in the form of language issue reports (LIRs) of which over 800 were received. LIRs from all over the world were processed into a set of proposed language changes that were thought to deserve consideration to bring the preliminary design up to the standard required for a working language.

After consideration of the proposed language changes, the language design team developed several revisions which resulted in the publication of the final Ada Reference Manual [1.3], dated July 1980 and launched at the 'Ada Debut' in Washington DC, September 1980.

Since that date work has continued on clarifying the language definition, including some minor modifications. A final revised version of the language reference manual is expected to be published by the end of 1982.

1.4 Environment Specification

From the original objectives of the HOLWG it can be seen that the project was conceived from the start as more than just the development of a language. Much of the progress in programming techniques is concerned with the support tools available to the managers, designers and programmers working on large projects. These tools range from the language translator and debugging aids through to comprehensive project management support facilities. Underlying all such tools is a database which can store all project relevant information.

In the current state of the art, software support tools are mainly ad hoc in nature, being developed independently for particular operating systems or projects. The concept of an integrated programming support environment (IPSE) calls for a machine independent user interface to the operating system with a suite of coordinated tools that will support a software system throughout its life cycle. The advantages of an IPSE are many: trained users may be switched between projects and support machines without the considerable retraining costs presently encountered; tools can be transferred between systems saving the "reinvention of the wheel"; and coordinated support for a project allows control and enables managers to predict and monitor progress. In addition, full life cycle support covers the expensive period of maintenance.

The DoD realizes that the major savings from the high order language project were to be made in the use of an integrated environment to support the use of Ada. Thus, in parallel with the language design phase, was begun the development of a requirements specification for the Ada Programming Support Environment, (APSE), through the documents SANDMAN, PEBBLEMAN (initially released in the summer of 1978 and revised in January 1979), and STONEMAN (several preliminary releases finalized in February 1980).

The requirements for an administrative framework to support the use of Ada were contained in PEBBLEMAN Part I and steps are now being taken to implement these. In the past many of the promised advantages of using high level languages have been lost due to the lack of standardization between implementations. The DoD is determined that this shall not be allowed to happen to Ada and administrative procedures are now being implemented to control the use and standardization of the language. An Ada Joint Program Office (AJPO) has been set up to coordinate all DoD Ada activities. The DoD has trade marked the name Ada when used in connection with programming. This is to enable the AJPO to exert control over all Ada material and thus prevent the establishment of subsets, supersets or Ada-like languages. SofTech have a contract to develop an Ada Compiler Validation Facility and no compiler may claim to translate Ada unless it passes a validation test.

The DoD has already added Ada to its list of approved languages and reduced the other members of the list to just a few languages already in wide use by the Military.

The requirements for the software environment for the support of Ada are contained in STONEMAN. This software has three proposed levels, the Kernel APSE (KAPSE) which provides the machine independent operating system and database, the Minimal APSE (MAPSE) which adds a minimal set of tools to the KAPSE, and a full APSE which may contain an open-ended set of tools. All tools are to be implemented as Ada programs running on the KAPSE interface.

Particular to the APSE is the proposed method of using Ada to implement embedded systems software. The target hardware for such systems, typically a processor with a few PROM memory chips and interfaces to external hardware, is clearly not suitable for the production of software. For this a host machine is used with main memory and secondary storage capable of supporting the use of program development tools. Programs are developed and tested on the host and then loaded down-line into the target. The APSE will run on the host machine but will also contain facilities for target loading, monitoring events in prototype targets, and maintaining a data base which records all significant target data.

1.5 Language and Environment Implementation

At the time of writing, numerous compiler efforts are underway in both industrial and academic establishments. Major projects are centred in the USA, the UK, and Europe, and there is also a considerable amount of work being undertaken in other parts of the world. There is clearly a major commitment to Ada in the defence industry but this interest can be seen to be extending into government and general industry through financial support for projects. The first production quality compilers with full host and target capabilities will probably be available by early 1983. However, at present, several implementors are experiencing difficulties in implementing efficiently all the features of Ada, especially in the absence of a final, unambiguous definition.

Any attempt here to list the state of implementations would necessarily be out of date by the time this book reaches the bookshops. However, an AdaTEC subgroup of SIGPLAN has been formed and their newsletter provides a regular comprehensive guide to all implementation efforts in the US and around the world.

The APSE requirements are currently the subject of several design studies and implementations. The USAF has funded three studies for an Ada Integrated Environment (AIE), the US Army has an Ada Language System (ALS) being designed and implemented, the US Navy has a commitment to introduce supported Ada by 1985, the UK Department of Industry has funded a Minimal APSE design from a consortium of British companies, and the European Commission is funding the development of a Compiler and an Environment by a multi-national European consortium. It is this work which offers the greatest potential for allowing Ada to be the vehicle for improved software engineering. An Ada compiler alone will provide just another language, albeit one that represents the state of the art in language design. An Ada compiler embedded in an APSE will provide an integrated workshop for the production and maintenance of large scale embedded computer systems. It is in the design of the APSE that new ground is being broken, in the provision of tools to support management and production based on concepts hitherto confined to the research and development laboratory. The next few years should see great advances in these areas.

The potential introduction of several APSEs presents a problem because the portability of tools may be hindered by the use of different KAPSE conventions, through which the tools must interact with the underlying machine. This problem has been recognised and KAPSE Interface Teams have been set up in the US to attempt to define a set of interface conventions.

1.6 Conclusion

Ada has been designed as a vehicle for applying software engineering practices to the programming of embedded computer systems. It also appears to be suitable for a wider range of scientific and commercial applications, although the latter will require the development of packages to support sophisticated file handling.

The introduction of a full APSE, and the training of staff in the methods of its use, present a very ambitious project which will occupy much of the software industry for the next decade. However, if the project is successful, considerable cost savings should begin to be achieved by the 1990s.

References

[1.1] "Candidate R&D Thrusts for the Software Technology Initiative"; Samuel T Redwine, Jr., Eric D Siegel, and Gilbert R Berglass; US Department of Defense, May 1981.

[1.2] "DoD's Common Programming Language Effort"; David A Fisher; IEEE Computer, March 1978.

[1.3] "Reference Manual for the Ada Programming Language"; Jean Ichbiah et al; United States Department of Defense, July 1980.

[1.4] "Preliminary Ada Reference Manual" and "Rationale for the Design of the Ada Programming Language"; J D Ichbiah et al; SIGPLAN Notices, Volume 14, Number 6, June 1979.

CHAPTER 2

THE ENGINEERING OF LARGE-SCALE SOFTWARE

The falling cost and increasing size and speed of computers during the nineteen sixties encouraged a proliferation of projects involving the construction of large programs. Unforeseen difficulties were encountered, caused by lack of experience on which to base working methods and from which to gauge the effort involved. There were many failures; projects over ran the budgets allocated; programs were delivered late, and were full of errors when they were delivered. Out of what became known as the 'software crisis' grew the new discipline of software engineering. It would be difficult to express the nature of the problem more eloquently than in the words of E W Dijkstra, whose work has contributed greatly to the progress of software design methodologies since that time. He wrote: [2.1]

> "As long as there were no machines, programming was no problem at all: when we had a few weak computers, programming became a mild problem, and now that we have gigantic computers, programming has become an equally gigantic problem. In this sense the electronic industry has solved not a single problem, it has only created them - it has created the problem of using its products."

The writing of small programs presents no real difficulty; the difficulties arise with programming 'in the large'. Anyone with a little education in the art can compose a program of a few tens of machine instructions; such a program contains about one 'headful' of complexity. Even if the program is written in the internal code of the machine, the programmer is able to grasp its behaviour in its entirety. The use of a higher level language, which expresses the solution of a problem rather than the detailed steps required to carry it out on some particular machine, enables somewhat larger programs to be successfully written with comparative ease. Many applications, however, involve the writing of programs with hundreds of thousands of machine instructions. Such programs specify details of action sequences whose complexity greatly exceeds the ability of a human head to comprehend it. At best, the human reader can study a small part at a time, and is powerless to understand its full potential complexity. Moreover, such a program takes many man-years to write, and is consequently constructed by a team of programmers who cooperate in writing the complete program.

Obtaining reliable programs on such a scale requires an approach to the design and construction which can be recognised as having much in common with large scale engineering in other fields. There is an element of art in the design. Some decisions are based on aesthetic considerations, and reflect personal style on the part of the programmer; there is no single correct solution. There are, nevertheless, guiding principles which reflect the outcome of past experience, and there are scientific and mathematical principles which can be brought to bear on the assessment of the adequacy and correctness of programs.

It is a strange fact that, in all these difficulties, the computer programmer has not made much use of the computer itself to help him. In spite of the fact that the computer is the supreme tool for handling complex systems with security, software engineering has been the last branch of engineering to benefit greatly from its use.

Ada, with its associated environment, has been designed in an attempt to correct this situation and provide the system designer and programmer with aids to the creation of high quality, reliable software, particularly in the field of embedded computer systems. This book is concerned with the Ada approach to the engineering of such large scale software systems.

2.1 The High Cost of Software

It goes without saying that a software system requiring many man years of effort is also expensive. Software construction is a labour intensive industry, and the falling cost of hardware does not help to reduce software costs. On the contrary, the cheaper hardware has encouraged the use of computers in new applications and the construction of more ambitious projects. Both these trends increase the urgency of improved methods of software production.

Software evolves during its life. Changes in existing programs during their life time are loosely called maintenance, and it is found that, during the life of a program system, the cost of such maintenance often exceeds the cost of the original construction. Moreover, changes made during such maintenance are liable to cause the original structure of the program to be impaired, and future changes become increasingly difficult to introduce. This is particularly true for programs written at the machine code level.

Software design must make provision for inevitable future changes: it is more important to ensure that a program is easy to read and change, than to pander to the lazy programmer by providing abbreviations, default options and other short cuts. This is a point of view taken by the designers of Ada. At times the language may seem verbose and repetitive, and the text will often be longer than the equivalent in some other languages. This must be accepted as the price to pay for the clarity and reliability of the finished product.

2.2 Managing Complexity - Decomposition and Abstraction

To overcome the difficulty of comprehending complex systems people commonly use two important devices, decomposition and abstraction. In decomposition, complex objects are viewed as composed of collections of simpler parts. So, for example, an army is decomposed into divisions, divisions into brigades and so on in a hierarchy of levels of description which ends with the primitive objects, in this case individual soldiers, tanks and other weapons. In a similar way complex actions are described in terms of simpler steps, which may be further reduced to reach eventually the atomic actions relevant to the area of discourse.

Each step in a decomposition involves the description of the system components in greater detail. Abstraction, on the other hand, involves conceptual simplification of a complex system by deliberately ignoring detail. The concept of a building ignores the fact that it is constructed from rooms, and eventually from bricks and mortar. The concept of a city ignores its construction from buildings and streets. The mere act of giving a name to a complex idea is an important element in the process of abstraction.

In a similar way, complex actions are conceived as elementary, by naming them and temporarily ignoring the wealth of detail which the name implies. In a hospital, the concept of 'operating' ignores all the detail implied about the behaviour of the surgeon and the theatre staff during the progress of an operation.

In the design of a large program these concepts of abstraction and decomposition are central to the ability of a system designer to specify a system which is to be constructed by the cooperation of a team of programmers. The problem represented by the complete system to be created may be decomposed into subproblems which can then be solved separately as program modules. The behaviour of each module must then be specified at an abstract level, to enable its implementation according to the requirements of the overall system. This has been recognised for a long time in the concept of modular programming, and in the provision made in programming languages for the specification of subprograms. The most important features of Ada, which will be new to programmers experienced in the construction of programs in earlier languages, lie in the provisions it makes for creating designs in terms of components more complex than procedures and functions, whose definition may initially be given in an abstract sense, with a careful specification of the interface presented to the other program components.

It would be difficult to over stress the importance of abstraction in system design. It enables the programmer to separate the concerns for what is to be done from the details of how these objectives will be achieved. This separation of concerns will be recognised as the motivation for many of the facilities provided by the new language.

Decomposition and abstraction are closely related to the approaches to program writing which are often referred to as 'top-down' and 'bottom-up'. Solving a problem from the top-down involves expressing its solution in terms of simpler problems, subproblems, whose solution is assumed to be possible, but which is postponed until a later stage. These, in turn, may be solved in terms of still simpler problems, assumed solvable, and so on until the problems remaining can be trivially described as primitive actions expressible in the programming language in use.

Programming from the bottom-up, on the other hand, implies constructing program units, which in turn can be used as bricks to form more complex units. The choice of such units is often driven simply by a desire to get something achieved, to get on with the job. A system designer who yields to such pressure usually makes a grave mistake. Although powerful program modules may be constructed, there is little guarantee that the final product will meet the requirements of the project. It is generally recognised that top-down programming, which starts from those requirements, is the safer approach. Nevertheless, in its proper place, the bottom-up approach can be useful. The components created should be regarded as extensions of the language relevant to the problem, providing program objects to implement abstract concepts prevalent in the problem domain. A collection of routines to handle the calendar would be a case in point. If the problem on hand concerns itself with dates, it is certain that program units to implement the behaviour of the calendar will be required. The programs for this can be written without concern for how they will be used. The choice of such components is an example of the use of abstraction.

It is of interest to note also that classical discussions of problem solving introduce the ideas of analysis and synthesis as approaches to a problem solution. In fact, decomposition and abstraction, top-down and bottom-up, and analysis and synthesis are all examples of the same basic dichotomy.

2.3 Modular Programming

As remarked earlier, the need for modularity in the construction of software was recognised many years ago, and the introduction of modular programming greatly helped to reduce the problems in the following period. Nevertheless, it did not prove, of itself, a complete solution to the difficulties. Large systems constructed in modular fashion by teams of programmers frequently gave great difficulty when the separately composed modules were put together to form a complete system. These difficulties stemmed from two main causes.

Insufficient care was taken to define the interfaces between separate modules; this led to misunderstandings, so that the parts produced by different programmers were incompatible.

Components written by different programmers, each correct in itself, interfere with each other in execution. This can happen if shared data are incorrectly accessed by modules, or from inadvertent or deliberate use by one module of resources belonging to another.

These difficulties can be reduced by providing, within the compiler, software aids to control the use of components by other modules with which they interact, and to enforce 'information hiding', preventing program parts from accessing details of other components which are not relevant to their purpose. Such aids depend on the inclusion of sufficient information in the program to enable the compiler to control correct use of modules by others. The language must not only provide facilities to express 'encapsulation', the enclosure of a module behind a secure fence, preventing incorrect access, but must also provide a clear definition of those elements and features of the module which may be used by other components and constitute its interface with the rest of the program. In later chapters the Ada package will be recognised as the unit of encapsulation which serves the dual role of providing secure modularity, and at the same time aiding abstraction, separating the concerns of the programmer for the specification of what is to be done from the decisions as to how it is to be done. This was identified, above, as an important element in providing a framework for logical system design.

2.4 A Program as a Model

It is important also to recognise the role of a computer program as a model of the problem domain. Objects in the real world are represented in the computer by data structures devised to model the structure of the objects they represent, while the program operations model their behaviour. The data objects and operations are conceived to reflect the abstract behaviour of the world objects. Axioms relevant to the problem area must be valid also for the objects in the computer which represent them. Most systems consist of collections of parts which co-exist and interact in well defined ways. The computer model may, therefore, contain software items which run concurrently and interact in a manner which mirrors the interactions of the real world system parts.

External objects are represented in the computer by values of program variables representing attributes relevant to the problem area in question. It should be noted that the same object may be described by different attributes when considered in relation to a different problem area. The weight of a person may have no relevance to his employer, and would not appear in the database of that organisation. On the other hand it would be crucial to the model of the person of interest to his medical practitioner. A model is a simplification of the totality of the real world, and different simplifications may be appropriate to different observers. Such simplifications are often referred to as abstraction. In the sense of the word used here, it is not correctly so called. Abstraction hides relevant detail by temporarily ignoring it; disregarding irrelevant detail is not the same process. If the model provides a complete description of all relevant aspects of the external world, then it is not more abstract than the world it models.

Each external object belongs to a class with corresponding attributes, distinguishable from objects in other classes. The current state of a pressure vessel, for example, may be represented by a temperature and a pressure. The instantaneous state of a rotating machine is represented by an angle and an angular velocity. In each case there are two state variables, yet these variables represent values from unrelated sets. It is meaningful to compare the states of two pressure vessels, or to control the state of such a vessel to a state represented by a pair of set point values. It would be meaningless, however, to compare the states of a pressure vessel and a rotor.

Very few of the numerical values with which a program is concerned are pure numbers in the sense of mathematics. Each has physical dimensions, and possibly other attributes defining the class to which it belongs. Moreover, many objects belong to sets whose values are not numeric at all. A switch or relay may, for example, be open or closed, and these will be values of the variable representing the state of the switch in a program. Arithmetic on such a variable would be meaningless.

Each object class, then, has its own 'essence', its private set of attributes defining its characteristics, its possible set of values and the legal operations. Realistic programs will not compare a temperature and a pressure, or assign the value of a length to a variable representing a mass.

A powerful aid to program correctness utilises this feature of program objects, to detect illegal use of variables. The compiler for the language can help to ensure that a program containing logical errors cannot execute and produce nonsensical results. Errors can be detected when the program is compiled. This is done by allocating to each variable a **type**, defining the class of object to which it belongs, and the operations which are legal on it. The information provided to the compiler can be used to construct run time checks that variables do not acquire values which would be nonsense for objects of their type.

Perhaps even more important than the detection of logical errors in the use of variables in a program is the role of object types in preventing incorrect interactions between program components. Types form part of the specification of module interfaces, and checks by the compiler and loader during program assembly can ensure that program components are not misused by those with which they interact.

Thus careful control of the correct use of variables according to their types is an important aid in ensuring program correctness. A language enforcing such correct use of objects according to their type is said to be strongly typed. Ada is a strongly typed language.

2.5 The Engineering Approach

In common with practice in other engineering fields a program must be:

specified,
designed,
constructed,
validated,
evaluated.

The chief role of the Ada language is in the areas of design and construction. Nevertheless, specification of the application requirements should precede the construction of any program. This stage involves careful systems analysis, and the provision of a specification document which serves as a guide to the programmer during his work, as well as the terms of contract with the customer. This is an important area of study, and one which is the subject of a great deal of current research. Methods of specification of systems and software do not form a central part of this book. Nevertheless, programming of secure systems cannot be achieved without a sound approach to specifying the problem. This topic will be addressed in connection with the case study in chapter 4.

As will become clear in later chapters of this book, it is a feature of Ada program units that they have separate specifications and bodies. The specification part provides the definition of the program interface of the unit, defining all those structural features which must be known by the other parts of the program in order to use it correctly. This includes the syntax and type information relevant to the rest of the program: it is not a specification of the effect of the program unit in execution. The separation is nevertheless an important one, and permits the program design to be checked by the compiler, before the programs detailing the internal operations of the components is written. This greatly reduces the risk that errors will be discovered after large amounts of effort have been invested.

The same separation permits bodies of units to be changed in complete certainty that there can be no unintended side effect on the behaviour of other units. This means that performance can be tuned up by rewriting inefficient parts of the program with great confidence that this will not have adverse effects on other parts of the program. This independence of program components also enables them to be adapted to changing requirements during the life of the program, with the same assurance.

Similarly, validation of a component, whether by test or by proof, cannot be subsequently invalidated by incorrect use of the module by other parts of the program. It is a confident belief of Jean Ichbiah, the chief language designer, that Ada will permit the emergence of a software components industry, which will sell components according to specification from a catalogue, permitting users to construct systems satisfying their needs.

Reference

[2.1] "The Humble Programmer"; E.W.Dijkstra: Turing Award Lecture, CACM Vol 15 Number 10, October 1972.

CHAPTER 3

EMBEDDED COMPUTER SYSTEMS

3.1 The Nature of Embedded Systems

The considerations of the previous chapter concerned the problems of constructing large scale programs, and set the scene for appreciating the purpose of some of the most important features of Ada. These considerations would apply equally to programs intended for any problem area, such as commercial data processing or scientific problem solving. Ada was primarily designed, however, to fill the special needs of embedded systems. As explained in chapter 1, an embedded system is one in which the computer and its software form part of some larger system, with which the program interacts and exchanges data and control information. Programming such systems requires facilities beyond those described earlier. These additional requirements are reviewed in this chapter.

In most cases the wider system consists of a collection of distinct objects whose behaviour is of concern to the program in the embedded computer. Such items include, for example, electromechanical devices whose states are observable through special purpose interfaces. These transfer to the computer store values of physical variables captured by suitable transducers. They often include, also, human beings, the system users, who interact with the program through terminals or other specially adapted hardware. Typical of such a system would be the software of an avionics control system which interacts not only with the hardware of the aircraft but also with the pilot.

Though they are not usually regarded as belonging to the class, systems where the external world is entirely human, such as an airline reservation system which consists of a collection of offices and sales outlets, possess some of the properties regarded as special to embedded systems.

The special needs of embedded systems fall into four main categories, as follows:

Concurrent control of separate system components.

Real-time facilities to specify times at which actions are to occur in absolute terms, and to synchronize actions at different points in a system.

Facilities to interact with the special purpose hardware interfaces involved.

Facilities to specify actions to be taken in the event of erroneous behaviour of hardware or software.

There are some additional considerations which also apply. Programs are frequently very large (50,000 to 100,000 lines is quite normal). Consequently large teams are engaged in the work, and there is often a big turn-over of staff.

Typically, embedded systems last for many years. A system life of 10-15 years has been usual in the past and longer lived systems may be expected to be constructed in the future. This makes important demands on maintainability of the software. During that life the requirements may change significantly, and the staff responsible for maintenance will change several times during the life of the software. Even the hardware will often be renewed and replaced by more modern versions once or twice during those years.

Reliability of the programs is even more important than in the case of programs for commercial data processing. It will often be vital that software should be error free at the first delivery to a user's site. This is not usually expected with commercial systems, where fixing a few errors after delivery would be a normal expectation.

Since embedded systems are time critical, efficiency of implementations will be more important than in other systems. It is claimed by the language design team that the design of the Ada language included only features which it was believed could be implemented reasonably efficiently on most computers.

The consequences of these special requirements are discussed in the following sections.

3.2 Concurrent Programming

A characteristic of an embedded system is the collection of coexisting external elements which comprise the system. The computer program must interact 'simultaneously' with all these items in order to maintain the necessary control. Fortunately, typical computer execution speeds are such that actions carried out in sequence can produce the illusion of simultaneity, relative to the comparatively slower time scales of the external world objects. A collection of separate objects can, therefore, be controlled 'concurrently' by a corresponding collection of program components whose execution is interleaved on a single processor to produce an effect of true concurrent execution[+]. Responsibility for organising such behaviour, which is often referred to as 'pseudo concurrency', is sometimes left to the programmer constructing the system, who writes a program involving cyclic operation of program sequences to handle the various tasks. However, there are three reasons why this is undesirable. First, it complicates the programmer's already difficult task by placing on him responsibility for a concern which is irrelevant to the control tasks being created. Secondly, it runs counter to the need to permit modular decomposition, and possible allocation of the separate components to different programmers. Lastly, left to the system, it may be possible to utilise true concurrency when the program is run on a computer with multiple processors.

One of the program units available in Ada is the **task**. These may be used to compose logically separate program units and the responsibility for organising their pseudo concurrent execution is left to the Ada system.

[+] If, indeed, the computer possesses several processors, it may be able to execute several programs truly concurrently. With present hardware technology this is usually limited to a rather small fixed number.

Tasks are equivalent to what are called processes in an operating system. Readers familiar with the design of operating systems will be aware that concurrency is managed by an executive kernel, which schedules eligible tasks for the use of the available processor or processors. In past practice programmers writing programs for embedded computer systems have been required to enable concurrent execution of their programs by interacting with the operating system, or when the overheads of a general purpose operating system have been considered too heavy, special purpose executive kernel programs have been written. Consequently, such programming has been a highly specialised domain. A general purpose executive is usually not able to take account of the types of values passed as messages during task interaction, so part of the security offered by strong typing is lost. Ada provides concurrent tasking as a feature of the language, to be used by the programmer at the application level; a run time system including an executive kernel program is automatically loaded into the object program by the Ada system.

3.2.1 **Task Interactions**

The elements of a system are not usually entirely independent. There are interactions arising from their use of shared resources on the one hand, and from the need to synchronise their actions, on the other. The tasks in the computer model must reflect these interactions by corresponding accesses to shared data and by obeying some laws concerning the order of execution of critical statements. Correct behaviour of concurrent tasks which share a resource usually require that the tasks in question observe some protocol in their accesses to it. In simple cases it will usually be necessary to enforce 'mutual exclusion', making the access by one task a primitive indivisible act, so that simultaneous access by the other is impossible. Without such control, a task consulting a data structure may obtain an inconsistent set of values from a structure which has only partially been updated by some other task.

Sharing of resources can also be the cause of the condition known as deadlock or the 'deadly embrace'. This condition arises when two communicating tasks get into a situation in which each is waiting for the other to complete its use of a shared resource. Ada has no features explicitly to prevent deadlock, and it is quite possible to write Ada programs which seize up in this way. However, the 'rendezvous', Ada's main method of task interaction, is easy to understand, and free from the dangers of the erroneous use of semaphores, which can be a cause of deadlock in many less sophisticated languages.

The present work would not be the place to expand fully on the difficulties of programming concurrent systems: readers are referred to textbooks on operating systems [3.1],[3.2]. The full account of Ada tasks and the use of the rendezvous, will be found in chapter 9.

3.3 Real-time Facilities

Embedded computer systems typically have very stringent time restrictions on the rate at which data must be processed. They are real-time systems, that is systems which must be able to receive continuously changing data from external sources and process that data sufficiently rapidly to be capable of influencing the sources of the data. In such systems, there must be some limit on the amount of time that can be spent on processing before control decisions are made. The programmer of an embedded system will also require to control the time at which some action is to occur, or to specify a delay before the execution of some program step. If a task is waiting for a response from an external source, or from another task, it must also be able to detect when a delay exceeding that expected occurs, so that provision can be made for possible malfunction of the external hardware, or software failure in some other task.

The times in such measures must be absolute. The computer system must include a 'real-time clock', enabling the program to discover the current time of day, by reading the state of some register which is regularly incremented on a time basis, and capable of causing an interrupt to reactivate a task at the end of a specified delay. The language should include features to manage the interactions with the clock.

When the time comes that a task, awaiting the critical instant at which it must carry out some action, needs the use of the processor, there may already be other tasks also waiting to use it. It will often be unacceptable that a long delay should ensue before it can be scheduled to have its turn. "Worst case" behaviour cannot be permitted to produce delays in execution beyond a certain tolerance. Thus, a characteristic of a real-time system will often be the need to have an processor with considerable spare capacity.

3.4 Interaction with Hardware

Embedded systems often interact with special sensors or actuators in the external system. Because of the time critical nature of the interaction, the program must interact directly, and not through a layer of operating system functions. The devices are connected to the computer through interface circuits whose properties are special to the particular system. It is, therefore, necessary to provide means by which the programmer can access I/O registers, and relate them to named variables and types in the program. Where I/O is address mapped, particular store addresses must be related to particular variables, and access to individual bits within a word must be possible. These are aspects which have usually been handled in machine language in past practice. It was an objective of the DoD effort to bring these programs within the scope of the new language.

Inevitably such specifications are machine dependent. However, Ada provides features to express the required representation enabling the compiler to ensure correct logical behaviour and reduce machine dependent aspects to a minimum.

Some external devices use interrupts to communicate with the user's program, and this is another feature which a language for embedded systems must handle. Scheduling must enable an interrupt handler to be invoked with high priority when an interrupt is detected by hardware.

3.5 Exception Handling

When a program to compute the solution to some scientific problem fails due to the failure of the program, or of the hardware, it is reasonable to abort the program. There will be no serious consequences. In the case of an embedded system, however, it is not acceptable to abandon control of a plant because a minor error occurred in some part of the program. Frequently human life will be involved, and highest standards of safety must be observed. On failure of part of the system there must be provision for human take over. An avionics system must at least allow the pilot to eject before permitting the plane to crash! The programmer must specify the actions to take in the unexpected case of a failure in some part of the system. His aim must be to raise, if necessary, appropriate alarm signals to other parts of the program, and to take, if possible, local action to handle the error condition without disturbing the normal operation of the rest of the system. Such alternative actions can be defined using standard programming techniques, but they often lead to inelegant program structures, where provision for an error condition clutters the text of the program for normal behaviour.

As required by the STEELMAN specifications, Ada designers included facilities to enable programmers to switch control to special exception handlers when an error occurs. These exception handling facilities have been the source of some controversy [3.3]. Raising an exception in Ada corresponds to a discontinuous jump of control to a new program sequence, in a potentially unstructured way. Discussion of the use of exceptions will be deferred to the appropriate section of chapter 13.

References

[3.1] "Operating Systems Principles"; Per Brinch Hansen; Prentice-Hall, 1973.

[3.2] "Operating Systems Theory"; Edward G Coffman Jr. and Peter J Denning; Prentice-Hall, 1973.

[3.3] "The Emperor's Old Clothes"; C A R Hoare; Turing Award Lecture CACM Vol 24, Number 2, February 1981.

Exercise 3

3.1 List the main features which constitute the special requirements of a language to serve for programming embedded systems.

3.2 Why do embedded systems have more need for concurrent program execution than commercial systems?

3.3 Explain the way in which deadlock can occur in interacting concurrent programs. Invent examples of deadlock in real life, arising from rigorous applications of the rules of conduct (the highway code, rules of etiquette, etc.).

CHAPTER 4

CASE STUDY - PROBLEM SPECIFICATION

The central theme of this book is a description of the way Ada can be used to implement the software for real embedded computer system applications. This is developed by using a case study and the chosen application is based, to a large extent, on an existing computer assisted hospital patient monitoring system +. This case study has been chosen to demonstrate the main features of Ada in the context of the type of application for which the language has been designed.

The present chapter starts with an informal description of the case study and then gives a more formal specification of the requirements of the software. At this stage in the analysis of the system there need be no reference to the details of the implementation language, since the requirements must be language independent. However, before the program design for a solution of the requirements can be developed, the facilities of the language have to be understood. These facilities are described in chapters 5 to 14 where many of the examples used are drawn from the problem area of the case study. Using the full power of Ada, the systematic design of the program is developed in chapter 15 with a rationale given for each design decision. Chapter 15 also outlines the steps that would have to be followed in producing a 'live' system from the final program design, a full source listing of which is given in chapter 16.

+ Patient monitoring systems have been used before to illustrate programming concepts. The first paper using such a system was by Stevens, Myers and Constantine [4.1], and there have been several more recent papers which have used this example to discuss specifications [4.2, 4.3, 4.4]. The present study is an extended definition of the problem, to provide a richer case study .

Section 4.1 gives an overview of the problem tackled by the case study. The rest of this chapter, which gives the more formal requirements specification, may be omitted at a first reading.

4.1 An Overview

The Westminster Hospital in London has a cardiac surgery unit where open heart operations are performed on patients using the technique of profound hypothermia [4.5]. After such a procedure there is considerable danger to the patient as his body readjusts to normal temperature control. In particular, post-operative patients have a large excess of body fluid. During the period of adjustment it is essential that the patient's body functions and vital signs be carefully monitored and, where possible, adjustments be made in time to preserve life.

The hospital has installed in its post-operative intensive care unit an on-line computer system which is used to monitor patients' life functions, such as blood pressure and heart rate, record data concerning the patients in a database, and raise an alarm when any of the monitored parameters lies outside acceptable critical limits. The case study is concerned with the software for controlling this system.

The Westminster Hospital system was first used in 1970 and, although it has undergone several subsequent enhancements, it is still in use today. This long-lived feature is typical of embedded systems where a useful system life-cycle of 20 years is not unusual. However, the case study is not a simple copy of the existing system. Rather, it is an exercise in understanding the nature of the problem and then engineering a design that would be suitable for a re-implementation of the system. This design will use the programming facilities of Ada and, in addition to features of the original implementation, will include enhancements to take advantage of the possibilities offered by improvements in hardware capabilities and power since 1970.

The intensive care unit in this study has sixteen beds. Each bed is equipped with a visual display computer terminal (VDU) and a set of monitoring sensors that can be attached to a patient. There is also a central monitoring station where a VDU is provided for use by hospital staff. The system is controlled by a single processor with disc storage and a magnetic tape unit.

All interactions with the system are by hospital doctors and nurses and there are no special purpose computer staff employed, except for on-call maintenance engineers. The system is thus embedded within the normal functioning of the cardiac unit and has the real-time response problems of interacting with the automatic monitors.

When a new patient is admitted to the unit a member of the medical staff is responsible for activating the monitoring system and initializing the patient's data. The first step is to prompt a bedside VDU. This causes the system to respond with instructions which are followed by the hospital staff. Initially, the system prompts on the VDU for input data such as the patient's identity, the initial values of parameters that are not sensed directly and the acceptable upper and lower limits that are to be monitored on each parameter. After this phase, the sensors are connected by a nurse or doctor, the system responding after each connection to indicate either that the function is correct or that the sensor should be adjusted. The actual functions monitored are detailed in chapter 15.

Once the patient has been successfully connected to the system the terminal displays a menu of actions available to hospital staff. This menu includes possible data inputs and enquiries about the patient's condition. On-line monitoring continues until the patient is disconnected.

The monitoring data on patients is collected in two ways. Firstly, the sensors attached to each patient detect values such as blood-pressure and temperature. These are polled at regular intervals and their readings recorded. Secondly, the VDU by each patient's bed is used for manual input of data by hospital staff. This data relates mainly to fluid inputs and outputs. From the measures given, the system calculates the fluid balance for the patient. Manual input can also be used to replace expected data from a failed sensor, an essential safety requirement. The upper section of the VDU screen is used to display the latest monitored readings and the last item of manually input data. The system raises an alarm either when no reading is obtained, due to a fault in the apparatus, or when readings show that the patient's vital signs have moved beyond the acceptable limits.

If the values detected by the system fall outside the limits set for a particular patient, then the system will activate a light over the patient's bed and a buzzer and light in a central monitoring booth. Information on the nature of the particular emergency will be displayed on the bedside VDU. These alarms will continue to function until a member of the medical staff types a code at the patient's VDU. During the alarm the system will still continue to record the patient's data for subsequent analysis.

In addition to the on-line monitoring, the system supports other functions. Hospital staff can use a bedside VDU to request that the system produce analyses of the historical data held on a patient. This can be displayed in a graphical form either on a VDU or using a hard copy printer. A doctor can note the drugs that a patient is to receive, and this information can be used to prompt the nursing staff who administer the drugs. Doctors can also alter the acceptable limits for the factors associated with a patient. There is one central VDU that is located at the nurse's monitoring station. This can be used to obtain information on any patient and will also display warning messages concerned with any patient. The system also stores historical data on each patient which is used to produce regular report summaries.

When a patient ends his stay in the unit, either by being discharged back to the ward or by dying, a member of the hospital staff will disconnect his sensors and type any final data into the system using the bedside VDU. This patient's data will remain available on-line for a further 48 hours, after which time it is archived onto tape and responsibility for it passed to the hospital's central data processing unit. Again, the system will prompt the actions that have to be taken at this stage.

4.2 Formulation of the Requirements Specification

The first stage in the construction of a program consists of an analysis of the requirements of the system and the derivation of a specification of these requirements in terms suitable for guiding the program design. In realistic systems, of even modest scale, the complexity of such analysis is sufficient that errors can arise in this early stage which, if they are not detected immediately, will plague the system throughout its future development. Time used carefully checking the consistency of the specifications is not ill spent; it will be more than recovered later.

Many analysts will initially use manual methods at this stage. However, formulation of specifications and their checking process is greatly aided if some formal methodology is used to guide the analyst. There are already available certain software aids, mostly proprietary, which provide for automatic analysis of formal specifications for consistency, and for some types of completeness. They may ensure, for example, that all concepts are defined before they are used. In future years aids of this kind should become commonplace, and indeed tools to support system specifications may appear as early components of the Ada support environments. The methods in use at different centres may not be the same, however, as in this area of the APSE it is not currently intended to force Ada users to adopt particular standards.

The importance of this stage of system development has been recognised by the UK Department of Industry, who funded a study of the use of existing methodologies for Ada program development [4.6]. The report produced provides a survey of most of the existing techniques, and case studies demonstrating the use of several of them.

In the following section, which deals with the requirements for the patient monitoring system, the approach used is based on the method CORE (COntrolled REquirement specification) [4.7]. This method seems to bring the right degree of formality into the process for the specification of a system of modest scale such as the present one. At the same time,CORE should be readily comprehensible to the reader without a detailed tutorial since the present treatment is based to a large extent on the application of sound common sense.

The remaining sections of this chapter give the details of how CORE has been applied to produce a combined diagrammatic and narrative description of the required system. These sections have been included to emphasize the authors' belief that the use of a formal methodology for the requirements analysis is an important stage in software engineering. Section 4.3 gives an informal account of the system's requirements, leading to a more formal analysis in terms of CORE in section 4.3. The latter can be omitted by readers without prejudice to their comprehension of the chapters which describe the Ada language.

4.3 Requirements Summary of the Patient Monitoring System

The CORE method allows the analyst some degree of choice in the way in which the concepts proposed in CORE are applied. This is one of the advantages of CORE, allowing it to be applied in a variety of different problem areas. However, once standards are agreed, they are enforced throughout a particular project. The details of the approach used here include interpretative decisions made by the authors.

At this stage in the CORE analysis, the system is examined to identify 'viewpoints' from which the requirements may be considered. These are the requirements as seen by the various parties who interact to form the total system. The viewpoints form a hierarchy where each successive layer is concerned with the details of a sub-system. The hierarchy of viewpoints for the patient monitoring system is shown below:

- The Patient Monitoring System
  - The Hospital
    - Doctors in charge of each patient
    - Nurses caring for patients
      - at the bedside
      - monitoring a central console
    - Hospital Records
  - The Patient
  - The Patient's Medical Practitioner (Indirect)
  - The Computer System
    - Maintenance and Support (Indirect)
    - Actions (Sensors, Data Monitoring, Displays and Reports)

The viewpoints marked as 'indirect' are included in the hierarchy for completeness but will not contribute directly to the requirements analysis.

The next stage in the CORE analysis is to specify the requirements that each viewpoint has from the system. In general, such an analysis can only be formed after data-gathering by consultation with the customer for each viewpoint. The present problem was chosen for the case study partly because each reader will be sufficiently familiar with the concepts of hospital patient care to be able to accept the analysis without actual data gathering. The remainder of this section contains an informal description of the requirements of the various clients.

4.3.1 The Doctor's Viewpoint

Following notification of an abnormal excursion of the readings outside the acceptable range for a particular patient, the doctor will give emergency treatment and record details of the treatment.

In addition, the doctor in charge of the treatment of a particular patient wishes to be able to:

> enter details of a patient's treatment to be given by the nurses;
>
> obtain, on the bedside console, a display of the patient's current critical factors;
>
> alter the acceptable critical limits for the patient's factors;
>
> set the frequency of measurement of each patient's factors;
>
> obtain, by request, on the bedside console displays of:
> fluid balances,
> a record of the drugs administered,
> graphs of data trends;
>
> reset alarm status after emergency treatment and enter details of treatment given;
>
> obtain every 12 hours a print-out of of the record of the patient since admission, and, additionally, on request.

4.3.2 The Nurse's Viewpoint

At the bedside console the nurse must be able to:

> log in a new patient;

disconnect a patient;

consult the doctor's instructions regarding medication and nursing care;

input information concerning intake and loss of fluids; this cannot easily be made fully automatic, since it must include loss by vomiting, urine, bleeding, etc. on the one hand, and gains by injections, blood-transfusions and drip feeding on the other;

input a record of drugs administered;

check monitor readings;

when a malfunction of a monitoring sensor is indicated, input replacement reading by hand.

At the central console the nurse must be able to:

receive warnings of emergency conditions by visual and audible signals, with copy of the relevant message on the central console;

request reports on a patient who is currently in the unit or has been disconnected within the last 48 hours.

4.3.3 Hospital Records' Viewpoint

Maintenance of the hospital records requires the ability to:

initialize a new patient's records in a database;

update records at regular time intervals during treatment;

when a patient is discharged, or dies, produce a report for patient's medical practitioner and archive the records;

provide reports for individual patients on request;

4.3.4 **The Patient's Viewpoint**

The patients are the reason for the system's existence, but their needs are, nevertheless, fairly simple. In the intensive care unit they are not active parties to the proceedings. Their main requirements are that they receive correct treatment, both according to a doctor's instructions and in response to emergency conditions.

4.3.5 **The Patient's Medical Practitioner (Indirect)**

The doctor who refers the patient to the hospital has an indirect view of the computer system being specified. He will supply technical details which may form part of the patient's initial records. When the hospital care is completed he will require a summary report.

4.3.6 **The System Viewpoint**

Maintenance and Support (Indirect):

> During the life time of the system it will require maintenance in the form of servicing and enhancements. For a full analysis of the system this aspect should be specified right from the start of the project. This will allow the design of the system to cater for scheduled maintenance. However, this part of the system is considered indirect for the purposes of this case study.

Sensors:

> The sensors for each patient are to be polled at a regular time interval which is set by the doctor;
>
> Automatic checking is required of the instrument status at each reading in order to confirm the correct operation of the sensor. In addition, exhaustive checks are to be initiated from time to time by nurses or system service engineers.

Data Monitoring:

Data from sensors and manual input is to be checked against acceptable limits.

Displays:

Display data when requested;

Raise emergency displays when dangerous conditions are detected.

Reports:

Generate summary reports at regular time intervals and on request.

4.4 Analysis of the Requirements

Having established the informal requirements of each viewpoint, the CORE analyst constructs a diagrammatical representation of the actions required as seen by each viewpoint in isolation. As a first step towards these diagrams, a table is drawn up showing the operations and the flow of data neccessary to satisfy these requirements. The table has five columns, headed 'sources', 'inputs', 'action', 'outputs' and 'destinations'. The actions are those associated with the particular viewpoint. For each action there must be at least one input, and each input must have a source. Likewise, each action must generate at least one output and each output must have a destination.

It is through their inputs and outputs that the actions make themselves known to the observer. Thus, these tables can be used to check the consistency of the viewpoint; all inputs must lead to an action and all outputs must stem from an action. The tables also show, by the use of arrows, the data flows implied by the viewpoint.

Separate tables are drawn up for each of the viewpoints and samples of these are shown in Tables 4.1 and 4.2 for the doctor's and system actions'

Table 4.1 - Tabular Analysis of the Doctor's Viewpoint

SOURCES	INPUTS	ACTIONS	OUTPUTS	DESTINATIONS
System Patient Monitor	Alarm	Give Emergency Treatment	Reset Alarm	System
	Display of Abnormal Readings		Treatment Given	Database
Doctor	Treatment Schedule	Set Treatment	Updated Data Record	System Data Records on Patient
	New Critical Limits/timing	Change limits/ Timing	Changed Data Record	
Doctor	Request Display	Generate Display	Graphic Display	VDU
Doctor	Request Report	Generate Summary Report	Printed Report	Doctor
Clock	Time Signal			

Table 4.2 - Tabular Analysis of the System's Viewpoint

SOURCES	INPUTS	ACTIONS	OUTPUTS	DESTINATIONS
Clock	Signal	Poll Sensors	Signal	Sensors
Sensors	Readings	Check Readings	Fault Report	Nurse
			Request Manual Replacement	Doctor/ Nurse
Nurse	Manual Replacement	Check Levels	Alarm	Doctor/ Nurse
			Vital Signs Data	Data Records
Doctor/ Nurse	Fluid Levels			VDU
Doctor/Nurse	Information Request	Prepare Report/ Display	Report	Doctor
			Display	
Clock	Signal Report			
	Signal Treatment	Retrieve Treatment Due	Treatment to be Given	VDU
Doctor/Nurse	New Data on a Patient	Update Data Records	New Data Records	Database
Doctor/Nurse	Final Data	Archive Patient	Archive Data	Hospital Records

viewpoints. The requirements for different viewpoints may well duplicate information about the system. Such redundancy in the requirements is desirable since it assists the analyst in checking the consistency of the various viewpoints.

4.4.1 Using CORE Diagrams

After the tabular analysis, CORE action diagrams are used to describe the implied action sequencing for each viewpoint. The design of CORE allows the analyst some flexibility in the format of these diagrams; the interpretation used here has been chosen by the authors. CORE has been successfully used elsewhere with slightly different rules of interpretation.

The symbols used in the diagrams are described as follows. A rectangle is used to indicate an action.

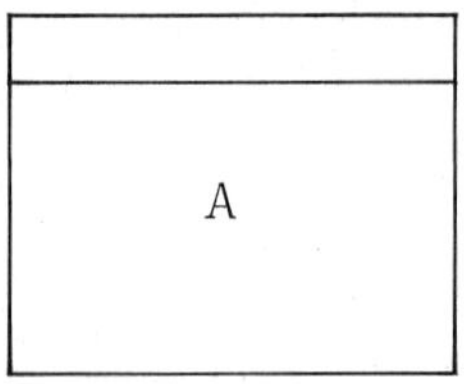

Action A

The layout of actions from left to right indicates sequencing. Arrows indicate dataflows between actions. Often dataflows are drawn from left to right, but that is not a requirement in CORE; the direction of flow being indicated by the arrow head.

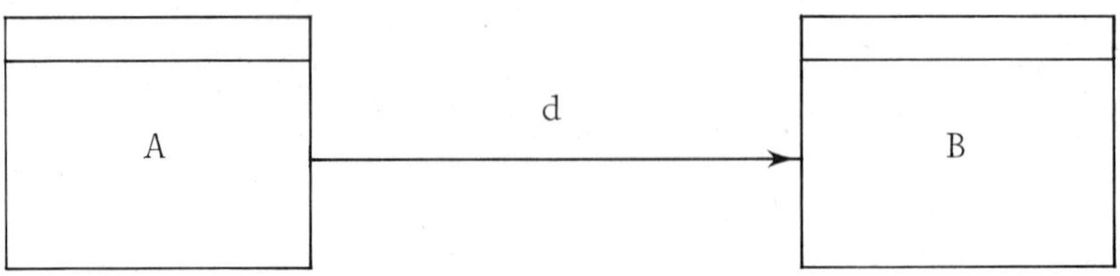

Action A is followed by action B, and there is a dataflow, d, from A to B.

A dataflow may be critical, meaning that each value supplied by A **must** be consumed by B. This is shown as:

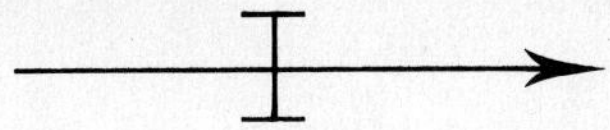

Actions with the same vertical alignment, such as A1 and A2 below, have no implied ordering and may be executed in parallel. To avoid ambiguity, no action boxes may overlap vertically.

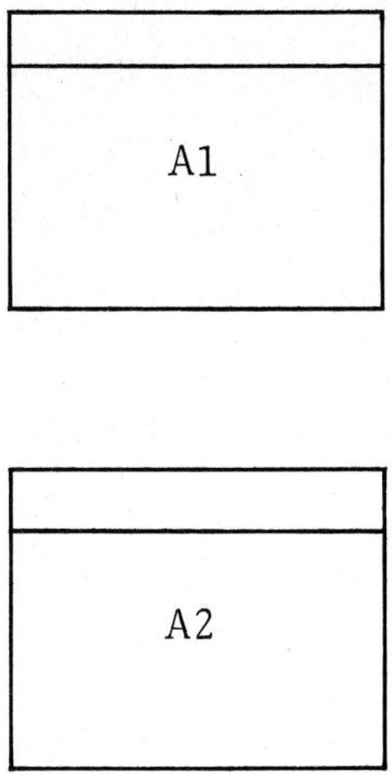

Actions A1 and A2 may execute in an indeterminate order.

They may, but do not have to, execute concurrently.

Several instances of the same action may exist is parallel and this is shown by 'shadow' boxes.

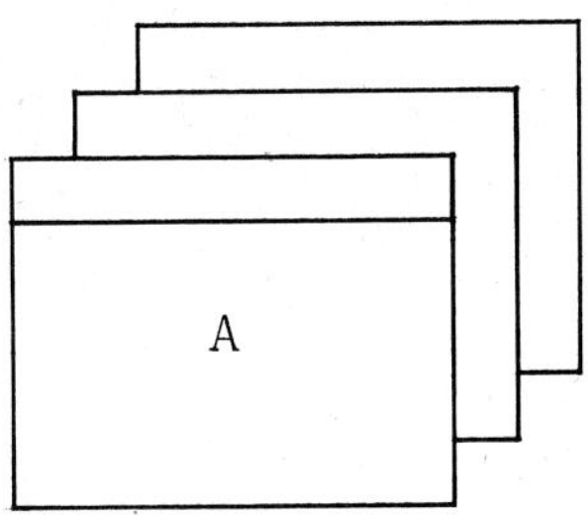

Action A occurs several times in parallel

Various symbols are used to show conditions for actions to occur or be repeated. A choice of actions may be made conditionally:

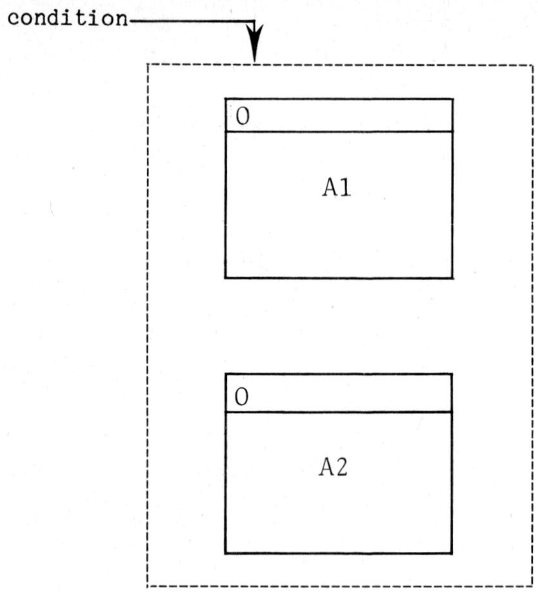

An action may be iterated on a pre-condition or until a post-condition:

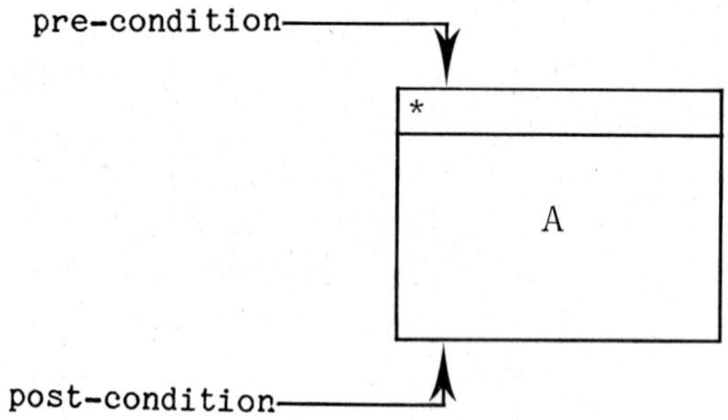

Action diagrams are drawn up using the information contained in the tabular analysis. For a large system, such as the patient monitoring system, the complexity of the actions may call for a hierarchical decomposition. Each level is numbered, with the highest level being called level 0. Within each level the actions are labelled numerically and any action that is further decomposed is shown with an arrow at the bottom of its box. The full analysis process involves the drawing of diagrams for each viewpoint. These are then combined into a single system diagram. During the combination of viewpoints, inconsistencies may come to light and the process is repeated until a consistent combined system is produced. In this case study, only the final systems diagrams produced by this process are presented.

4.4.2 **Requirements Diagrams for the Intensive Care Unit**

The CORE notation described above has been used to draw viewpoint diagrams for the system, shown in figures 4.1 to 4.8. Figure 4.1 shows the highest level of system viewpoint, with interactions with the environment external to the intensive care unit. These are the input of data on a new patient, received from the patient and his medical practitioner, and the output of reports and archive data. This level is called level 0, it contains actions which are numbered 0.1, 0.2 and 0.3, and each of these actions are further decomposed in later figures.

The action BED-SIDE PATIENT MONITOR (0.1) is performed for each of the beds in the unit and this is indicated by the shadow boxes. For each bed, the action is repeated for each new patient assigned to the bed and it is at the start of each iteration that the data on a new patient is processed. When a patient leaves a bed his monitor data is still available for system actions for a further 48 hours. During this time each detached patient is represented by a MONITOR FOR DETACHED PATIENT. A single CENTRAL CONTROL MONITOR is active all the time and deals with central response to alarms and data requests. Figure 4.1 shows the data flows between the actions, alarms from the bedside monitors to the central control monitor, requests for data from the central control to the patient monitors with report data being sent in response. The layout of the actions indicates that they can all be happening asynchronously.

FIGURE 4.1 INTENSIVE CARE UNIT - LEVEL 0 VIEWPOINT

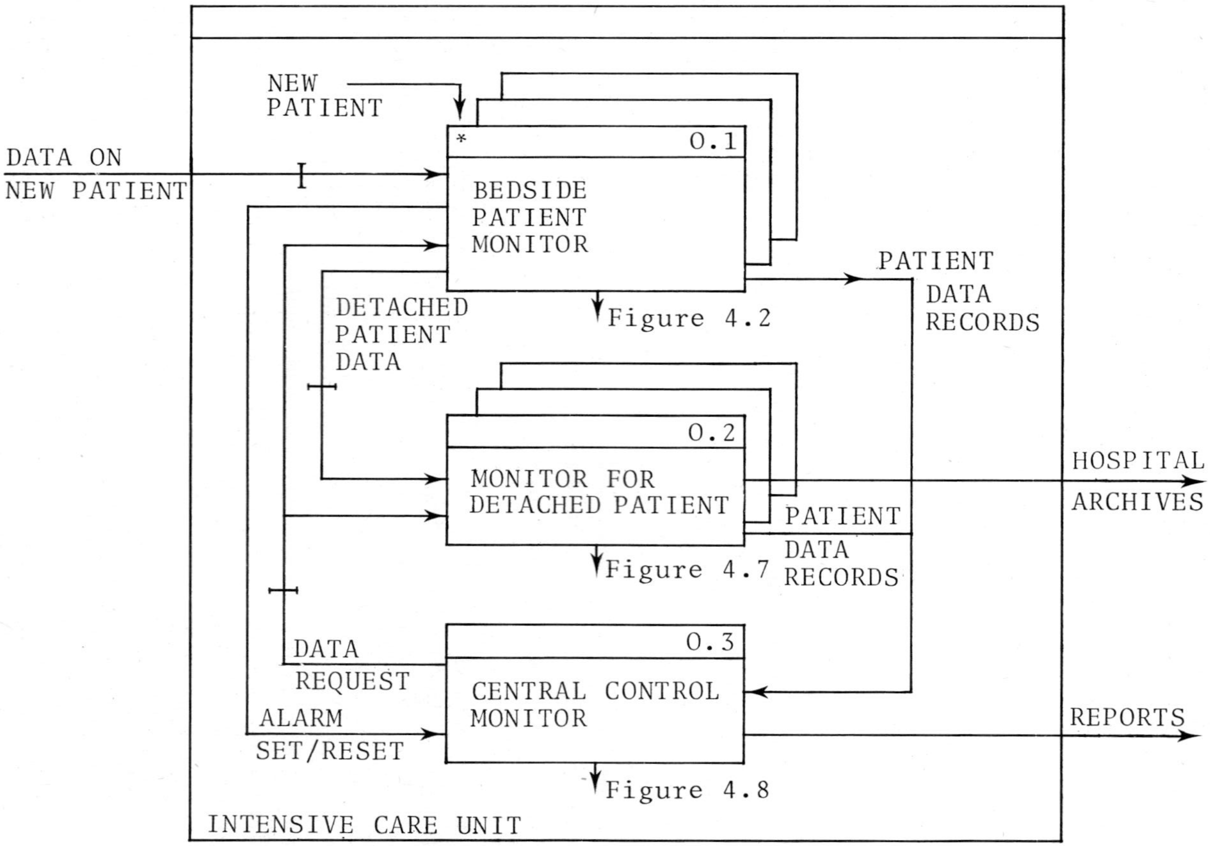

FIGURE 4.2 BEDSIDE PATIENT MONITOR (O.1)

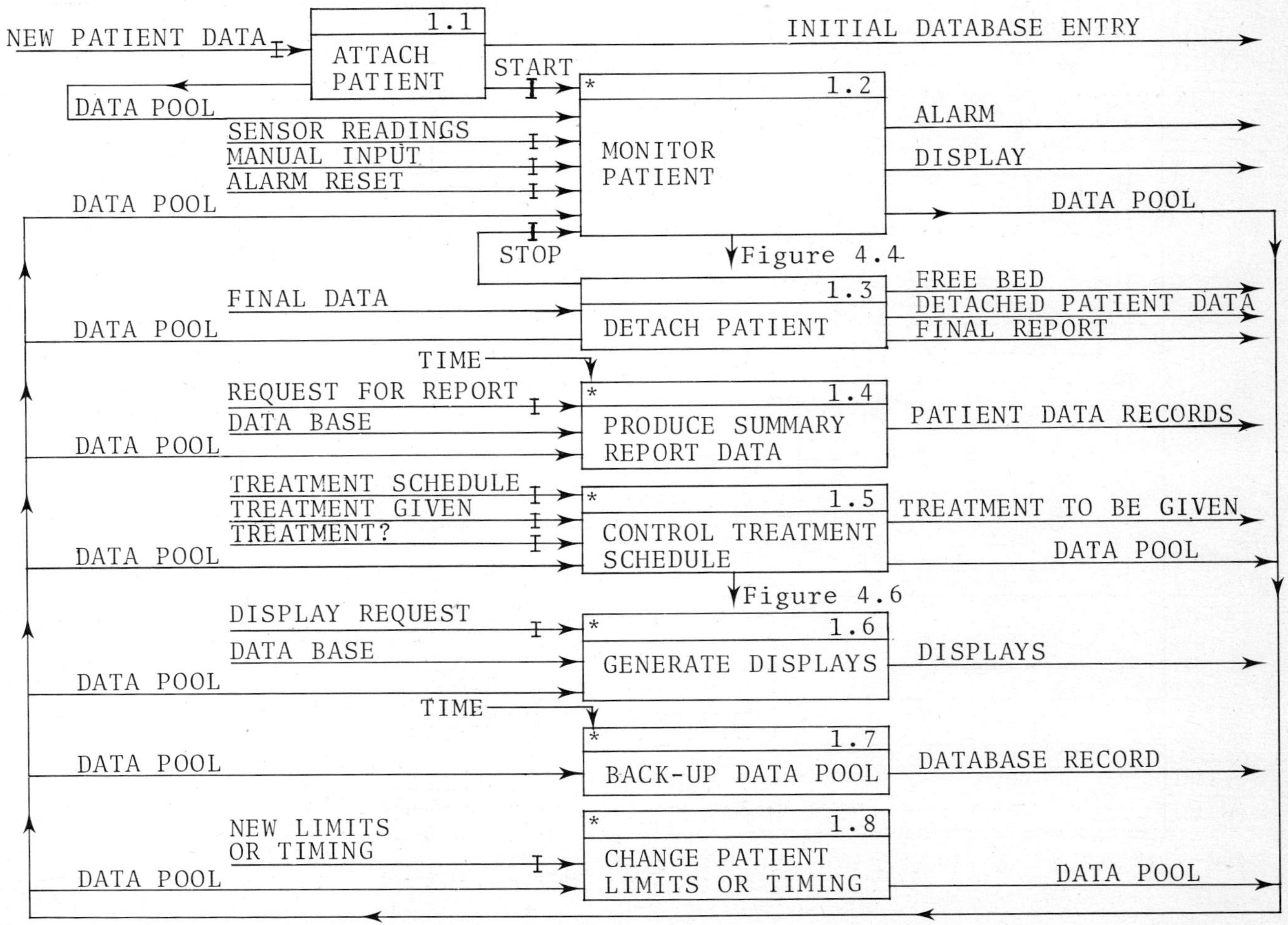

FIGURE 4.3 'ATTACH PATIENT (1.1)

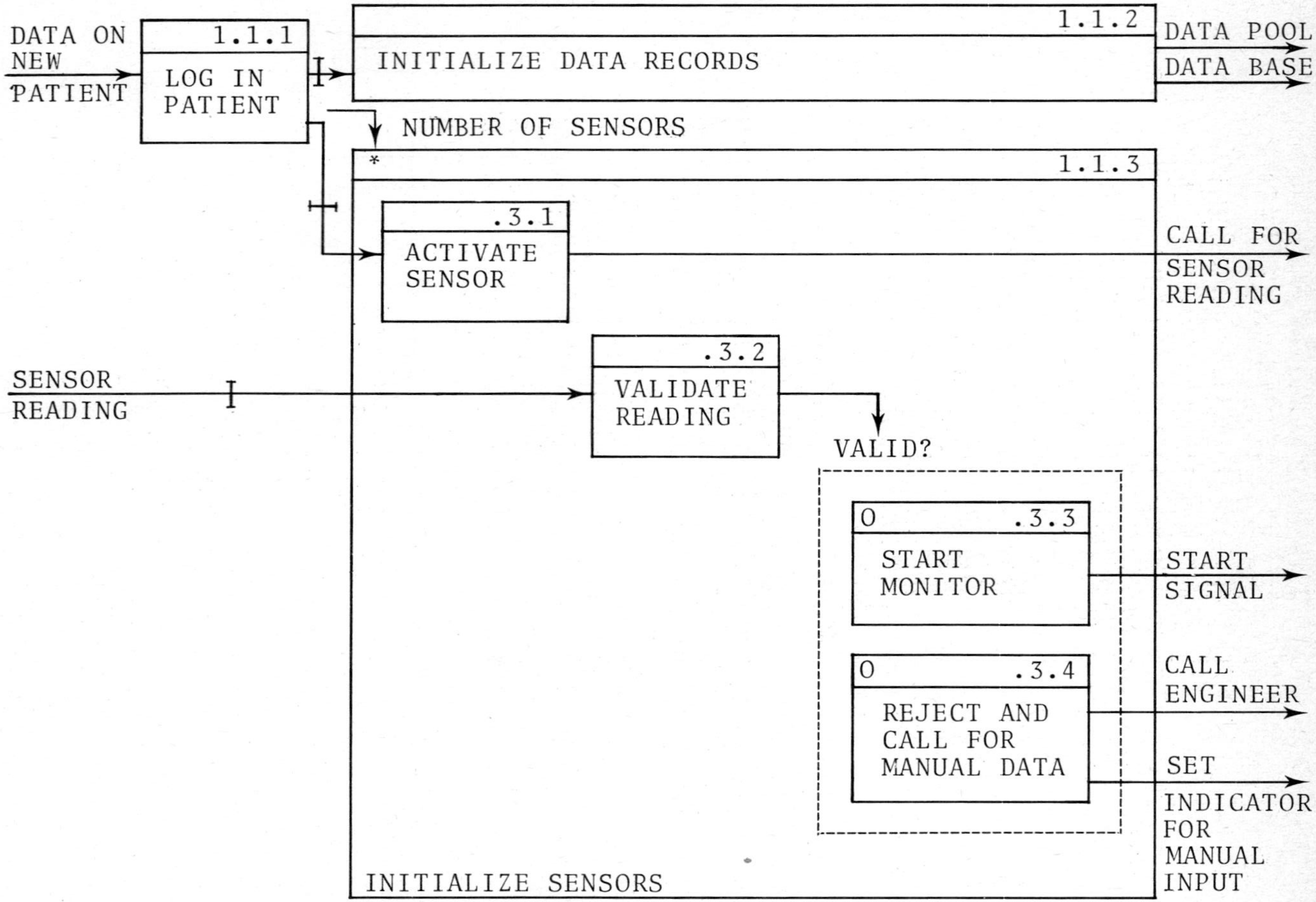

FIGURE 4.4 MONITOR PATIENT (1.2)

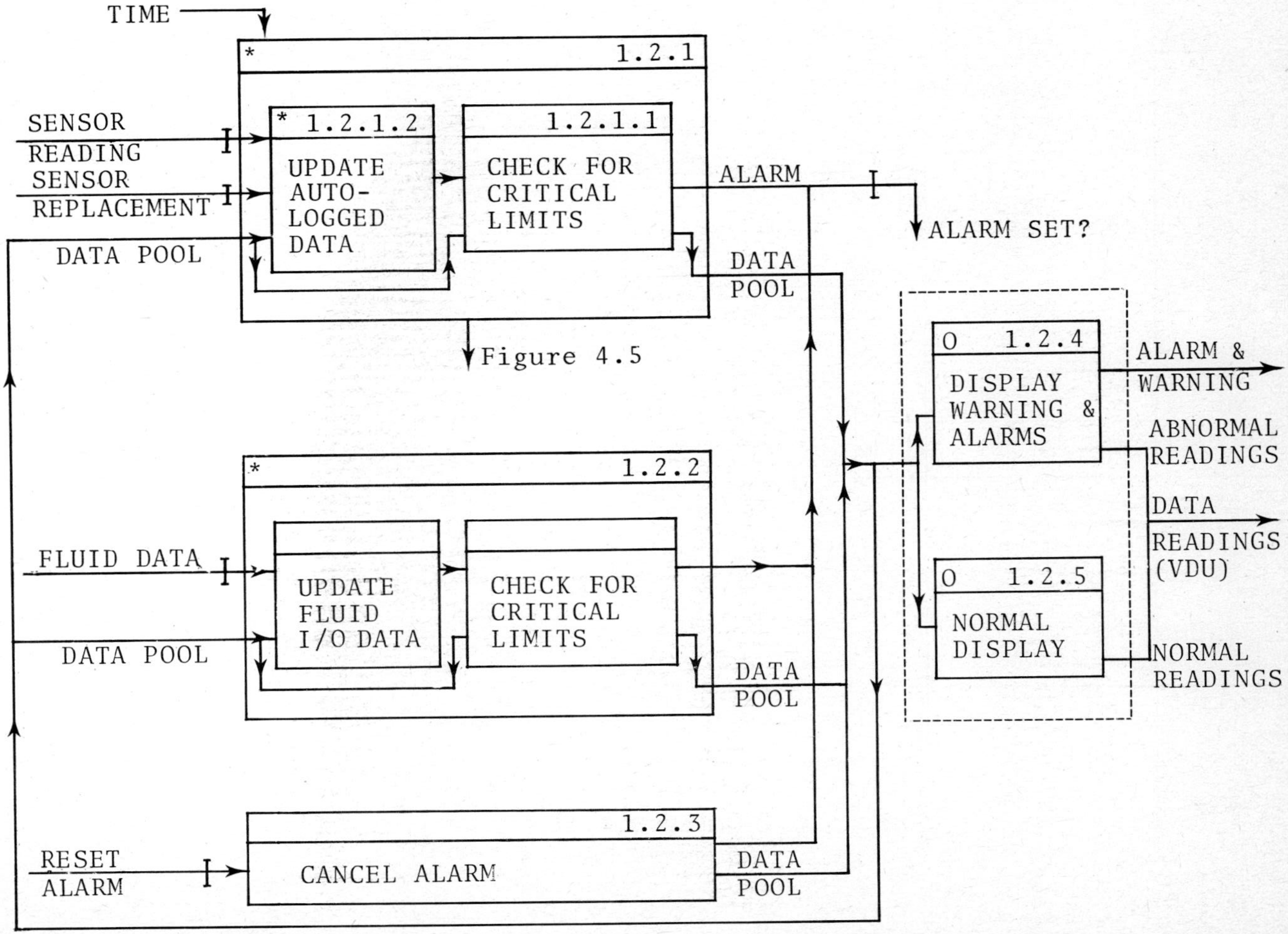

FIGURE 4.5 AUTOMATIC MONITORING (1.2.1)

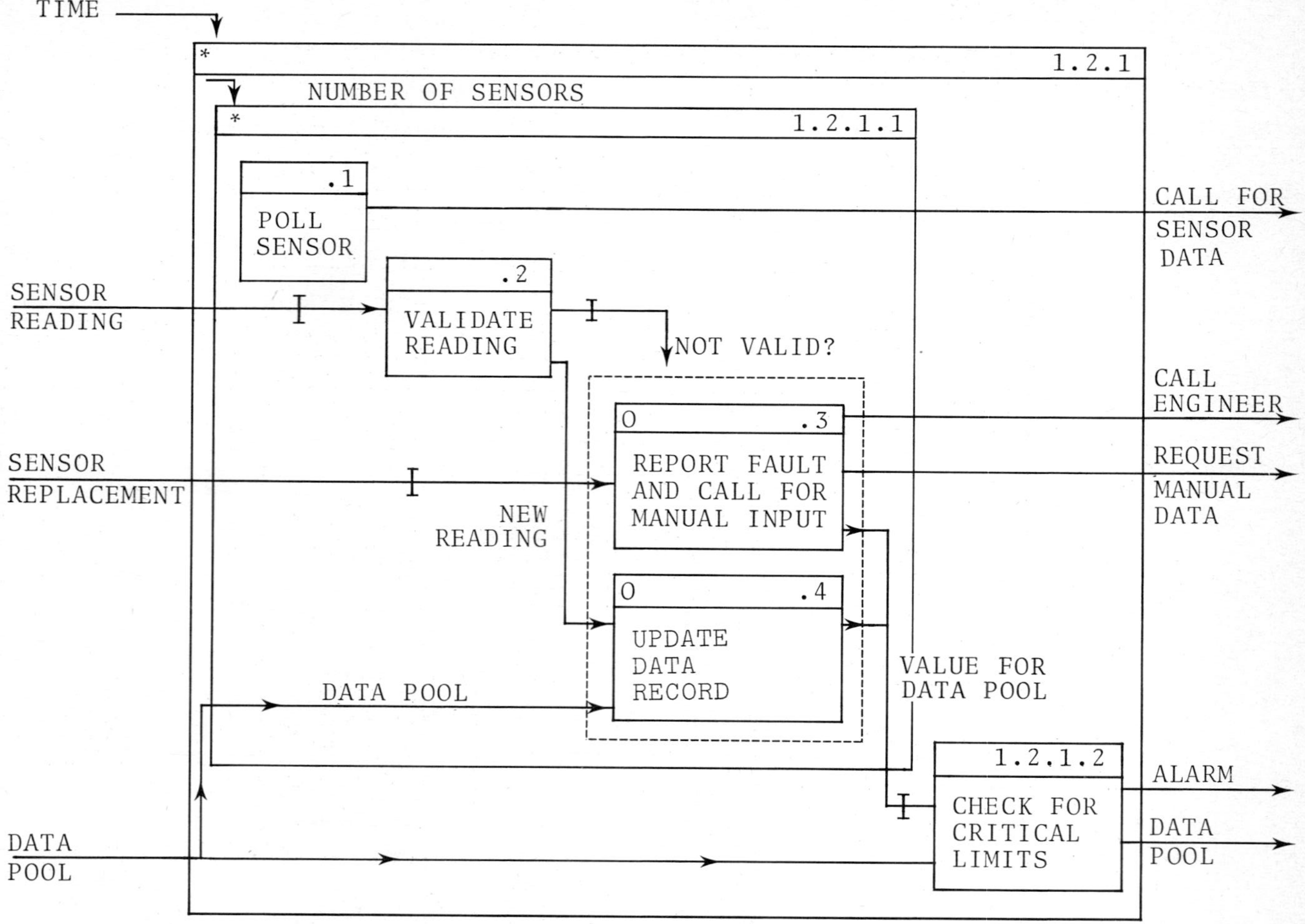

FIGURE 4.6 CONTROL TREATMENT SCHEDULE (1.5)

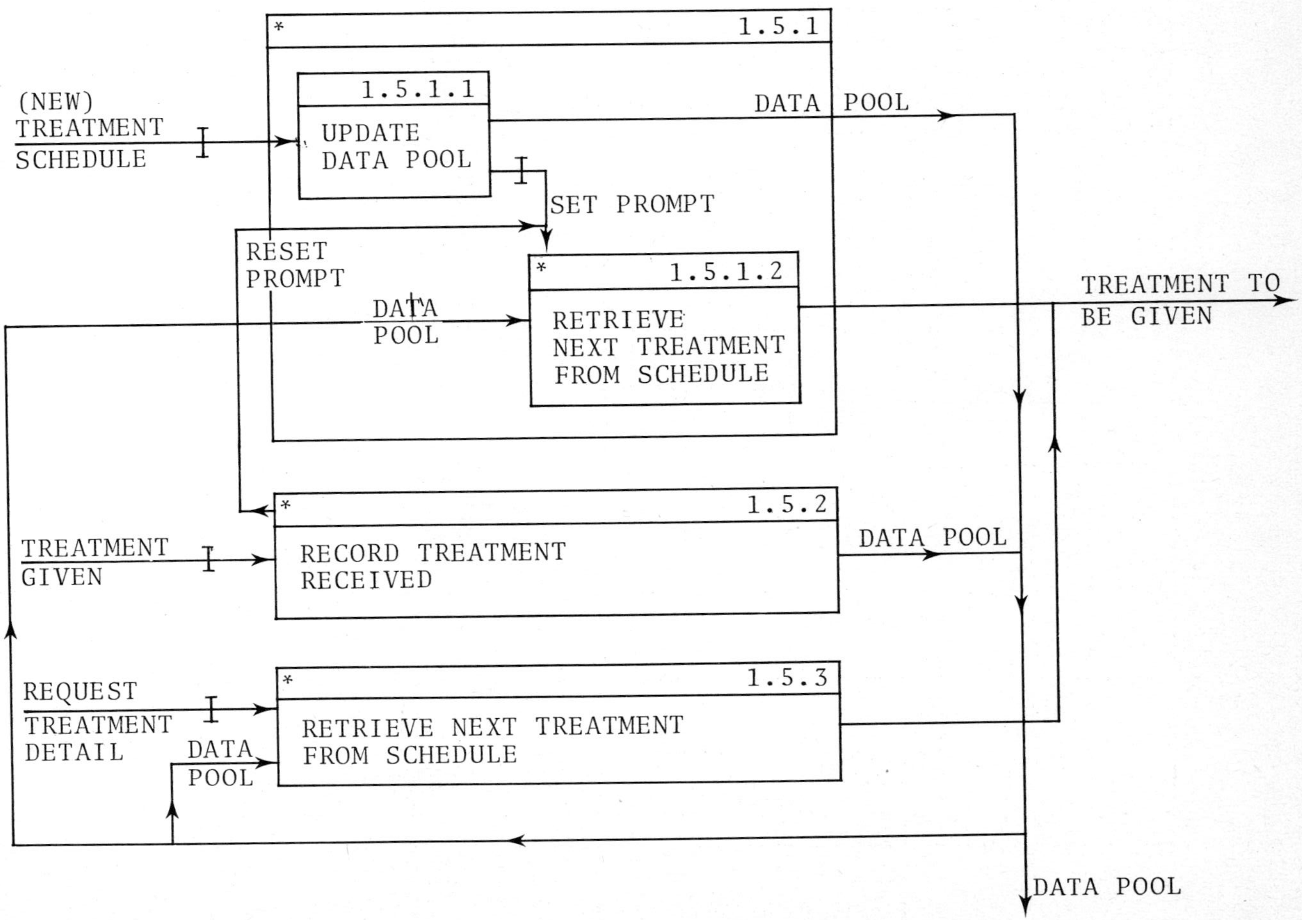

FIGURE 4.7 MONITOR FOR DETACHED PATIENT (0.2)

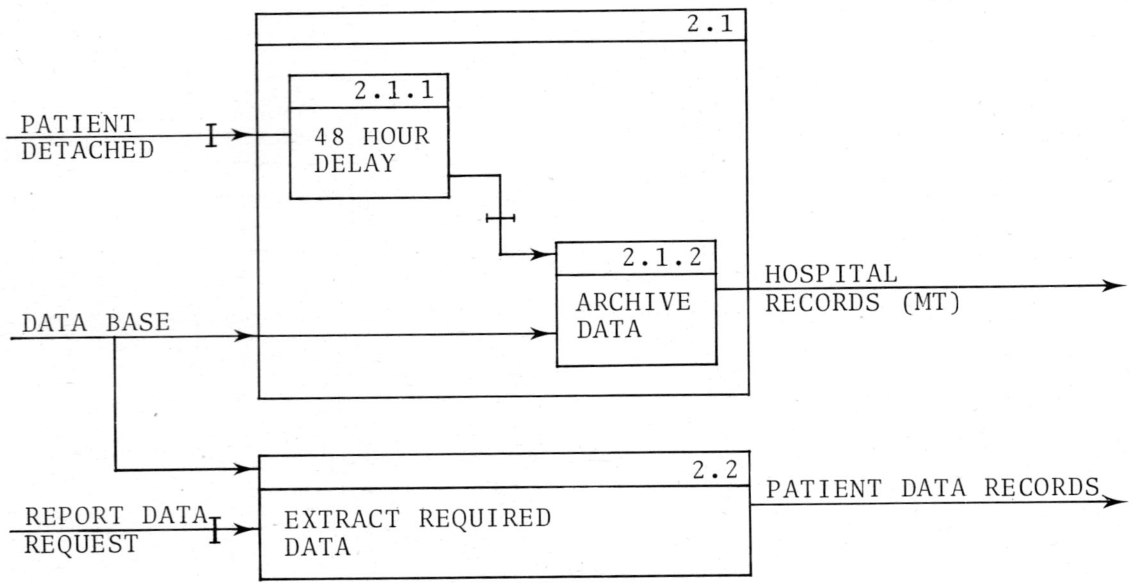

FIGURE 4.8 CENTRAL CONTROL MONITOR (0.3)

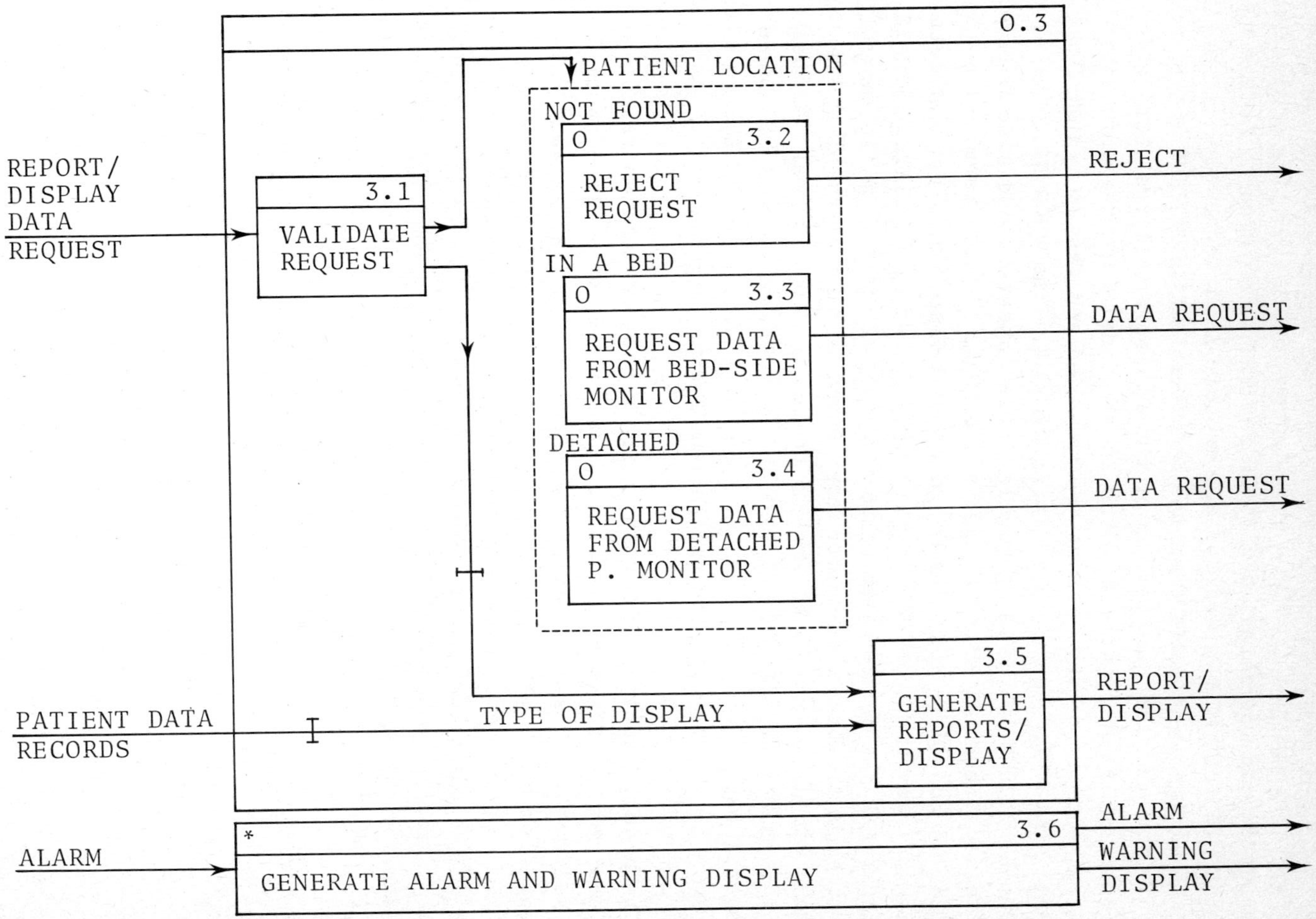

Figure 4.2 gives a decomposition of a bedside patient monitor. The action of attaching a new patient must happen before any other actions in this monitor, and the detail of ATTACH PATIENT is covered in figure 4.3. The other actions of the monitor all execute asynchronously. At any time a patient may be detached from the bed, this DETACH PATIENT action happening only once for each activation of the monitor. All the other actions are repeated, either following the input of data or on a time signal. The vital factors of the patient are recorded and tested by MONITOR PATIENT which is described further in figure 4.4. The PRODUCE SUMMARY REPORT action will take place at regular time intervals and also following an explicit request, either made on the local bedside terminal or from the central console. Requests for graphical displays of patient data can be made at any time, and these will be produced by GENERATE DISPLAYS on the local VDU. The monitor also helps the medical staff with the control of the patient's treatment. A doctor may record details of the drug treatment to be given and these can be used to prompt nursing actions. Further details of this CONTROL TREATMENT SCHEDULE process are given in figure 4.6. A doctor may also activate CHANGE PATIENT LIMITS OR TIMING to alter the levels used in monitoring the patient's vital signs.

The bedside monitor actions require a pool of data which holds all the information on the patient that is required for on-line monitoring and treatment. This is shown in the requirements diagram as a non-critical dataflow called DATAPOOL. For security and archive reasons this data is backed up into a database at regular intervals. The database is to contain a unique entry for each patient. This entry is initialized when a patient is attached, up-dated while the patient is under treatment, and completed when the patient is detached. After detachment the datapool is destroyed, but the database entry is passed to the MONITOR FOR DETACHED PATIENT.

Figure 4.3 shows the detailed requirements for ATTACH PATIENT. In response to data on a new patient being entered at the local terminal, the LOG IN PATIENT is activated and the bedside monitor is ready for use. Two further actions then take place asynchronously. The data records for the patient are initialized, both in the database and in the creation of a local data pool. The sensors used to monitor the patient are initialized. Each of the sensors in turn is activated and checked for a valid reading. If a faulty reading is detected then a maintenance call is generated and an indicator set on the local VDU to show that manual replacement readings will be required for that particular value. When all the sensors have been activated then the monitoring process can be signalled to start.

Figure 4.4 specifies the functions of the process to MONITOR PATIENT. Three actions can take place in response to external data. The first, numbered as 1.2.1, is concerned with the automatic data collection and checking and is described further in figure 4.5. The second, 1.2.2, is concerned with checking the fluid level of the patient every time new data is input giving amounts of fluid input or output. The overall fluid level is updated in the datapool and then checked for critical limits. If either of these checking actions detects an error an alarm condition will be set, and will remain set until 1.2.3 is activated by an external request to cancel the alarm. Actions 1.2.4 and 1.2.5 are alternatives, chosen on the status of the alarm. When set, alarm signals are sent to the central console and displayed locally, together with data readings giving the cause of the alarm. When the alarm is not set, the latest data readings are displayed at the top of the local VDU.

The automatic monitoring of the sensors is shown in detail in figure 4.5. The whole process is repeated at fixed time intervals and, for each monitoring, the action is repeated over all the sensors. Each sensor is polled and its reading validated. A valid reading is used to update the datapool. If the reading is not valid, indicating a sensor failure, the fault is reported and a manual replacement reading used. When all the sensor readings are available they are passed on for checking.

Figure 4.6 illustrates the requirements for the control of the treatment schedule, a decomposition of the action of 1.5 in figure 4.2. A treatment schedule may be given to the system at anytime and this is used to update the datapool and set a prompt timing for the next treatment to be given. In parallel with this, data may be input at anytime giving details of treatment actually given. This is recorded in the datapool and the next treatment prompt re-set. From time to time nursing and medical staff will wish to refer to the treatment schedule and obtain a display of the treatment to be given. This may be followed by treatment or an update of the treatment schedule.

Returning to the first level of specification shown in figure 4.1, the actions 0.2 and 0.3 are detailed in figures 4.7 and 4.8 respectively. The

MONITOR FOR DETACHED PATIENT exists for 48 hours. It is set up when a patient is released from a bed, during the next 48 hours data on the patient may be extracted from the data base and at the end of the time delay the patient's data is archived to the hospital records. The CENTRAL CONSOLE MONITOR exists throughout each activation of the patient monitoring system. It has two functions, it will accept details of alarms from any of the individual monitors and display them on a central console, and it will also generate reports on any patients whose records are still in system. Figure 4.8 shows that patient data requests must first be validated and then routed to the correct monitor.

4.4.3 Data Items

The CORE diagrams introduce a number of data objects, some input from viewpoints external to the computer system, some generated internally, and others sent on to other viewpoints. These are summarized for reference in tables 4.3, 4.4 and 4.5.

4.5 Conclusion

A combination of informal description and CORE analysis has been used to describe the requirements for the embedded computer system in an intensive care unit. This same approach can be used to fully specify the entire system, not just its software components. However, such an analysis would be beyond the scope of the aims of this book. Sufficient information is given here only to allow the reader to understand the design of the Ada program in chapter 15.

Table 4.3 - Summary of Input Dataflows

DATA NAME	SOURCE	DESCRIPTION
DATA ON NEW PATIENT	Patient, Hospital doctor, Patient's Medical Practitioner	Personal information, Medical history
NEW LIMITS	Doctor	Critical limits for sensed factors
NEW TIMING	Doctor	Timing for sensor poll
SENSOR READINGS	Sensors	Automatically logged vital signs
MANUAL INPUT:-		
SENSOR REPLACEMENT	Nurse or Doctor	Vital signs
FLUID DATA	Nurse or Doctor	Fluid input and output
ALARM RESET	Doctor	Cancels alarm
FINAL DATA	Doctor	Details of release of Patient
REQUEST FOR REPORT	Doctor or Nurse	Details of type of report required
TREATMENT SCHEDULE	Doctor	Treatment to be given
TREATMENT GIVEN	Nurse or Doctor	Log of treatment
REQUEST TREATMENT DETAILS	Nurse or Doctor	Query treatment

Table 4.4 - Summary of Internal data

DATA NAME	DESCRIPTION
DATAPOOL	Details directly relevant to the monitoring and treatment of a patient
DATABASE	Information on patient, in store and on disc; contains personal data, medical history and a log of data recorded in the intensive care unit
DETACHED PATIENT DATA	Information on patient released from bed including location of related database entry
START/STOP	Conditional signal to activate monitor (1.2)
ALARM	Signals alarm condition, until cancelled

Table 4.5 - Summary of Output Dataflows

DATA NAME	DESTINATION	DESCRIPTION
REPORTS:-		
SUMMARY	Doctor	Progress reports
FINAL	Doctor, hospital records, Patient's Medical Practitioner	Last report
HOSPITAL ARCHIVE	Hospital records	Final data on Magnetic Tape
DISPLAY:-		
DATA READINGS	Doctor and Nurse	Vital signs
GRAPHS	Doctor	Analysis of data
TREATMENT TO BE GIVEN	Nurse or Doctor	Prescribed treatment
CALL FOR SENSOR READING	Sensor	Polling
INDICATOR FOR MANUAL INPUT	Nurse	Sensor data must be substituted
CALL ENGINEER	Nurse	Indicates system fault
ALARM	Nurse and Doctor	Indicated patient in danger

References

[4.1] "Structured Design"; W P Stevens, G F Myers and L C Constantine; IBM Systems Journal, Vol 13, 1974.

[4.2] "A Requirements Engineering Methodology for Real-Time Processing Requirements"; M Alford; IEEE Transactions in Software Engineering, SE-3; 1977.

[4.3] "The use of formal asynchronous process specifications in a system development process"; D R Fitzwater and P Zave; Texas conference on Computing Systems, 2B; 1977.

[4.4] "Invariants in the Application-orientated Specification of Control System"; S J Goldsack and J Kramer; Automatica Vol 18, No 2; 1982.

[4.5] "Three Years of Experience with Computer-Assisted Patient Monitoring"; Anna Mikolajczuk; Medinfo 1974.

[4.6] "Ada-based Systems Development Methodology Study Report"; Augusta Consortium report for the UK Department of Industry; 1981.

[4.7] "Controlled Requirements Specification (CORE)", Seminar Manual; Geoff Mullery; Systems Designers Limited, Camberley, England.

CHAPTER 5

PROGRAM CONSTRUCTION

5.1 Introduction

Programming language designers have traditionally followed one of two approaches to the development of complete programs from subunits; the 'flat' approach of using stand-alone subprogram segments linked by single level calls, or the hierarchical approach of separating code into functional modules nested within other units according to context.

The first of these methods is analogous to information stored in an encyclopaedia which can be accessed by a one-level look up of a key name. It has several advantages. The internal declarations of one program unit are not visible to any other unit. Subprograms can communicate only by parameter lists or access to an explicitly declared common data area, thus minimizing the side effects that can be caused by erroneous code accessing information with which it should not be concerned. In addition, subprogram functions and subroutines can be separately developed and complete programs built using precompiled library units. However, because calls and declarations may be compiled in any order, this approach has the disadvantage of not requiring that the compiler to check that all calls on subprograms have the correct parameters and context of use.

The second approach of nested procedures, functions, and blocks, allows programs to be structured so that resources are declared only when they are required. If a data area or function is required within an inner block of the program then it can be declared at the start of that block. Subprograms can communicate not only by parameters, but also through any variables visible to both the called and calling unit. However, the visibility of resources within their scope cannot be controlled and, in large programs, this leads to the problem of name space invasion in inner blocks. Moreover, all program units must be declared and fully specified before they are used, so that the compiler can check that every call is compatible with the corresponding declaration. This technique gives important support for programmers but is unsuitable for the construction of large and complex programs, because it requires that programmers first implement the full detail of the coding of the units at the lowest level of problem decomposition before the code of the higher levels of the program. This form of program construction is also less suited to the inclusion of standard library routines.

Ada offers a framework for using both methods with an extended concept of the program unit. It provides the full facilities of block structure but allows the programmer to delay implementation of the details of nested program units so that coding can follow the course of problem decomposition. Ada also provides a mechanism for the construction of stand-alone units and has the potential for the implementation of comprehensive and powerful libraries of software components.

5.2 The Ada Design Philosophy

The program units of Ada are subprograms, packages and tasks. The form of each of these program units reflects the philosophy that program development should separate the concern of what is to be achieved from the detail of how it is to be achieved. The specifications of Ada program units can be used to construct a program design that can be tested for consistency by the compiler. After agreement on this program design, the bodies of the units can be coded in isolation since all inter-unit communication is made via the specifications. There are several advantages of this approach: program design can be checked for consistency before detailed coding is started; teams of systems implementors can work on different components knowing that their only interfaces with other components are well defined; the details of the coding of any unit body can be altered without the rest of the program having to be recompiled and any pre-existing software component matching a required specification can be used.

Ada provides the traditional Algol-like subprogram units of **functions** and

procedures. Acknowledging that these have been shown to be inadequate for fully modular development, since they provide limited control over inter-module communication and are too tightly bound into the overall program structure, they are not offered as the main units of program modularity. The language unit provided for the structuring of modularity and abstraction in complex program systems is the **package.** This reflects the fact that Ada has been designed for a modular approach to large software development with systems being constructed from independently produced components. The package can be used to enclose a group of logically related declarations to be used by other program units, to group together logically related subprogram units, and to provide encapsulated data types. In each case, there is a package specification of the interfaces served and a separate, possibly void, package body which gives the detailed coding.

The concurrent requirements of embedded systems are provided for by the **task.** Here, there is also a specification and body, but the specification of a task contains only the details its entry points, calls on which provide the communications interface with other program units. The body of the task contains the code of a logically independent process of the system, included in which will be statements that accept calls on the communication entries and executes code in a rendezvous with the calling unit.

5.3 Some Preliminaries

There are some basic facts about the way in which Ada programs are represented that must be understood before fragments of the language can be presented. Programs are represented by using a set of 57 printing characters to form lexical units. This character set uses only upper case letters. However, on systems where lower letters are available they may be used but with the same meaning as the corresponding upper case characters. There are 62 key words in the language and these are not distinguished from user defined words in the text of a program by any textual convention. They are reserved words which may be used only in their Ada defined context. The preferred convention of the language reference manual [5.1] will be used in this book to distinguish between key words and identifiers. This is that lower case, bold face, type be used for key words, for example

begin, and upper case be used for identifiers.

Ada identifiers are constructed from any string of letters and digits, starting with a letter. They may contain internal single underscores to improve readability and they may not cross a line boundary. This gives a maximum identifier length limited to the length of a line, although, in practical use, they will be much shorter. Some valid identifiers are:

```
BED   PATIENT_MONITOR_SYSTEM   MAXIMUM_CAPACITY   RS232
```

The underscore is significant, so MAXIMUMCAPACITY is also a valid, but different, identifier.

Identifiers are used to name variables, constants, types, program units, and other objects. Every identifier must be introduced by a declaration, for example a variable is declared by:

```
OBJECT_NAME : TYPE_NAME;
```

such as:

```
BED_NUMBER : INTEGER;
```

or a constant:

```
PI : constant FLOAT := 3.141_592_653;
```

This latter declaration shows the use of the assignment symbol := to give a value to the constant. It also shows that the underscore may be used to improve the readability of a number. In this case it has no significance.

Variables may also be given an initial value:

```
BED_FREE : BOOLEAN := FALSE;
```

Comments can be inserted in Ada text by using a double hyphen. The compiler will ignore all text between the -- and the end of the line; comments continuing over more than one line must start each line with the -- symbols. The convention for comments is to use upper and lower case letters as they would normally be used in English text.

The space character is significant in Ada as a separator. No lexical item may contain an internal space and at least one space or non-alphanumeric character must separate adjacent words.

Thus, the spaces in

```
if BED_FREE then .....
```

are necessary but they are not needed in PATIENT(BED_NUMBER). The end of a line is also significant, acting like a space and thus limiting the length of any single lexical item.

Additional spaces and line ends have no significance, so an Ada program may be written in completely free format with the semicolon being used to indicate the end of each statement. However, the language reference manual [5.1] advocates a comb-like layout for the reserved, or key, words that delimit the components of language units. This approach is illustrated in the outline program shown in figure 5.1 below. The main unit of an Ada program, where the sequence of execution will start, is a procedure. In the example this procedure is identified by the name MAIN_PROGRAM. However, there is no requirement for the programmer to use any special identifier for this procedure.

figure 5.1 - Outline of an Ada Program

```
procedure MAIN_PROGRAM is

   -- The declarative part of the program containing the
   -- declarations of resources used throughout the  procedure.

begin

   -- The imperative part of the program containing code that uses
   -- the resources  declared above;
   -- may contain nested declare blocks with  their own resources.

exception

   -- Handlers for any exceptions raised during
   -- the execution of the imperative part.

 end MAIN_PROGRAM;
```

Any program unit has three parts, divided in a comb by four key words. The first part, introduced by the key word for the class of the unit, (in this case **procedure**), is the declarative part and it contains declarations of variables, constants, user defined types and other program units. These form the resources that are required throughout the main program and all such resources must be declared before they are used. The word **begin** marks the start of the imperative part of the program. This contains the program statements that use the resources of the declarative part to perform the required actions of the program. Next, **exception** marks the exception handlers which deal with any exceptional failures that occur during the execution of the imperative part. The unit is closed by an **end**, after which the identifying name of the unit, and only this name, may optionally be repeated. One, or more, of these parts may be omitted if not required.

Other kinds of program unit are distinguished by a different initial key word but have the same comb structure dividing them into three parts. Packages and tasks have their declarative part split into an externally accessible specification and a private part. These units can be embedded within a single program, forming a top-down structure, or constructed as stand-alone library components used in bottom-up program system design. These approaches, which both have their merits, are described in the next two sections.

5.4 Top-Down Construction

At the simplest level, a small Ada program can be submitted as a single procedure unit containing nested program units, as shown in the program in figure 5.2.

Here the MAIN_PROGRAM has declarations of a variable identified by BED_NUMBER and of type INTEGER, a constant identified by MAXBEDS also of type INTEGER, and a user defined type PATIENT. The details of how users may define types are described in chapter 6. The MAIN_PROGRAM also contains the declarations of three program units, a **procedure** LOG_NEW_PATIENT, a **function** DAYS_IN_USE, and a **package** USEFUL_THINGS. Subprograms are specified by a signature. This gives the formal identifiers for any parameters that are to be provided, the type and modes of transfer for each parameter and, in the case of functions, the type of the result. The specifications of these program units are visible throughout the body of the program unit in which they are declared but the internal workings of the subprograms are not visible. Thus, in this example, LOG_NEW_PATIENT may be called with a single PATIENT parameter from any point in the code of the MAIN_PROGRAM.

figure 5.2 - Skeleton of an Ada Program

```
procedure MAIN_PROGRAM is
    -- examples of resource declarations

    -- variables and constants:
    BED_NUMBER : INTEGER;
    MAXBEDS : constant INTEGER := 16;

    -- a user defined type, see chapter 6;
    type PATIENT is .....

    -- a procedure, see chapter 8:
    procedure LOG_NEW_PATIENT (P : in out PATIENT) is
       -- declarations local to LOG_NEW_PATIENT;
    begin
       -- body of code of LOG_NEW_PATIENT;
    end LOG_NEW_PATIENT;

    -- a function, see chapter 8:
    function DAYS_IN_USE (BED_NUMBER : INTEGER) return INTEGER is
       -- declarations local to DAYS_IN_USE;
    begin
       -- body of code of DAYS_IN_USE;
    end DAYS_IN_USE;

    -- a package, see chapter 10:
    package USEFUL_THINGS is
        -- Visible specification of the resources provided by the package.
        -- These may be data areas, types or program units.
    end USEFUL_THINGS;
```

```
    package body USEFUL_THINGS is
        -- Declarations of resources local to the package.
        -- These can only be used in the package body.
    begin
        -- Imperative part of the package which contains the bodies
        -- of any program units declared in the specification.
    end USEFUL_THINGS;

begin
    -- Imperative statements of the main program.
    -- This uses the resources  declared above.
end MAIN_PROGRAM;
```

The package USEFUL_THINGS encapsulates facilities provided by the package. There are two parts to this package - the specification which will contain the declarations of constants, variables, data types or program units, and the body which contains the hidden internal details of the package. In the case of program units only their signatures will appear in the package specification; their bodies will be hidden in the package body which contains the resources and code private to the package.

The package USEFUL_THINGS could be declared as follows:

```
package USEFUL_THINGS is
    type NEW_TYPE is -- type details;
    C : constant NEW_TYPE  := -- expression giving a value;
    procedure USE_NEW_TYPE (X : in out NEW_TYPE);
end USEFUL_THINGS;
```

This would provide a declaration of the type NEW_TYPE, a constant identified by C and a procedure that is called USE_NEW_TYPE. The procedure acts on a parameter with the formal name X and of type NEW_TYPE. These resources would be available in any part of the MAIN_PROGRAM.

The package body could have the form:

```
package body USEFUL_THINGS is
    Y : NEW_TYPE;
    procedure USE_NEW_TYPE (X : in out NEW_TYPE) is
        -- declarations local to this procedure
    begin
        -- statements of the procedure
    end USE_NEW_TYPE;
begin
    -- initialization code of the package
end USEFUL_THINGS;
```

Objects declared within the body of the package are not visible outside that body. Here, the variable Y and the details of the code of USE_NEW_TYPE are private to the package body and cannot be accessed by the program unit enclosing the package declaration.

The declarations of the declarative part are said to be 'elaborated' in the order that they appear in the text. For simple declarations, such as types, this makes the names available for use later in the program. For variables, it implies the allocation of storage space. For a package body, elaboration will include execution of its imperative part. Objects cannot be used before they have been elaborated.

The above approach to program construction, whilst suitable for problems of programming "in the small", is not appropriate for programming "in the large", and does not use the full power of Ada. Since the bodies of the subunits are not semantically visible in the main program there is no need for them to be physically visible. The main program can be compiled into a library with stubs replacing the unit bodies. The bodies can then be included later as separate compilation units. The outline of the main program revised to show this approach is shown in figure 5.3.

The missing bodies are later compiled with a leading **separate** followed by the name of the program unit in which they belong in the overall program structure.

```
separate (MAIN_PROGRAM)
procedure LOG_NEW_PATIENT (P : in out PATIENT) is...
```

figure 5.3 - Skeleton of an Ada Program with Stubs

```
procedure MAIN_PROGRAM is
    BED_NUMBER : INTEGER;
    MAXBEDS : constant INTEGER := 16;

    type PATIENT is.....

    procedure LOG_NEW_PATIENT (P : in out PATIENT) is
    separate; -- a stub

    function DAYS_IN_USE (BED_NUMBER : INTEGER) return INTEGER is
    separate; -- a stub

    package USEFUL_THINGS is
      -- specification as before;
    end USEFUL_THINGS;

    package body USEFUL_THINGS is
    separate; -- a stub

begin
     -- body of main program
end MAIN_PROGRAM;
```

These separate bodies of the main program may themselves also contain stubs, giving a hierarchical structure.

This method of program construction allows top-down development of a complete program initially set out as specification stubs. The compiler can be used to check the consistency of the specifications of program units with their uses. Once this is established, the details of the separate units can be developed in isolation, thus allowing teams of program designers to work on a common project with well-defined interfaces.

The use of separately compiled bodies also has the advantage of allowing a body to be replaced, for example by an improved algorithm, without the necessity of recompiling the whole program.

5.5 Bottom-up Construction

The top-down design technique does not allow the system designer to make full use of the distributed nature of Ada. An additional, bottom-up, approach to program construction allows a system to be built from independent program units. Free standing program units, with the exception of tasks, may be compiled into a library file. These units can later be incorporated into Ada programs that require the facilities that they offer. Where units make use of other units the latter must have been pre-compiled into the library and the dependency shown by a **with** clause.

The package of USEFUL_THINGS may provide resources that can be used in a number of Ada programs. To provide this package in a library file its specification would be compiled as a single unit:

```
package USEFUL_THINGS is
       -- specifications
end USEFUL_THINGS;
```

A common requirement for a library package might be a collection of file handling declarations such as:

```
package FILE_HANDLER is
  type FILE is -- type details for a file;
  type DATA is -- structure of file record;
  procedure OPEN (NAME : in FILE; OK : out BOOLEAN);
  procedure READ (INFO : out DATA);
  procedure WRITE (INFO : in DATA);
  procedure CLOSE (NAME : in FILE);
end FILE_HANDLER;
```

Even without the corresponding bodies, units using the specified resources could subsequently be compiled into the library preceded by a **with** clause. The compiler would then check that all calls on the package interfaces are consistent with its definition.

```
with USEFUL_THINGS, FILE_HANDLER;
procedure A_PROGRAM is
  -- declarations using the specifications of  the packages;
  -- this can be obtained by the dot notation:
      RECORD : FILE_HANDLER.DATA;
  -- or by the use clause
      use FILE_HANDLER;
    MY_FILE : FILE; -- declaration of a file
begin
  -- code using the resources of the packages;
end A_PROGRAM;
```

The code of A_PROGRAM cannot, of course, be executed until the bodies of the packages that are used have also been compiled into the library files.

Given the compilation units:

```
package body USEFUL_THINGS is
        -- body of package
end USEFUL_THINGS;
```

and

```
package body FILE_HANDLER is
        -- code for procedures to OPEN, READ, WRITE and CLOSE;
end FILE_HANDLER;
```

then A_PROGRAM can be executed.

The library packages listed in the **with** clause of any program will be elaborated in the order given, with this causing the elaboration of any packages named in their **with** clauses. In the above example A_PROGRAM can 'see' the resources of both USEFUL_THINGS and FILE_HANDLER. However, FILE_HANDLER cannot 'see' USEFUL_THINGS. This method of separate compilation gives much greater control over visibility between units than the nested structure.

The package specifications must be compiled before any units that use them. However, the bodies can be compiled later and this again allows alterations in the details of how a specification is implemented without recompilation of the rest of the library. Although, if the specification of a unit is changed all the other library units depending on it must be recompiled.

Multiple dependencies can be used as long as the units are compiled in the correct sequence. Several procedures may be compiled into the same library file and make use of the same packages, such as the file handler. On linking, the name of the required main procedure is given to the language translation system and all the units upon which it depends are linked into the executing program.

The **with** relationship is not transitive and units may only use those other units on which they directly depend, although other indirectly used units will be included in the object program.

It is this method of using Ada that will promote the production of general software components, as first suggested by M D McIlroy in 1968 [5.2]. It is suggested that an Ada components industry will develop where general purpose packages are offered for sale to guaranteed specifications. The machine independent support environment, the APSE, will help to ensure that these packages can be used with any Ada system. Tailoring of these components to the needs of particular customers - say for precision or typing - can be achieved by using generic units, as described in chapter 11.

5.6 Concurrency

The program unit used to specify concurrent activity within an Ada program is the **task**. At the first level of decomposition tasks may not be independent compilation units but must be contained within a package, procedure or function. However, tasks may then be declared within other tasks.

A task has a specification part, which can only contain entries which other tasks may call, and a body of private resources and code. The code below shows a procedure which contains two tasks identified by the names FIRST and SECOND. The two tasks will be executed in parallel with the imperative part of the procedure TWO_TASKS. Any objects declared in the procedure before the tasks, such as the type MESSAGE, will be visible to both the tasks.

The tasks may communicate asynchronously by sharing access to any global variables of the procedure or synchronously by the rendezvous caused by one task calling an entry in the other.

```
procedure TWO_TASKS is
     type MESSAGE is ......
     -- a user defined type visible to both tasks

     -- specification of the first task
     task FIRST is
        entry QUERY (X : in MESSAGE);
        -- this is an entry call specification with parameter signature
     end FIRST;

     -- specification of the second task
     task SECOND is
        entry ANSWER (X : in MESSAGE);
     end SECOND;

     -- the body of the first task is separate
     task body FIRST is separate;

     -- the body of the second task is also separate
     task body SECOND is separate;

     -- any further declarations in the procedure not visible to the tasks

begin
     -- Imperative part of the procedure, this is executed in
     -- parallel with the bodies of the tasks FIRST and SECOND.
end TWO_TASKS;
```

The body of FIRST shows that it expects a call on its QUERY entry with a MESSAGE parameter. It will subsequently call the ANSWER entry of SECOND with a reply.

```
separate (TWO_TASKS)
task body FIRST is
   -- declarations local to FIRST
   Y : MESSAGE;  -- type declaration visible in TWO_TASKS
begin
   -- Imperative part of FIRST,
   -- this will include an accept of calls on QUERY
   accept QUERY (X : in MESSAGE) do
      -- code of the rendezvous of SECOND with FIRST
      Y := X; -- takes a copy of the message
   end QUERY;
   ...........
   -- and a call to ANSWER
   SECOND.ANSWER(Y);  -- entry visible in specification of SECOND
   ...........
end FIRST;
```

The task SECOND initiates a call on the QUERY entry of FIRST and then waits for a call on its own ANSWER entry.

```
separate (TWO_TASKS)
task body SECOND is
   -- declarations local to SECOND
   Z : MESSAGE; -- type declaration visible in TWO_TASKS
begin
   .....
   FIRST.QUERY(Z); -- entry visible in the specification of FIRST
   .....
   accept ANSWER (X : in MESSAGE) do
      -- code of rendezvous of FIRST with SECOND
      Z := X; -- takes copy of reply message
   end ANSWER;
   .....
end SECOND;
```

The code of each task is initiated when its body is elaborated. They then execute 'concurrently' with the imperative part of the program unit in which they are declared.

The Ada tasking mechanism offers a way of providing for the concurrency of execution frequently required in embedded systems programs, and the rendezvous provides a secure method of enabling them to communicate. The full power of these mechanisms is explained and demonstrated in chapter 9.

References

[5.1] "Reference Manual for the Ada Programming Language"; Jean Ichbiah et al; US Department of Defense, July 1980.

[5.2] "Mass Produced Software Components"; M D McIlroy; Proceedings of the Software Engineering conference sponsored by NATO Science Committee, 1968.

Exercise 5

5.1 Which of the following are not valid Ada identifiers?

X   4_SIGHT   DAYS_IN_THE_YEAR   X3H1   LENGTH-OF-RUN

5.2 What are the program units of Ada?

5.3 Which program units can be compiled as stand alone components?

5.4 What are the advantages of using stubs for unit bodies?

CHAPTER 6

MODELLING THE PROBLEM DOMAIN

6.1 Types, Variables and Constants

As explained in chapter 2, an Ada program models the problem domain by the use of data items and operations. The data items, which may be constants or variables, represent values and properties of the objects they model. Each such object has its characteristic attributes, which it usually shares with a class of similar objects. Such attributes are represented in a program by giving to each data value a characteristic **type.** The type of a data object defines the set of values which it may take, and the set of operations in which it may participate. The concept of type is extremely important in Ada programming. Ada being a strongly typed language, it is a role of the compiler to ensure that only legal operations are performed and that values are not transferred between objects of logically unrelated classes. Many logical errors may be detected during the process of compilation. Logical errors in the program may cause a value to be computed and assigned to a variable which lies outside that set legal for the type. The compiler will normally insert code to check the legality of each operation; any violation may cause an error to be reported during execution of the program.

Each data item and each type is referred to in the program by an identifier, a name chosen freely by the programmer. Good programming practice requires that the names chosen should be meaningful in the context of the problem, not ugly mnemonics and abbreviations. In this way the text of the program is made as clear as possible to read, the names conveying to the reader the concepts represented by the named items.

If T is the name chosen for some type, a variable of type T is introduced to the program by a 'variable_declaration' of the form:

```
VARIABLE_NAME: T;
```

Some types are predefined in the language. Such predefined types are those familiar in many other languages. Thus, variables may be declared to belong to any of the following types, without defining its meaning.

```
INTEGER
FLOAT
BOOLEAN
CHARACTER
STRING
```

These are primitive types of the Ada language. Types INTEGER and FLOAT correspond to the numeric types; their properties are those of the numbers of mathematics, restricted to subsets by the finite number of bits in the internal machine representation. They are, therefore, machine dependent.

Variables of BOOLEAN type are suitable to represent truth values, TRUE or FALSE. The type CHARACTER is used for variables whose values may be characters from the ASCII character set. STRING type is for variables whose values are text items, strings of characters from the ASCII character set. These will be described later.

Variables are not automatically initialised at the time of their declaration. The declaration:

```
PATIENT_AGE: INTEGER;
```

creates a variable whose value depends on the accident of what happens to be lying in the store which is allocated to the new variable. However, initialisation can be included by writing, for example:

```
PATIENT_AGE: INTEGER := 0;
```

which ensures that, initially, PATIENT_AGE is zero. (Appropriate for a newly born object, presumably). Of course any value of the type integer would be legal. The symbol := , called the assignment operator, is used whenever a value is to be assigned to a variable or constant.

The variable PATIENT_AGE may be given new values by assignment operations during the course of the program execution. However, data items may also be declared which are constants of some type. These are declared by writing a declaration of the form:

```
PI: constant FLOAT := 3.14158;
```

The compiler will control the correct use of such a constant, not permitting the program to change the value by assignment. In other respects it behaves like any variable of type FLOAT.

Facilities are provided, however, to enable programmers to define types for data objects which are members of distinct classes in the problem domain. The maximum benefit is obtained from strong typing, as an aid to program correctness, if a special type is declared for objects of a distinguishable class, even if they share most or all of the properties of some existing type.

Data objects may be simple objects or they may be composite. Simple data objects possess at any time a single value from the possible values of the type. Such objects are called scalars, and corresponding types are scalar types. Composite types are described by collections of values of simpler types. The standard types, with the exception of strings, are scalar types. In general scalar types may be:

- enumeration types
- numeric types

while composite types are constructed in terms of :

- array types
- record types

These classes of types are described in the following sections.

Access types, which are discussed in chapter 12, may be regarded as a special class of scalar type.

6.2 Enumeration Types

Very many items to be described in a program are not numeric in nature: rather, they take one of a set of values which have conventional names in the problem area. In a car body shop, an important variable in defining the paint to be used for painting some car body is the colour. A colour does not have values 1,2,3 ... but values red, green, blue, etc. The programmer can introduce a variable to represent the body colour as follows:

```
type COLOUR is (RED, GREEN, BLUE, YELLOW, WHITE, BLACK);
BODY_COLOUR: COLOUR;
```

This new variable may be given a value in an assignment statement:

```
BODY_COLOR:= BLUE;
```

The names given to the set of possible values are called 'enumeration literals'. The rules for choosing these names are the same as for other identifiers, except that they may also include character literals. Of course operations of arithmetic on such items are meaningless, and illegal.

Some further examples of types with suggestive meanings are:

```
type DAY is (MONDAY, TUESDAY, WEDNESDAY, THURSDAY,
                                    FRIDAY, SATURDAY, SUNDAY);
type SWITCH_STATE is (OFF, ON);
type LANGUAGE is (FORTRAN, COBOL, ADA);
type NEWSPAPER is (SUN, STAR, TIMES, EXAMINER);
type HEAVENLY_BODY is (SUN, STAR, COMET);
type VOWEL is ('A', 'E', 'I', 'O', 'U');
type FLUID_INTAKE is (DRINK, DRIP_FEED, TRANSFUSION, INJECTION)
type SEX is (MALE, FEMALE);
type FACTOR is (TEMPERATURE, BLOOD_PRESSURE, HEART_RATE, FLUID);
```

Identical enumeration literals, such as SUN and STAR, in different type declarations are not errors. The meanings are distinguished by context. In real life, a customer in a newspaper shop asking to buy the SUN would not cause any ambiguity; so it is with types. A variable declared:

```
JOURNAL: NEWSPAPER;
```

may subsequently be assigned a value

```
JOURNAL:= SUN;
```

which cannot refer to the HEAVENLY_BODY since JOURNAL is of type NEWSPAPER.

The names SUN and STAR are said to be 'overloaded'. This is a technical term for the use of the same identifier with more than one meaning. It is used also with procedures, as explained in chapter 8. It is considered preferable to allow reuse of a name, to be distinguished by context, rather than cause the programmer to invent artificial alternative names. There are very few circumstances in which any ambiguity is possible: one situation involves parameters of an overloaded function, as described in chapter 8. When there is a need to make a distinction, either to resolve such an ambiguity, or to make the program more readable, the value on the right of the assignment can be qualified by the type name using the notation:

```
NEWSPAPER'(SUN);
```

Values of an enumeration type are considered ordered in the order in which they are specified. Thus, in type LANGUAGE as defined above the relations FORTRAN < COBOL < ADA hold. In that example the order does not correspond to any natural ordering, so may be ignored. On the other hand in type DAY the order corresponds to a fundamental property of the type in question.

The types BOOLEAN and CHARACTER are considered to be predefined enumeration types:

```
type BOOLEAN   is (FALSE, TRUE);
type CHARACTER is (nul, ...  'A', 'B', ..  'Z' etc.);
```

These types have special properties provided by the language. However, variables of user-defined enumeration types have a somewhat restricted set of standard operations available. It is usually one of the purposes of the program to generate appropriate special operations for the objects being modelled. These must be constructed from the rather restricted set of primitive operations supplied by the system. These are as follows:

Variables of like type may be assigned to each other.

Values from the set of literals of the type may be assigned to variables.

Values may be compared, using the ordering which is implicit in the declaration.

It is possible to enquire as to the next and the preceding values in the declared set. If, for example YESTERDAY, TODAY and TOMORROW are of type DAY then the assignment:

```
TOMORROW  := DAY'SUCC(TODAY);
YESTERDAY := DAY'PRED(TODAY);
```

create the expected relationships[+].

The position in the ordered set corresponding to the current value of some variable can be similarly discovered. Thus, DAY'POS(TODAY) returns the integer value corresponding to the position of the current value in the week, starting from zero. Thus DAY'POS(FRIDAY) has the value 4. Conversely DAY'VAL(4) has the value FRIDAY.

6.3 Attribute Enquiries

The expressions such as DAY'SUCC(TODAY) are examples of 'attribute enquiries'. Several properties of objects according to their types may be accessed by the program in this way. In general if T is any enumeration type, and X is a variable of the type, then

```
T'FIRST, T'LAST
```

yield respectively the values of the first and last values as specified in the enumeration. Similarly

```
T'SUCC(X), T'PRED(X)
```

yield, as explained above, respectively the values following and preceding the value X in the enumeration. If X = T'LAST then the evaluation of T'SUCC(X) leads to an error, the raising of a CONSTRAINT_ERROR exception, while evaluation of T'PRED(X) leads to the same error if X = T'FIRST.

[+] Note, however, that such a type is not cyclic. The evaluation of DAY'SUCC(SUNDAY) is an error, as explained below for a more general case.

The use of attribute enquiries must be regarded as an important technique in Ada programming. It relieves the programmer of the obligation to know or to remember details of the all the types in the program, so reducing the probability of error. The written form of the program becomes less dependent on those details decreasing its vulnerability to changes in the type specifications in the course of maintenance of other program parts. Types are effectively more abstract.

Other types also have relevant attributes, for which enquiries are possible. Many of these will be described in connection with the types in question, but the language reference manual should be consulted for the full list.

6.4 Numeric Types

Variables may be declared to belong to the standard types INTEGER or FLOAT. Consider, for example:

```
BED_NUMBER : INTEGER;
TEMPERATURE: FLOAT;
```

This has a number of disadvantages. First, as remarked earlier, the maximum sizes of both variables, and the precision in the case of the TEMPERATURE, are machine dependent. There are other reasons, however, why it would be better to introduce special types. Assuming the variables have the meanings suggested by the names, both TEMPERATURE and BED_NUMBER are non-negative. By defining types for which negative values do not exist, program errors leading to the calculation of a negative bed number or temperature could have been automatically detected as errors equivalent to overflow of the INTEGER type. In Ada programming, programmers are encouraged to introduce special types for objects of logically distinct classes. Consider first the integer values.

6.4.1 Integer Types

Possibly, in addition to the bed numbers, the hospital requires the program also to keep record of a patient's age, which might be done using:

```
PATIENT_AGE: INTEGER;
```

There is now nothing to prevent PATIENT_AGE being used in an operation intended for BED_NUMBER. Moreover, arithmetic would be legal. If CRAZY is also a variable of type INTEGER then

```
CRAZY := BED_NUMBER + PATIENT_AGE;
```

would be valid, even though it is surely nonsense. An opportunity has been lost to utilise the automatic error checking provided by the compiler, through strong typing. A better solution would be to recognize the intrinsic difference between the objects being counted, and introduce special types for counting ages and bed numbers. They clearly belong to different classes.

```
type BED is range 1 .. 16;
type AGE is range 0 .. 100;

PATIENT_AGE: AGE;
BED_NUMBER : BED;
```

BED_NUMBER, and PATIENT_AGE cannot now take values outside their expected ranges; moreover the above nonsensical calculation would now be illegal, and would be rejected by the compiler.

It may seem unlikely that a programmer would be so foolish as to write such a statement in the first place. However, this is a very simple illustration of the way in which strong typing can help to prevent errors. Control of correctness of the use of types extends to the parameters of procedures and functions, and task entries, for example, which form the main mechanisms of exchange of information between separate components of a program. In a complex program, written by a team of programmers, the opportunities for error are numerous; a well known law of nature can be paraphrased, 'If an error can happen, it will'. Strong typing is a powerful aid to correctness which, if used fully, can make a large group of errors impossible.

A type defined by the use of the reserved word **range** as in the above examples, has all the properties of an integer, but with a programmer specified range. This is therefore not machine dependent, and the program is guaranteed to have the same behaviour on all machines. Each separate type definition introduces a different type, even if the ranges specified are the same.

Arithmetic is valid on user-defined numeric types, but unless special provision is made in the program, as explained in section 8.8, the operations of arithmetic must receive operands of the same type, and they then produce results which are also of the same type.

As with enumeration types, the smallest and the largest values of other discrete types may be discovered using the attribute enquiries 'FIRST and 'LAST. In the above examples AGE'FIRST and AGE'LAST have the values 1 and 100 respectively. INTEGER'LAST reveals the largest whole number which can be stored in the hardware representation of the integer type.

Collectively, enumeration types, including BOOLEAN and CHARACTER, and integer types, including both the predefined type INTEGER and types defined by the use of **range**, are referred to as discrete types. This is in contrast to the real types, which are sets approximating the continuum of values from the real number set.

6.4.2 Real Numbers

Variables to represent real numbers, whose possible values include fractional parts, may similarly be given unique types. These specify both the range of variables of the type, and their precision. However, the precision can be specified in one of two ways, floating and fixed point. Floating point types use the reserved word **digits** to define the number of significant digits with which the values must be represented.

```
type KILOS  is digits 6 range 0.0 ..  1.0E10;
type POUNDS is digits 6 range 0.0 ..  1.0E10;

MASS: KILOS;
QUANTITY: POUNDS;
```

These are floating point variables stored to a precision of six significant figures. Since POUNDS and KILOS have been defined separately, they are distinct types and the erroneous mixing of variables with different units would be prevented by the compiler.

Fixed point types are declared:

```
type AZIMUTH   is delta 0.001 range  0.0 ..  360.0;
type ELEVATION is delta 0.01  range -90.0 ..  90.0;

THETA: ELEVATION;
PHI: AZIMUTH;
```

These define variables whose precisions are given to fixed accuracies in decimal digits. It should not be assumed, however, that the values are multiples of the specified delta. The compiler is required only to ensure that the precision is at least as high as that specified, and a nearby binary value may be used. The arithmetic is still approximate.

Attribute enquiries relevant to floating and fixed point types include the evaluation of the smallest and largest values of the type using 'FIRST and 'LAST and also, in the case of some fixed point type, MY_FIX, the actual value used for delta, which may be accessed by referring to MY_FIX'ACTUAL_DELTA. Other enquiries can reveal details of the machine representations.

6.5 Constraints and Subtypes

A type defines a set of values. It is frequently appropriate to create variables whose properties are those of some existing type except that the possible set of values is restricted to a subset of the values for the type in question. This can be done using a 'constraint'. All discrete types constitute ordered sets of values, which can be restricted by the use of a 'range constraint', to define a subtype. For example:

```
subtype LETTER    is CHARACTER range 'A' ..  'Z';
subtype WEEK_DAY  is DAY       range MONDAY ..  FRIDAY;
subtype SUBSCRIPT is INTEGER   range 0 ..  100;

INDEX   : SUBSCRIPT;
ALPHA   : LETTER;
WORK_DAY: WEEK_DAY;
```

A variable such as INDEX, of type SUBSCRIPT, is now a variable with all the properties of an integer variable, except that its possible values are restricted to the specified range. It can participate with other integer types in the operations on integers, and assignments of INDEX to a variable of integer type is valid. If, for example, TOTAL is a variable of type INTEGER then

```
TOTAL:= INDEX;
```

is a valid assignment. Assignment in the opposite direction

```
INDEX := TOTAL;
```

is valid also, provided the current value of TOTAL is within the range specified for the subtype SUBSCRIPT. A CONSTRAINT_ERROR exception will be raised if this condition is violated at run time.

Similarly, TODAY of type DAY can be given a value by assignment from WORKDAY:

```
TODAY := WORKDAY;
```

On the other hand, the assignment

```
WORKDAY := TODAY;
```

requires a run time check that the current value of TODAY is within the restricted range.

Note that the assignment

```
WORKDAY := SATURDAY;
```

always produces an error, recognised by the compiler. However, all values of the parent type may be used in comparisons. Thus

```
WORKDAY < SATURDAY;
```

is legal, but always true.

It is perhaps helpful to emphasise the difference between INDEX defined in this way, and the variable, PATIENT_AGE previously defined

```
type AGE is range 0 .. 100;
PATIENT_AGE: AGE;
```

Although PATIENT_AGE is also derived from INTEGER, it is a distinct type, and assignments

```
TOTAL := PATIENT_AGE; and  PATIENT_AGE := INDEX;
```

would be illegal. Explicit type conversion is, however, possible. Thus

```
PATIENT_AGE := AGE(INDEX)+ ;
```

is valid. In general, type conversions are permitted between logically related types, which includes all numeric types. Run time checks may often be introduced by the compiler to ensure that the conversion is possible.

Constraints may also be applied to floating and fixed point types, producing subtypes. These may change the precision or the range of the base type, but only towards smaller ranges or less precision. For example:

```
type LENGTH is digits 10 range 0.0 .. 1000.0
subtype APPROXIMATE_LENGTH is LENGTH digits 5;

type BEARING is delta 0.125 range 0.0 .. 360.0;
subtype DIRECTION is BEARING delta 1.0;
            --same range as BEARING, accuracy one degree
```

It may be helpful to consider the standard types INTEGER and FLOAT as subtypes of the infinite base types consisting of the corresponding sets of true numbers, the constraints being those imposed by hardware.

Further examples of constraints and subtypes will appear in later sections.

+ Note the difference between, say,

```
            AGE'(5)        --a qualified expression
and         AGE(INDEX)     --a type conversion
```

The first clarifies that it is the 'age' of value 5 to which the expression refers, but does not change the type. The second is a type conversion, returning a value of type AGE numerically equal to the value of the INDEX.

6.6 Derived Types

Each new type definition defines a new type, though when the types are numeric, explicit conversions are permitted. If, however, types are declared, say:

```
type SWITCH_STATE is (OFF, ON);
type LIGHT_STATE  is (OFF, ON);
```

These declarations introduce logically unrelated types. Thus variables

```
SWITCH: SWITCH_STATE;    LIGHT: LIGHT_STATE;
```

are from unrelated sets, and the assignment

```
LIGHT := SWITCH;
```

is illegal. Even type conversion is illegal. It is, however, possible to create types which, though distinct, are logically related. Thus

```
type SWITCH_STATE is (OFF, ON);
type LIGHT_STATE is new SWITCH_STATE;
```

When declared in terms of the existing type using the reserved word **new**, LIGHT_STATE is said to be derived from SWITCH_STATE. With this alternative definition of the types, the assignment

```
LIGHT := SWITCH;
```

is still illegal, but conversion is possible.

```
LIGHT := LIGHT_STATE(SWITCH);
```

will assign corresponding values to the two variables.

User defined numeric types are regarded as derived from the parent numeric type. Thus type AGE could have been declared

```
type AGE is new INTEGER range 0 ..  100;
```

with the same effect as before.

6.7 Composite Types

Few items of interest are sufficiently described by a single value. An adequate model of any real object usually involves a collection of values. In most cases these values bear some structural relationship to each other. The representation of such structures in a program, therefore, requires a data structure. In Ada such structures are treated as generalisations of the concept of a type. The value of an object of composite type is a collection of values of simpler type. The latter, simpler, objects may themselves be composite; so a complex data type may be decomposed in a hierarchy ending with a collection of primitive objects, objects of scalar type, which cannot be further decomposed.

Composite types provide a level of abstraction in the description of data. Naming a structured type separates, in the programmer's mind, the concern for the concept which it models from the details of its computer representation.

Structured types belong to two main classes. These are

array types
record types

which are described in the following sections.

6.8 Arrays

An array is a collection of items of equal type accessible by an index. In its simplest form the concept models a subscripted variable in mathematics. Consider the following definitions:

```
type VECTOR is array (1 .. N) of FLOAT;
A,B: VECTOR;
```

These define a type, VECTOR, whose properties are those of a vector in linear algebra, and variables A and B, objects of the type. Each of the variables A and B now consists of a collection of N values of type FLOAT. The elements of an array variable are selected using the subscript notation. The Jth element of A is written A(J). (More generally J may be an expression of type INTEGER). In the program A(J) names an item of type FLOAT.

Space for arrays is allocated during program execution: index ranges may be specified in terms of variables whose values are known at the points in the program where the declarations appear. In the present case the lower bound is given as 1, a common case in practice, but not essential. The bounds could also be given as expressions.

```
type MY_VECTOR is array (N .. N+M) of FLOAT;
```

In the case of **type** VECTOR the index is a subtype of INTEGER. This is implied by the fact that the range of the index has been specified in terms of integer values. It is common, however, to represent data in arrays whose appropriate index is not numeric.

Consider, for example, the use of a table giving the rainfall in each month of the year, drawn from weather statistics of some observatory.

```
type RAINFALL is delta 0.1 range 0.0 .. 200.0;
type MONTH is
     (JANUARY, FEBRUARY, MARCH, APRIL, MAY, JUNE,
         JULY, AUGUST, SEPTEMBER, OCTOBER, NOVEMBER, DECEMBER);
type WEATHER_DATA is array (MONTH) of RAINFALL;

RAIN_DATA: WEATHER_DATA;
```

The variable RAIN_DATA is now an array indexed by the months in the year. An element of the table, say RAIN_DATA(JULY), gives a value of type RAINFALL which is a number, stored to the nearest 1/10th inch, as a fixed point variable.

In general the syntax for an array definition allows the index to be a discrete range, while the components may be of any type. This generality permits arrays to be constructed from collections of other arrays, records, access variables, or tasks, and so gives great power to describe complex objects.

The specification of a 'discrete range' for the index implies that it may be of any discrete type, though type INTEGER is permitted only with a range constraint. Permitted index specifications may thus be

an enumeration type
any discrete type constrained to a range

The MONTH in the above example is a case of the first alternative. Perhaps, however, a table is required only for the summer months JUN .. SEP.

```
type SUMMER_RAIN is array (MONTH range JUNE .. SEPTEMBER) of
                                    RAINFALL;
```

defines a table with four elements, one for each month in the given range.

For INTEGER ranges only, the abbreviated form obtained by omitting the type name and the word 'range' is permitted. Thus, the type VECTOR used as the first example could have been spelt out as

```
type VECTOR is array (INTEGER range 1 .. N) of FLOAT;
```

Array variables of identical type may be assigned to each other. This involves making a complete copy. In the case of the variables A and B declared above

```
A := B;
```

is a valid assignment. Values may also be given to every element of an array in an array aggregate assignment. There are many ways of specifying an aggregate, which are given in full in section 7.2. As an example, if all the elements of A are to be set to zero, this can be done by writing

```
A := (1 .. N => 0.0);
```

Though the index of an array variable must be a constrained discrete type, the specification of the range constraint may be deferred until the variable is declared.

```
type LIST_TYPE is array (INTEGER range <>) of ITEM;
```

The symbol <> is used to indicate a range to be specified later. The type is now said to be unconstrained; the range of the index must now be given when a variable of the type is declared

```
LIST: LIST_TYPE(10 .. 100);
```

creates a variable of type LIST with the index range given.

In general, arrays may be multi-dimensional. Thus

```
type MATRIX is array (1 .. N,1 .. M) of FLOAT;
```

is an obvious generalisation of the type VECTOR.

The indices may again be of any discrete types, and may be of mixed types. They may again be left undefined by the use of the symbol <>, but all dimensions must be unconstrained or all constrained.

```
type UNCONSTRAINED_MATRIX
    is array (INTEGER range <>,INTEGER range <>)of FLOAT;
```

The application of a constraint generates a subtype, which can be named:

```
subtype SHORT_LIST is LIST_TYPE(1 .. 5);
subtype WORLD_TENSOR is UNCONSTRAINED_MATRIX (1 .. 4, 1 .. 4);
```

6.8.1 Attribute Enquiries for Array Types

Just as it is possible to write program sequences which access the properties of a simple type by attribute enquiries, so a programmer writing a program to operate on an array may do so without full knowledge of all its properties, by using array attributes. For example, if A_TYPE is an array type, and A is a variable of the type, then the enquiries A_TYPE'LENGTH or equivalently A'LENGTH returns the number of elements in the array. A_TYPE'RANGE or A'RANGE returns the range of the index. Note that its value is the **range**, including the type and its limits. Finally, A_TYPE'FIRST and A_TYPE'LAST give the first and the last values of the index. A(A_TYPE'FIRST) is the first value in the array. Examples of the use of these enquiries are given in chapter 7.

6.8.2 Strings

The predefined type STRING is an array of characters. Its definition is equivalent to

```
subtype NATURAL is INTEGER range 1 .. INTEGER'LAST;
type STRING is array (NATURAL range <>) of CHARACTER;
```

For a constant of type STRING the index range is deduced from the value given in the definition. A variable of type string must be declared with the range of its index. Thus:

```
GANGSTER: constant STRING := "Al Capone";
                      --a string of 9 characters
PRESIDENT: STRING(1 .. 20);
```

The latter declares a variable suitable for storing a name of twenty characters. Later it may receive a value in an assignment

```
PRESIDENT := "GEORGE WASHINGTON   ";
```

A string literal in quotes should be regarded as a special kind of array aggregate, for character arrays.

6.8.3 **Anonymous Array Types**

In the case of arrays only, variables may be associated with a type in an anonymous type definition. For example

```
SCHEDULE: array (DAY) of HOURS;
```

creates a variable with the properties of the specified type, without naming the type.

This is equivalent to the declarations:

```
type X is array (DAY) of HOURS;
SCHEDULE : X;
```

but where the name X is invisible to the program.

The use of anonymous arrays is often convenient, to avoid introducing extra names in the program. However, the type of SCHEDULE is different from that of any other variable, and SCHEDULE could never form an actual parameter in a procedure call, as described in chapter 8.

Another variable

```
PLAN: array (DAY) of HOURS;
```

is not of the same type.

This is another instance of the general rule that each new type definition introduces a new type. Variables of equal type are always derived from the same type definition, which implies either that they are declared in the same declaration statement,

```
PLAN, SCHEDULE: array (DAY) of HOURS;
```

or else the type must be named.

Of course, components of SCHEDULE are referred to, for example, as SCHEDULE(MONDAY) and are objects belonging to the named type HOURS.

6.9 Record Types

An array collects into a single logical unit a set of values of equal type. Records provide named collections of items of possibly mixed types. Such a collection is commonly required to provide a representation of a world object. Perhaps the most familiar case of a concept which is constructed in this way in every day life is a date. Thus the declarations:

```
type MONTH_TYPE is
     (JANUARY, FEBRUARY, MARCH, APRIL, MAY, JUNE,
         JULY, AUGUST, SEPTEMBER, OCTOBER, NOVEMBER, DECEMBER);
type DATE is
     record
         DAY: INTEGER range 1 .. 31;
         MONTH: MONTH_TYPE;
         YEAR: INTEGER range 1901 .. 2999;
     end record;
```

create a type consisting of three components, forming together a date in the conventional calendar. The subsequent declaration:

```
BIRTH: DATE;
```

creates a variable of the type. The fields of a record are referred to by the dot notation, yielding a 'selected component'

```
BIRTH.MONTH
```

This can be thought of as equivalent to the apostrophe s which denotes a possessive in English. BIRTH.MONTH means the month of birth, or birth's month. A value can be assigned to the selected field:

```
BIRTH.MONTH := JANUARY;
```

Three separate assignments could be used to fill the fields of the record, but a record aggregate may be used to give values to all the fields of the record at once.

```
BIRTH := (5, JANUARY, 1982);
```

A full account of the use of record and array aggregates is be given in chapter 7.

A record type defines a structure consisting of a collection of fields, each a variable definition, describing a component part of any object conforming to the type. Thus, in the DATE record there are fields of appropriate type for the year, for the month and for the day. In general the fields may themselves be of structured type, other records, arrays or indeed, as discussed in chapter 9, a record field may be a variable of some task type. As remarked in connection with arrays, records permit the programmer to take an abstract view of complex objects, structured as a hierarchy of simpler elements.

The declarations in the fields of the record may include initialization assignments. In that case every variable declared to be of the type is created with that field already initialized.

The following declarations describe a control panel consisting of a set of ten toggle switches, a potentiometer controlling some speed on a continuous basis, and a decade switch in one of ten positions.

The panel called PLANT_CONTROL is created with all its switches set to OFF or to zero.

```
type POTENTIOMETER is delta 0.1 range 0.0 ..  360.0;
type SWITCH_STATE  is (OFF, ON);
type DECADE         is range 0 ..  9;
type SWITCH_ARRAY is array (1 ..  10) of SWITCH_STATE;
    type CONTROL_PANEL is
        record
        KEYS: SWITCH_ARRAY := (1 ..  10 => OFF);
        SPEED_CONTROL:  POTENTIOMETER := 0.0;
        DECADE_SWITCH: DECADE         := 0;
    end record;
PLANT_CONTROL: CONTROL_PANEL;
```

6.9.1 **Variant Records**

In considering complex objects, it is common to recognize situations in which a class of related objects are described by the same collection of values in most respects, but that sub classes can be recognized which differ in some details. To permit the modelling of this kind of variation Ada typing includes facilities to declare record variants. Consider a system of communicating control centres which interact by passing messages. There are three types of message, to provide emergency transmission of an alarm signal, to send a message to all other centres, not requiring a reply, and to send a message to a particular destination, requesting the reply containing some information. Such a message could be contained in a record whose type is defined as follows:

```
type CENTRE_NUMBER is range 1 ..  10;
type MESSAGE_CLASS is (ALARM, REQUEST_REPLY, BROADCAST);
type MESSAGE (CLASS: MESSAGE_CLASS) is
  record
    DATA: STRING(1 ..  1024);
    LENGTH: INTEGER range 0 ..  1023;
    SOURCE: CENTRE_NUMBER;
    case CLASS is
        when ALARM          =>
              URGENCY: INTEGER range 1 ..  5;
        when BROADCAST      =>
              null;
```

--continued

```
-- MESSAGE continued

                    when REQUEST_REPLY =>
                              DESTINATION: CENTRE_NUMBER;
                              TIMEOUT: DURATION;
               end case;
          end record;
```

CLASS, although given special prominance in the syntactic structure of the record, behaves in many respects like a normal field. Additionally, however, it is a discriminant, serving as a parameter selecting one of the three message variants. The choice is determined by the current value of the discriminant field of the record, according to the possibilities listed in the case clauses. Each possible value of the discriminant must be covered by some case, though unmentioned cases may by covered by **'others'**. The rules for cases in a variant record are exactly the same as for case statements described in full in chapter 7.

```
          COMMUNICATION: MESSAGE(CLASS => BROADCAST);
```

declares a variable with the structure of a MESSAGE constrained to a BROADCAST variant.

When a record is declared with a discriminant, the value of the discriminant must be defined by the time a variable of the type is created. In the above example this was done at the declaration of the variable. The value of the discriminant cannot now be changed, and the variable COMMUNICATION can only contain a BROADCAST message.

If, however, a default value for the discriminant is given in the declaration of the type:

```
          type MESSAGE(CLASS: MESSAGE_CLASS := ALARM) is
               record
                    -- as before

          UNIVERSAL_COMMUNICATION: MESSAGE;
```

now creates a variable which is a message of the variant suitable for an alarm message. However, that is now not immutably fixed. The field of the record corresponding to the discriminant can be changed by assignment, provided the whole record is being changed, in an aggregate assignment, or by assigning another record of the other variant. e.g

```
UNIVERSAL_COMMUNICATION := COMMUNICATION;
```

switches it to the BROADCAST class.

In this form the type is unconstrained, and can be used to generate subtypes:

```
subtype BROADCAST_MESSAGE is MESSAGE (CLASS => BROADCAST);
subtype ALARM_MESSAGE is MESSAGE (CLASS => ALARM);
```

A discriminant may also be used to control the size of an array within a record. In the following MAX is a previously declared constant (>50):

```
subtype POINTER is INTEGER range 1 ..  MAX;
type QUEUE(SIZE: POINTER := 50) is
   record
      INPOINT, OUTPOINT: POINTER := 1;
      STORE: array (1 ..  SIZE) of ITEM;
   end record;

QUEUE_FOR_TAXI: QUEUE;
                        -- a default of 50 entries
QUEUE_FOR_BUS : QUEUE(25)
                        -- a maximum of 25 entries
```

6.10 Operations on Variables of User Defined Types

The operations relevant to a given type depend on the properties of the objects being modelled in the problem domain. These are defined by appropriate program segments, also constructed by the programmer, in the form of functions and procedures, named program subunits taking parameters of specified types. An account of the rules for writing and using subprograms is given in chapter 8. Earlier in the present chapter it was emphasised that the full concept of a type includes the associated set of operations. In a type definition statement:

```
type T is ....;
```

the possible set of values is specified. The full concept of a type, including its defined operations, is obtained by constructing a package, encapsulating the definition of the type(i.e its value set) with the definition of its associated operations. This more complete notion of type is discussed more fully in chapter 10.

6.11 Storage allocation and Dynamically Variable Structures

This chapter has described the main facilities offered by Ada for the construction of data types and data structures. Variables of the types defined are declared in declaration statements, which give rise to allocation of storage for the objects declared on the system stack. This space is released when the items in question go out of 'scope'. The rules for the scope of variables are described later in section 8.3.

The size of an array, and the range constraints of a subtype, may be determined at 'run time' from expressions involving variables whose values are known at the point of declaration.

The data structures created in this way are static, in the sense that, following an activation of the unit in which an object is declared, space has been allocated for it, and its size cannot subsequently be changed. An array, for example, once created has a fixed number of elements.

Ada provides facilities, also, to create structures which are dynamically variable, by the use of access variables. This will be described in full in chapter 12.

6.12 Example of a Complex Data Structure

This completes the present account of the facilities offered in Ada for defining types and structures. Careful use of these facilities will enable programs to be written using data definitions which are elegant, easy to understand, using meaningful names from the problem area. To give an example in full of a fairly complex structure, consider the description of a patient in the patient monitoring system. This is close to the definition in the package SYSTEM_TYPES in the programs presented in chapter 16.

```
-- types for personal details of patients

subtype NAME_TYPE       is  STRING (1 ..  20);
subtype ADDRESS_TYPE    is  STRING (1 ..  50);
subtype PHONE_NO        is  STRING (1 ..  15);
subtype RELIGION        is  STRING (1 ..  20);
subtype RELATIONSHIP    is  STRING (1 ..  20);
type SEX is (MALE, FEMALE);
type KIN is
   record
     NAME             : NAME_TYPE;
     ADDRESS          : ADDRESS_TYPE;
     TELEPHONE_NUMBER: PHONE_NO;
     KINSHIP          : RELATIONSHIP;
end record;
type PERSONAL_INFO is
   record
     NAME             : NAME_TYPE;
     ADDRESS          : ADDRESS_TYPE;
     GENDER           : SEX;
     TELEPHONE_NUMBER: PHONE_NO;
     NEXT_OF_KIN      : KIN;
     BELIEF           : RELIGION;
   end record;
```

```
--types for patient factors

type CENTIGRADE       is digits 2 range  0.0 ..  50.0;
type MILLIMETRES      is digits 2 range  0.0 ..  200.0;
type PER_MINUTE       is digits 2 range  0.0 ..  200.0;
type LITRES           is digits 3 range -5.0 ..   5.0;
type FACTORS is
   record
     BODY_TEMP        : CENTIGRADE;
     RIGHT_ATRIAL,
     LEFT_ATRIAL,
     DIASTOLIC,
     SYSTOLIC         : MILLIMETRES;
     PULSE_RATE       : PER_MINUTE;
     FLUID_LOSS       : LITRES := 0.0;    --default for fluid balance
   end record;
type LIMITS is
   record
     LOWER,UPPER: FACTORS;
   end record;

MAXBEDS: constant := 16;                  --initially
type BED is range 1 ..  MAXBEDS;
type PATIENT is
   record
     PERSONAL_DETAILS: PERSONAL_INFO;
     MEDICAL_FACTORS : FACTORS;
     SAFE_RANGES     : LIMITS;
     POLL_INTERVAL   : DURATION := 30.0; --default half minute
     BED_NUMBER      : BED;
   end record;

INTENSIVE_CARE_UNIT: array (BED) of PATIENT;
```

This structure defines an array of patients, each of which possesses a set of attributes, many of which are themselves complex. To access, for example, the field of the 13th patient which represents the upper limit of the acceptable SYSTOLIC pressure, the program must refer to

```
INTENSIVE_CARE_UNIT(13).SAFE_RANGES.UPPER.SYSTOLIC
```

However, as explained in section 6.14, there exists a short hand method for simplifying accesses of this kind.

The data structures used to model a patient in the programs given in chapter 16 are in fact somewhat simpler than this, because it has proved convenient to distribute some of the parts of the structure in different program units.

6.13 Choosing Names

A difficulty with a strongly typed language, especially with one like Ada which encourages the creation of many different types, is the large number of extra names to be introduced to define the types involved. In many programs there may be almost as many types as there are variables. This often leads to a dilemma when a programmer is obliged to decide whether to give the obvious, meaningful name to the variable or to the type. In fact, a little thought will show that in most cases the common noun used to name a concept in everyday speech is the name of the class of objects, the type, rather than the name of a particular object. If it is possible to use a noun with the indefinite article, a or an, then the name refers to the class. Thus consider, for example, a date, a newspaper, a light_state. A particular instance of the class is named by qualifying the class name in some way; today's date, my newspaper, the kitchen light_state. The programmer should not be surprised, therefore, if the variable name, describing an instance of a type, being more strongly specialised, is longer than the type name itself.

On the other hand, the variable name will usually appear more often in the program, so there is a temptation to try to use a short name for the variable. In general good taste should be sufficient to ensure that meaningful names are used rather than ugly abbreviations. Proper names refer, of course, to instances of the type to which they belong.

```
JOHN, MARY: STUDENT;
```

Truth values, variables of type BOOLEAN are frequently adjectives in english:

```
        GOOD, VALID: BOOLEAN;
```

Pocedures, described in Chapter 8, name actions, so should usually be verbs.

In view of the strong mathematical tradition, the use of I,J for index variables is reasonable, for short lived variables in local scope, but the likelihood of obscuring some existing meaning of such a common name must be borne in mind. Abbreviations may be used to help simplify the expression of some algorithm, but they should not usually be used for names of objects which are known in several program units. So far as possible, when an abbreviation is used, the same abbreviation should be used consistently for the same objects. In the programs of the case study B has been freely used for the patients bed number, where it appears as a formal parameter in the definition of a procedure or function.

Difficulties become even greater when access variables are involved. It is then necessary to invent names for the basic type, the access type, and the variables of the type.

It is difficult to give much further advice on the choice of names except to recommend the selection of names which are meaningful in the problem area, as far as possible of the right part of speech, and in general to exercise good taste. In particular, avoid lazy options which make the program ugly to read.

6.14 **Renaming**

Ada permits renaming of objects, where that can help to make a program clearer. In general, giving a second name, an alias, to an object must be deplored. Nevertheless, there are many cases where it is preferable to writing a long, complex name, which is unlikely to be read in full by the reader. Thus, to access the upper limit of the systolic pressure, given above, the following declaration could be introduced

```
    S_MAX: MILLIMETRES renames
                      INTENSIVE_CARE_UNIT(13).SAFE_RANGES.UPPER.SYSTOLIC;
```

Within the scope of this declaration the concise name S_MAX could be used instead of the complex name. Note that the declaration allocates a type to the new name, and the compiler will, of course check that this agrees with the type of the object renamed.

Such renamings can be almost essential in making algorithms involving complex structures. Anticipating the use of **for** loops and **declare** blocks, (chapters 7 and 8), consider the program segment:

```
for B in BED loop
     declare
          S: MILLIMETRES renames
               INTENSIVE_CARE_UNIT(B).SAFE_RANGES.UPPER.SYSTOLIC;
     begin
          S := S + 1;
     end;
end loop;
```

Here, the very localised use of the renaming is surely clearer than writing the complete expression twice. Notice that the renaming declaration comes into effect on entry to the declare block, and S renames a different object on each cycle of the loop.

Renaming can be applied to variables, procedures, and functions and tasks. It may also be applied to task entries, which are renamed as procedures. The value of this will be seen later. Examples of most of these renamings will be found in later chapters.

A type may be renamed as a subtype, in which the subset of the values is the complete set; i.e. there is no additional constraint. In the patient monitor will be found the following declarations:

```
package PATIENT_IO is new INPUT_OUTPUT (UNIT_RECORD)
```

This generates a package containing a type INOUT_FILE, which is accessed by the dot notation as PATIENT_IO.INOUT_FILE. For clarity and simplicity this is <u>immediately</u> renamed as

```
subtype TRANSACTION_FILE is PATIENT_IO.INOUT_FILE;
```

Exercise 6

6.1 Choose types suitable for variables to represent the following

a) A state in the USA
b) The population of a state in the USA
c) A table of population, state by state
d) A state of New England
e) The temperature of a water bath, measured to an accuracy of 1/10th of a degree Farenheit
f) The speed of a vehicle measured to an accuracy of 0.1%. Vehicles often exceed the speed limit, but may be assumed not to exceed 100 MPH.
g) A position on the earth's surface, measured in longitude and latitude, to the nearest 1/100th of a degree in either direction.

6.2 Develop a model of a company, in terms of its name, address, etc. the type of its business, its departments, the staff on its payroll in each department etc.

6.3 A 'bus' consists of twelve wires, each carrying an analogue signal consisting of a voltage in the range 0 to 10 volts. Construct a type to model such a unit.

6.4 The collection of lifts serving a building, controlled by a computer, is a typical example of an embedded system, in which the collection of lifts is concurrently controlled to provide the service to passengers originating and leaving at one or other of a set of floors. The system consists of an array of lifts, each described by a set of variables giving the current state of the lifts themselves, together with a panel of buttons on which passengers record their destinations. There is also a collection of button pairs, up and down, to record requests from passengers awaiting service. Develop a model of such a lift system using the Ada data structures.

CHAPTER 7

EXPRESSIONS AND STATEMENTS

7.1 Manipulation of Data Objects

The previous chapter has shown how the Ada type facilities can be used to describe objects that are abstract representations of the problem domain. A program is concerned with the manipulation of these abstract objects in ways that model the behaviour of the system. Language features are required that allow the construction of new values from existing object values and this section describes how such constructions are written in Ada.

7.1.1 Arithmetic Expressions

An expression defines a rule for deriving a new value. The simplest expressions are those of arithmetic, and for these Ada provides the usual operators with the following order of precedence:

exponentiation	**
multiplication	*, /, **mod**, **rem**
unary operators	+, -
adding operators	+, -

The expression:

```
-X**N - A*B + C/E**4
```

would be evaluated in the order shown by the brackets:

```
(((-(X**N)) - (A*B)) + (C/(E**4)))
```

however, brackets may be used to overrule the precedence laws:

```
(-X)**N - (A*B + (C/E)**4)
```

and these expressions may be as complex as required.

Exponentiation is defined only between left-hand operands of the types INTEGER, FLOAT, or their subtypes, and right-hand operands of type INTEGER. The other binary arithmetic operators of Ada are only defined for operands of matching type or subtypes and there are no automatic type conversions. However, explicit type conversion can be used as explained in sections 6.5 and 7.1.6 below.

The **mod** operator allows the construction of expressions which use modulo arithmetic. Thus, given COUNT initially equal to 9 and MAX_SIZE to 10, the value of

```
(COUNT + 1) mod MAX_SIZE
```

is 0. The **rem** operator gives the remainder on integer division.

Arithmetic operations on enumeration types or structures are, of course, meaningless and illegal. However, operations may be 'overloaded' to include arithmetic between elements of whole arrays, or slices, of equal size (see section 8.8).

Given the declarations:

```
A, B : array (1..10) of INTEGER;
```

then:

```
A - B -- subtracts each element of B from
      -- the corresponding element of A,

A(1..5) + B(6..10) -- A(1) is added to B(6), A(2) to B(7),
                   -- and so on, to A(5) and B(10).
```

All arithmetic expressions may contain constants. Pure numbers may be used with types derived from integer, fixed, or floating point numbers, as with the '48.0' in:

```
NEXT_TIME + 48.0*HOURS
```

For arrays, constants are formed by aggregates given as a bracketed list of values.

```
A - (2,2,2,2,2,2,2,2,2,2),     B(2..4) + (1,1,1)
```

The full rules for aggregates are covered in section 7.1.5 below.

In the case study, some arithmetic is performed on values that represent a patient's vital signs and strong typing is used to ensure that values are compatible so that, for example, a temperature reading for a patient is not added to his fluid balance. Modulo arithmetic is used, for example, in updating pointers to an array used as a circular buffer of records for file transfer.

7.1.2 Logical Expressions

Operators, in order of precedence, that can be used in boolean expressions, are

unary	**not**
relational	=, /=, >, <, >=, <=, **in**
logical	**and, or, xor**

Note that the logical operators **and, or** and **xor,** have equal precedence - an unusual situation compared with the majority of programming languages.

Given

```
P, Q, R: BOOLEAN;
```

then in the expression

P **or** Q **and** R

normal evaluation will be from left to right. Brackets are essential if the **and** is to be evaluated first.

P **or** (Q **and** R)

Boolean expressions include the standard comparisons such as

```
X <= Y
```

and these may be applied to numeric and enumeration types, such as:

```
TODAY >= WEDNESDAY
```

Logical expressions also include checks on subtype membership where the operator **in** (and **not in**) is used to determine whether or not a value of a parent type is within the constraints of a subtype.

For example, given the declaration of

```
type DAY is (MONDAY, TUESDAY, WEDNESDAY, THURSDAY,
             FRIDAY, SATURDAY, SUNDAY);
subtype WEEKDAY is DAY range MONDAY..FRIDAY;
TODAY : DAY;
```

then the following tests may be made:

```
TODAY in WEEKDAY -- true if the value of TODAY is in MONDAY..FRIDAY
TODAY in DAY range MONDAY..FRIDAY -- same test
TODAY not in WEEKDAY -- true if D is SATURDAY or SUNDAY
```

A shorthand notation may be used for integers only is :

```
I in 1..100
```

Logical operations and comparisons between arrays, and array slices, are carried out element by element. An array used to flag error conditions:

```
ERROR : array (1..3) of BOOLEAN := (FALSE,FALSE,FALSE);
```

can be tested with the expression:

```
ERROR = (FALSE,FALSE,FALSE)
```

which will have the value FALSE if any of the error flags have been set. An extension of this concept is used in the case study to test for errors in the hardware interface.

7.1.3 Character and String Operators

The ordering relationships are defined for characters in accordance with the standard ASCII character set. In this ordering, letters are ordered in the standard alphabetic order, so that 'A' < 'B'.

Strings of equal length can be compared, in which case the ordering is determined by the first non-matching character. The ordering is, therefore, that used in a dictionary, so that "ADA" < "ADD" is true.

Strings may be concatenated with other strings to form longer strings, using the operator &. Thus the constant string "Al " & "Capone" has the same value as the string "Al Capone". If a string is written on the page on more than one line, then the lines must be joined in this way. Thus:

```
"Al " &
"Capone"
```

is another way of writing the same string. Note that the string would not contain the carriage control character, so it would be written on one line on output. In fact, although the carriage control character is included in the type CHARACTER it does not have a representation as an enumeration literal such as 'A'. However, the standard environment contains a set of definitions of constants with values corresponding to the control characters. The carriage return is named ASCII.CR and this may be inserted in a string by using the concatenation operator. The interaction between the staff and the system in the patient monitor uses a menu-driven dialogue in which the menu to be sent to the screen is written in the program:

```
MENU: constant STRING :=

"               Please Choose Operation:           "& ASCII.CR &
"                   1) Enter New Safe Ranges       "& ASCII.CR &
"                   2) Enter New Timing            "& ASCII.CR &
"                   3) Enter Fluid Data            "& ASCII.CR &
"                   4) Enter Treatment Information"& ASCII.CR &
"                   5) Generate Report             "& ASCII.CR &
"                   6) Log Out Patient             "& ASCII.CR;
```

7.1.4 Type Conversion

Expressions may include explicit type conversion between logically related types, thus, given the declarations:

```
X : FLOAT;          N : INTEGER;
```

then X*Y would be illegal. However, X*FLOAT(N) causes N to be converted to a floating point representation before multiplication, and produces a result of type FLOAT.

INTEGER(X) rounds X to the nearest whole number.

7.1.5 **Aggregate Values**

Ada extends the concept of expressions to include aggregate values. These provide values for all the elements of a record or array type variable.

Aggregates may be a list of values separated by commas. In this case, the number of values must equal the number of elements in any array, or record, with which they are used. The position of each value in the aggregate indicates which array element, or record component, it is to be associated with. Examples of aggregates are:

```
(1,1,1) -- three integer values,
(TRUE, FALSE, TRUE, FALSE) -- four BOOLEAN enumeration constants,
(26, JUNE, 1982)  -- a date record,
```

This form of aggregate is said to use a positional notation.

Aggregates can also be given in an naming notation. With arrays the name of each element is its index, with records names are the identifiers of the individual components. Each name is associated with a value by the '=>' symbol:

```
(1=>10, 3=>5, 2=>0) is an equivalent aggregate to (10,0,5)
(MONTH=>JUNE, DAY=>26, YEAR=>1982) is a named aggregate for the date.
```

In the naming notation elements may appear in any order; this can be used to avoid any problems over compatible ordering with declarations. (In the date example it supports both European and American conventions.)

The names of elements taking the same value may be grouped together as a range:

```
(1..5=>0, 6..10=>5) -- five zeros followed by five tens,
```

or as a discrete list of items separated by ¦

```
(1¦3¦5=>TRUE, 2¦4=>FALSE) -- five boolean values alternatively
                          -- TRUE and FALSE,
```

The key word **others** may be used to set a value to all names not specified directly, but this can only be used in a context where the type of the aggregate is unambiguous, as with the declarations:

```
HOURS_WORKED : array (DAY) of INTEGER :=
               (FRIDAY=>7, others => 8);
ERROR : array (1..5) of BOOLEAN := (others=>FALSE);
```

An aggregate may start with the positional notation and then change to the named notation but, once abandoned, use of the positional notation cannot be resumed.

In using an aggregate to represent a value belonging to a variant record the discriminant must always appear before any of the components of the record that depend on the discriminant. In the case study the following type declarations are used to represent transaction records for a patient's history file (user defined types are used):

```
typeTRANSACTION_CLASS is (START_UP, VITAL_SIGNS,TREATMENT_SCHEDULE,
          TREATMENT_GIVEN,FLUID_TRANSACTION,NEW_LIMITS, NEW_TIMINGS);
type UNIT_RECORD (CLASS: TRANSACTION_CLASS:=VITAL_SIGNS) is
     record
          T: CALENDAR.TIME; -- a system defined type for time of day
          case CLASS is
               when START_UP  =>
                                        null;
               when VITAL_SIGNS  =>
                                        DATA    : FACTORS;
               when NEW_LIMITS  =>
                                        RANGES  : LIMITS;
                                        FLUID_RANGES: FLUID_LIMITS;
               when NEW_TIMINGS =>
                                        INTERVAL: DURATION;
               when FLUID_TRANSACTION  =>
                                        WHICH_FLUID  : FLUID;
                                        VOLUME:   LITRES;
               when others  =>
                                        TEXT: LINE;
          end case;
     end record;
```

Here, the discriminant CLASS is used to determine the structure of an actual record. Aggregates are used to compose particular unit records:

```
(CLASS=>TREATMENT_SCHEDULE, T=>CALENDAR.CLOCK; TEXT=>TREATMENT_PRESCRIBED)
```

7.2 Assignment Statements

Values computed in an expression can be assigned to a variable in a statement of the form:

```
VARIABLE_NAME := -- an expression;
```

The variable named must be able to take the result of evaluating the expression. This means that it must either be of the same type or of a subtype for which the result of the expression satisfies the constraints applied to the variable; this may involve a run-time check and any violation will cause an **exception** to be raised.

For example, given the declarations:

```
type TERMINAL_INDEX is INTEGER range 0..16;
subtype BED is INTEGER range 1..16;
T : TERMINAL_INDEX;
B : BED;
```

then the assignment T := B is always legal but the assignment B := T-1 will be legal only when the value of T is greater than 1. This will be checked at run time and, on failure, a CONSTRAINT_ERROR exception will be raised.

7.2.1 Aggregate Assignments

Named and positional aggregates may be used to assign values to arrays. For example, given the declaration:

```
A, B: array (1..5) of BOOLEAN;
```

then A := B will assign the whole of array B to A,

```
A(2..4) := (TRUE,TRUE,FALSE);
```

uses positional notation to assign values to the slice of the array A from A(2) to A(4),

```
A := (1..4=>TRUE, 5=>FALSE);
```

uses index naming notation to assign TRUE to the first four elements of A and FALSE to the fifth,

```
A := (TRUE, FALSE, 3..4=>TRUE, 5=>FALSE);
```

uses a mixture of positional and indexed notation.

The key word **others** may be used to specify all unmentioned index values

```
A := (1,4=>FALSE, others TRUE);
```

is equivalent to the aggregate (FALSE,TRUE,TRUE,FALSE,TRUE).

Aggregates can also be used to assign values to record objects. Given the declaration

```
D1, D2: DATE;
```

then

```
D1 := (15,MARCH,1982);
```

uses positional assignment.

Whole records can be assigned or components may be selectively altered, using the dot notation :

```
D2 := D1;
  D1.MONTH := JULY;
```

Aggregates may be used to give initial values to arrays or records at their declaration and to form constant array values:

```
A : array (1..100) of INTEGER := (1=>1, others =>0);
```

will initialize a 100 element array to zeros, apart from the first element.

When forming aggregates, a multi-dimensional array is considered to be an aggregate of values of one less dimension. Thus :

```
NULL_MATRIX : constant MATRIX := (1..10=>(1..10=>0));
```

will initialize a 10 by 10 matrix to zeros.

Recognising that an array provides a representation of a mapping between the index value and the component value, it may sometimes be appropriate to use named associations, so as to display the relation in a table:

```
A:= (1 => TRUE,
     2 => FALSE,
     3 => TRUE,
     4 => TRUE,
     5 => FALSE);
```

7.3 Program Control Statements

The construction of algorithms that model the behaviour of a computer system requires statements that can be used to control the sequence of execution of a program. In some cases a choice may be made between alternative actions, in others groups of statements are to be repeated under some constraint. Ada provides an **if** statement for a binary choice of actions, a **case** statement for choices over a discrete range, and a **loop** statement for repetitions. Each of these statements is bracketed by key words which indicate the start and end of the statement.

7.3.1 If Statements

The **if** statement allows a selection of actions based on the result of a logical (boolean) test.

For example, given the declarations

```
D : DAY;    W : INTEGER;
```

the following code will change the value of D to its successor and increase a weekly count held in W

```
if D = SUNDAY then
   D := MONDAY; W := W+1;
else
   D := DAY'SUCC(D);
end if;
```

This example shows the preferred comb structure of the layout of the statement. There must be a **then** part but the **else** part is optional. Often a further choice is required in the **else** part of an **if** statement. In Ada, this may be incorporated into a single **if** statement by using an **elsif.**

```
type AGE is INTEGER range 0..120;
type WELFARE is (CHILD_BENEFIT, PENSION, NONE);
MY_AGE: AGE;  WHAT_I_GET: WELFARE;
........
if MY_AGE < 16 then
    WHAT_I_GET := CHILD_BENEFIT;
elsif MY_AGE >= 65 then
    WHAT_I_GET := PENSION;
else
    WHAT_I_GET := NONE;
end if;
```

The **if** condition may be any Boolean expression. This includes a 'short-circuit condition' which ensures that when evaluation of the condition from left to right has obtained an unambiguous result, the rest of the expression will not be evaluated. This is obtained using the notations **and then** or **or else** to replace the corresponding boolean operators. Thus:

```
if I=0 or else N/I>MAX then.......
```

will ensure that the division by zero does not occur if the first term has already yielded TRUE.

Similarly,

```
if I<MAX_RANGE and then A(I) = 0 else .....
```

will not test the value of the array element if I is greater than MAX_RANGE. Short circuits like these can be used to prevent the execution of code that could generate an exception, and to improve efficiency.

7.3.2 Case Statements

The **case** statement allows a multiple choice of actions determined by a discrete value. In the following example D is of the enumeration type DAY.

```
case D is
   when MONDAY..THURSDAY => WORK;
   when FRIDAY           => WORK; PLAY;
   when SATURDAY|SUNDAY  => null;
end case;
```

Note that the empty statement is expressed as **null**.

The value given after **case** is called the discriminant and all possible values must be covered in choices of the statement, if necessary with the 'catch-all' **others**. The choices in the **when** branches of the statement may be given as a single value, a range, a set of values separated by |, or **others**.

Extensive use is made of the case statement in the patient monitoring system. Interaction with a bedside VDU is directed by the use of menus and a case statement is used to select from alternative actions from a character input at the terminal. Below is the case which responds to a character choice made against the menu shown in section 7.1.3.

```
GET_REPLY (BED_NUMBER, CHOICE); -- a procedure call retuning the
                                -- character choice for a given bed
   case CHOICE is
      when '1'    => ENTER_NEW_LIMITS (BED_NUMBER);       -- procedure
      when '2'    => ENTER_NEW_TIMING (BED_NUMBER);       -- calls for
      when '3'    => ENTER_FLUID_DATA (BED_NUMBER);       -- actions
      when '4'    => ENTER_TREATMENT_INFO (BED_NUMBER);-- to be
      when '5'    => GENERATE_DISPLAY (BED_NUMBER);       -- taken on
      when '6'    => LOG_OUT_PATIENT (BED_NUMBER);        -- menu choice
                     exit;  --from loop containing the case statement
      when others => REQUEST_REPEAT (BED_NUMBER); -- error in choice
   end case;
```

7.3.3 **Loop Statements**

Repeated actions are controlled by loop statements. A simple loop is written:

```
loop
   -- sequence of statements;
end loop;
```

Entered from above, this will cause the program to cycle, repeating forever the actions specified by the sequence of statements.

In a real time program, a loop which cycles forever is not unusual within a process that is eventually terminated by some external action. This will be seen in many of the tasks in the case study. However, it is more common to require that the program controlling a repeated action should specify the conditions for loop termination. There are several methods available.

An **exit** statement can be used to control the ending of a simple loop as in the following example:

```
loop
    GET_REPLY(CHOICE);
    exit when CHOICE in CHARACTER range '1'..'4';
    PUT_STRING(" Try again ");
 end loop;
```

Here a character is accepted from a bedside terminal. If it is not a valid reply then a 'try again' message is displayed and this repeats until a valid character is received.

In general, there may be a sequence of statements before the **exit** and a sequence of statements after the **exit.** Either of these sequences may be null. Exit may be used to give the effect of a 'pre-test' loop or a 'post-test' loop, when one or other of the empty options is chosen. When the condition is satisfied, control passes directly to the end of the loop. The **exit** may also be used unconditionally.

An example of a situation when the use of the **exit** seems appropriate is suggested by the following fragment of program:

```
loop
    -- read next record;
    exit when --end marker;
    -- process input data;
 end loop;
```

In reading data from an input stream, terminated by a special last record, it is necessary to ensure that processing does not occur if the read returns the marker indicating that there is no more data. There is one more 'read' than 'process'.

An **exit** in the inner loop of a nested loop passes control only to the end of the inner loop.

```
loop
   ......
   loop
      ......
      exit;
      ......
   end loop;
   -- control passed here by exit in inner loop;
   ......
end loop;
```

To enable control to be passed directly out of an outer loop, a loop may be named, and the name can then be used with an exit to cause control to pass to the end of the named loop:

```
MAINLOOP: loop
                .......
                loop
                   .......
                   loop
                      .......
                      exit MAINLOOP when I=1;
                      .......
                   end loop;
                   .......
                end loop;
                .......
          end loop MAINLOOP;
          -- control passes to here on exit;
```

If a loop is named, its name must be repeated after the corresponding **end**.

For most purposes, a preferable means of expressing the condition for termination is by prefixing the loop with a control clause, and here Ada provides a **while** condition or a **for** count.

The statement:

```
while <boolean condition> loop
    -- statements;
end loop;
```

will cause the condition to be evaluated before entry to the loop on each cycle, repetition being terminated if the condition is false. Thus, the loop body is executed none or more times. However, there is still the possibility of an endless loop if the condition never becomes false.

An example of the **while** statement in calculating a factorial is shown below:

```
FACT : FLOAT;  N : INTEGER;
......
FACT := 1.0;
while N /= 0 loop
   FACT := FACT*FLOAT(N);
   N := N-1;
end loop;
```

If the number of cycles can be determined before entry to a loop it may be controlled by a **for** clause as in the following:

```
for I in <discrete range> loop
   -- sequence of statements;
end loop;
```

where the indexing parameter, in this case I, is implicitly declared. Its type is determined by the type of the specified discrete range, and may be any discrete type. The index variable is unknown outside the loop, and its value cannot be changed by assignment within the loop body.

A discrete type was defined in chapter 6 to be an integer type or any enumeration type, including character types. A 'discrete range' may be a complete discrete type or sub-type (except that the whole of the integers is not permitted) or it may be a specified range of some type. If a range of integers is required it may be written simply N..M, where N and M may, in general, be integer expressions.

Although the range of the indexing parameter is limited to a discrete range or a subtype, the order of use may be reversed:

```
for I in reverse 1..N loop....
```

Enumeration types may also be used to sequence the loop.

In the case study an enumeration type WARNING is used to name the possible causes of error:

```
type WARNING is (BLOOD_PRESSURE, TEMPERATURE, PULSE,
                           FLUIDS, INTERFACE_TIME_OUT, SENSOR_ERROR);
```

and an array of messages is defined to give on-screen alarms:

```
ALARM_MESSAGES : constant array (WARNING) of STRING :=
(" BLOOD PRESSURE ALARM in bed(s): ",
 " TEMPERATURE ALARM in bed(s):    ",
 " PULSE ALARM in bed(s):          ",
 " FLUID BALANCE ALARM in bed(s):  ",
 " INTERFACE TIME OUT in bed(s)    ",
 " SENSOR FAILURE in bed(s)        ");
```

At the central nurse monitor station a vector of vectors is used to indicate which alarm conditions exist:

```
type BED_ALARM is array (BED) of BOOLEAN;
ALARMS_SET : array (WARNING) of BED_ALARM
           := (others => (others => FALSE));
```

ALARM set allows an error condition to be identified by warning type and by bed. The same warning may, of course, have been generated by more than one bed. A combination of **if** and **loop** statements are used to display the warning messages:

```
for W in WARNING loop
    if ALARMS_SET(W) /= (others => FALSE) then
        -- display on screen ALARM_MESSAGE(W);
        for B in BED loop
          if ALARMS_SET(W)(B) then
            -- add bed number to screen display;
          end if;
        end loop;
    end if;
end loop;
```

Attribute enquiries may be used to make the limits of a **for** loop more general, either for enumeration types or for arrays. Given the enumeration type DAY the loop:

```
for D in DAY'FIRST..DAY'PRED(DAY'LAST) loop
```

will range over all possible values of DAY except the last. It will also be robust against any change of definition of DAY, say from MONDAY through SUNDAY to SUNDAY through SATURDAY.

Given a type VECTOR which represents an array of FLOAT elements, the declarations:

```
V:VECTOR;
SUM: FLOAT := 0.0;
MEAN: FLOAT;
```

followed by a code sequence:

```
     --give values to elements of V;
...

for I in VECTOR'RANGE loop
     SUM:= SUM + V(I);
end loop;
MEAN := SUM / FLOAT(VECTOR'LENGTH);
```

would produce the average value of the contents of the vector elements in MEAN.

The programmer writing this segment of code needs to know only that a vector is an array of elements of type FLOAT; he need not know how many elements there are, nor even the type of the index. This reduces the possibility of errors, and the program will not need to be changed if the type definition is changed during program maintenance. The programmer can take a rather abstract view of the meaning of the type VECTOR. Such an approach is particularly useful in writing procedures and functions which may take vectors as parameters. Values such as the number of array elements and the first and last index do not have to be passed as parameters.

7.3.4 The Goto Statement

This allows unconditional transfer of control. It is included here for completeness although, with the structure of Ada, it should never prove necessary to use it. It has not been used in the case study.

Goto allows the transfer of control within the scope of a label name, that is from the start of the imperative part to the end of the program unit in which the labelled statement occurs. A label must be placed in << >> brackets and may occur before any statement:

```
<<SOME_WHERE>> I := I+1; -- a labelled statement
```

Control may be transferred to the labelled statement in the same scope:

```
if I<=LIMIT then
    goto SOME_WHERE;
end if;
```

Even within the scope of a label the legal transfers are limited; it is not possible to jump into a compound statement or into or out of an accept statement (used in tasks), a subprogram, task or package body. When exception handlers are used it is not legal to jump into them, between them, or from them back into the body of the program unit in which the exception occured. Subprograms, tasks, packages and exception handlers are all covered in later chapters of the book.

Exercise 7

Write Ada program statements that will perform the following actions:

7.1 Given F1, F2 and F3 as three BOOLEAN variables, set F3 to TRUE if either F1 or F2 (but not both) are TRUE, to FALSE otherwise.

7.2 Given the INTEGER variables X,Y and Z, find the remainder on integer division of the smaller of the values in X and Y into the larger, and assign the result to Z.

7.3 Given the declarations:

```
subtype NAME is STRING(1..20);
CLASS_ROLL : array (1..N) of NAME;
STUDENT : NAME;
I : INTEGER;
```

check CLASS_ROLL for the student named by the value of STUDENT; if the student is in the roll then set I to the number of his index position, otherwise set I to zero.

7.4 Given the declarations:

```
type LIGHT_STATE is (ON,OFF);
type ROOM is (DINING,LIVING,KITCHEN,BED_1,BED_2,BATH);
HOUSE_LIGHTS : array (ROOM) of LIGHT_STATE;
```

check the status of each room light and then turn off any lights that are on.

7.5 Oysters should only be eaten when there is an 'r' in the month. Set the BOOLEAN variable SAFE_TO_EAT according to the value of THIS_MONTH, a variable belonging to the enumeration type MONTH.

7.6 The type USA_STATE represents the states of the USA, and the type TIME_ZONE represents world time zones. Given the declarations:

```
type STATE is record
     STATE_NAME : USA_STATE;
     TIME       : TIME_ZONE;
end record;
S : STATE;
```

set the correct time value for S, assuming a value has already been given to S.STATE_NAME.

CHAPTER 8

SUBPROGRAMS AND BLOCKS

8.1 Structure

Procedures and functions, which are referred to collectively as subprograms, form named program units. They are similar to units familiar in most programming languages under these names, or referred to as subroutines. They are declared separately from the place where they will be used, and 'called', or 'invoked', at points in the program where the composite actions they define are required. They may receive parameters supplying the data on which they operate; procedures may return altered values in their parameters, functions may not alter their parameters but must return a single result. Blocks are used to enclose a program part which is logically a sub-problem; they form a statement and are written in the place where they are used.

Figure 8.1 - Structure of a Subprogram or Block

```
"unit nature"

     declarative part

begin

     imperative part

exception

     exception handlers

end;
```

As described in chapter 5, all program units of Ada have a comb-like structure with key words delimitimg the parts of the unit. This structure is shown in figure 8.1.

Here the "unit nature" identifies the category of the unit. The declarative part contains declarations of resources that will be available for use throughout the unit. They are said to be local to the unit. These resources may be types, variables, constants or further program units. The imperative part contains the executable code of the subprogram unit. The exception handlers deal with any error conditions occuring during the execution of the imperative part. The declarative part or the exceptions handlers may be empty; in the latter case the keyword **exception** is omitted.

Ill-considered use of exception handlers can lead to programs whose behaviours are unpredictable and they should not be used lightly. A description of their capabilities is delayed until chapter 13 where they are considered in the context of real-time programming.

The block is used as a sequence of Ada statements textually enclosed as a unit with the status of a single statement. Its "unit nature" is **declare**, and it is used to couple declared resources with a statement group in which they are required. It is recommended that these should be restricted to temporary types and variables, use clauses and renamings [8.1]. The block can also be used to couple exception handlers to a group of statements.

Blocks are a little different from subprogram units. In all other cases, Ada distinguishes the specification of the unit, defining its interface with other parts of the system, from the body which defines its implementation. The reserved word **is** is used to couple a declaration to the definition of the body. The separation is clearer in the case of packages and tasks, but exists also for subprograms.

A subprogram may be either a **procedure** or a **function.** They are introduced by declarations of the form

```
procedure IDENTIFIER(PARAMETER_LIST)
```

and

```
function IDENTIFIER(PARAMETER_LIST)return TYPE_OF_RESULT
```

respectively, known as the specifications, or signatures, of the subprograms. The IDENTIFIER is a valid Ada name for the subprogram and it may optionally be repeated after the final **end** of the unit, a practice which improves the readability of an Ada program. The parameter list specifies the formal parameters of the subprogram. If there are no parameters then the brackets may be omitted. For a function, the type of the returned result must be given.

A subprogram may be a stand-alone library unit or it may be declared in the declarative part of another program unit. When the declaration of a subprogram is elaborated its name and the description of its parameters become 'visible' to the following code. It may then be 'invoked' by a call, referring to it by name, which has the status of a statement for a procedure and the status of an expression for a function.

8.2 Parameters

The bracketed list of parameters of a subprogram defines the formal names of the parameters, their types, and the mode of transfer that will be used when actual values are associated with the formal parameters on calling the subprogram.

For procedures there are three available modes of transfer:

in The value of the actual parameter at the time of call is supplied as the constant value of the formal parameter in the procedure body. The actual parameter may be an expression which is evaluated to give the value. Within the procedure the parameter can only be used with the semantics of a constant.

out The formal parameter has an undefined initial value. After the execution of the procedure the final value of the formal parameter will be found in the named actual parameter.

in out The formal parameter receives the initial value from the actual parameter at the time of call of the procedure and the final value is found in the named actual parameter after the execution of the procedure.

If the mode of transfer is not specified then **in** is assumed. For scalar types the language reference manual specifies that an **in** parameter will be copied into a storage location local to the subprogram. No assumptions may be made about the existence of local copies in the case of structured types and any program making such an assumption would be erroneous.

The actual parameters supplied on calling a subprogram must be of the same type as the formal parameters. For **in** parameters the actual parameter may be any expression that will deliver a result of the correct type or compatible subtype. This will be evaluated at the time of call and its value transferred as the parameter value. For **in** and **in out** parameters a variable must be provided that can receive the returned value from the procedure.

Procedures are allowed to modify their environments by changing the values of **out** or **in out** parameters. However, functions cannot cause such side-effects, since the parameter passing mode for the parameters of functions is restricted to **in.**

Some examples of procedure declarations are:

```
procedure SWAP (X,Y : in out INTEGER);
procedure QUADROOTS (A,B,C : in FLOAT; R1,R2 : out FLOAT);
procedure LOG_NEW_PATIENT (B : in BED);
procedure TRANSMIT (S : in STRING);
procedure ALARM;
```

Functions may use only **in** parameters, and must define the type of the result which will be returned when the function is evaluated. Some examples of function declarations are:

```
function FACTORIAL (N : NATURAL) return FLOAT;
function CONVERT (X : in SENSOR_DATA) return FACTORS;
function RANDOM return FLOAT;
```

Such declarations define only the way in which the subprogram can be called - which types of parameter must be supplied, and how many. There are situations when such a specification appears on its own, separated from the definition of the body. Most often, however, the program to implement the action is declared at the same point in the same declarative part. In this case, the body appears connected to the specification by the use of **is**.

```
procedure SWAP (X,Y : in out INTEGER) is
    TEMP: INTEGER := X;
begin
    X    := Y;
    Y    := TEMP;
end;
```

8.3 Scope Rules

That part of a program where a declared item can be accessed and used is called its 'scope'. On entry to a program unit the declarations in its declarative parts are elaborated in the sequential order in which they appear. Each is then in scope from the point of its declaration to the **end** of the program unit.

The scope includes the bodies of any program units subsequently declared within the unit. Scope is determined by the lexical structure, the text on the page; items are not visible within the bodies of called subprograms not declared within the scope.

Within a program unit there may be nested units and in these identifiers still in scope may be reused in declarations that name different objects. If this happens, the innermost declaration of a name is the one that is said to be visible and will be invoked when the identifier is used. However, earlier uses of the name which are still in scope may be accessed using the dot notation, naming the unit in whose declarative part the declaration appeared.

The Ada rules of scope are illustrated in figure 8.2.

8.4 Using Procedures

The elaboration of the declaration of a procedure causes it to be in scope until the end of its enclosing program unit. Anywhere in this scope it may be invoked, either directly or by using the dot notation. When it is

Figure 8.2 - Ada Scope Rules for Nested Procedures and Blocks

```
procedure OUTER is
   A, B, C : INTEGER;    -- A, B, C are in scope until end of OUTER
   procedure INNER is  -- INNER is in scope until the end of OUTER
      X, Y : FLOAT;  -- in scope until the end of INNER
      B : BOOLEAN;    -- in scope until the end of INNER, hides OUTER.B
      procedure INNER_MOST is  -- INNER_MOST in scope to end of INNER
         X, C : INTEGER;  -- in scope to end of INNER_MOST
                          -- hides OUTER and INNER declarations
      begin  -- start of imperative part of INNER_MOST
          -- in this code names may be used as follows:
          --    A  -  give access to OUTER declaration
          --    Y and B  -  give access to INNER declarations
          --    X and C  -  give access to INNER_MOST declarations
          --    OUTER.C  and OUTER.B gives access to OUTER declarations
          --    INNER.Y gives access to INNER declaration
      end INNER_MOST;
   begin  -- start of imperative part of INNER
      -- in this code X, Y, and B access INNER declarations
      -- A, C and OUTER.B access outer declarations.
      -- an enclosing block can have its local declarations:
      declare
          B : FLOAT;  -- in scope to the end of the block
      begin
          -- now B accesses the local FLOAT variable
          -- and INNER.B must be use to access the BOOLEAN
      end;  -- the block end
      -- B is now the INNER BOOLEAN again
      -- INNER_MOST is in scope and can be called as a statement
     INNER_MOST;
      ..........
   end INNER;
begin  -- imperative part of OUTER
   --  Only the declarations of A, B, C and INNER are still in scope
   --  INNER may be called from here as a statement
   INNER;
   ...........
end OUTER;
```

invoked a list of actual parameters must be provided that exactly matches the formal parameters in type and, except in the case of default parameters described in 8.6 below, in number. The association of formal parameters with their actual values can be shown by position, or by named association of the form FORMAL_NAME => ACTUAL_NAME.

For example, consider the procedure:

```
procedure QUADRATIC(A, B, C : in FLOAT;
                    R1, R2 : out FLOAT;
                    IS_COMPLEX : out BOOLEAN) is
    D: FLOAT := B**2 - 4.0*A*C;
begin
    IS_COMPLEX := D < 0.0;
    if IS_COMPLEX then
        R1 := 0.0; R2 := 0.0;
    else
        R1 := (-B + SQRT(D))/(2.0*A);
        R2 := (-B - SQRT(D))/(2.0*A);
    end if;
end QUADRATIC;
```

Given the declarations:

```
P, Q, R, X, Y : FLOAT;
           OK : BOOLEAN;
```

then QUADRATIC can be called in any of the following ways:

```
QUADRATIC(P, Q, R, X, Y, OK);
QUADRATIC(P, Q, R, R1=>X, R2=>Y, IS_COMPLEX=>OK);
QUADRATIC(R1=>X, R2=>Y, IS_COMPLEX=>OK, A=>P, B=>Q, C=>R);
```

with the same effect. It should be noted that, as with aggregates, once the positional notation has been abandoned it cannot be resumed since any sequencing count will have been lost.

When the flow of control reaches the **end** of a procedure it will automatically cause a return to the calling program sequence. However, earlier return can be explicity effected by the use of a **return** statement.

The QUADRATIC procedure could be rewritten as

```
begin
     IS_COMPLEX := D < 0.0;
     if IS_COMPLEX then
          R1 := 0.0; R2 := 0.0;  return;
     end if;
     R1 := (-B + SQRT(D))/(2.0*A);
     R2 := (-B - SQRT(D))/(2.0*A);
end QUADRATIC;
```

A procedure can alter its calling environment not only by assigning values to parameters but also by accessing directly variables declared in an outer scope that is visible from within its body. Objects of the latter kind are said to be non-local or global to the procedure. In fig 8.2, for example, A declared in procedure OUTER is accessible as a non-local object from the body of procedure INNER_MOST.

The procedure should be considered as a tool for modularizing small program segments. The logic of the segment should be decomposed into logically distinct components which can be designed, coded and tested as separate procedures, each small enough to be understood by a single programmer. Frequently used algorithms should be parameterized into procedures. The specification of the signature constitutes a contract between the implementor and the user of the procedure. The compiler can check that both parties comply with this contract.

8.5 Using Functions

Functions, like procedures, become available for use immediately after the elaboration of their declarations. However, they are invoked in the context of an expression and must return a value of the type defined in the specification. All functions must contain at least one return statement where the key word **return** is followed by an expression giving the value to be returned. The logic of a function may allow one of several paths of control to be followed, but each of these should lead to a valid return statement.

The function:

```
function TEMP_CONVERT (F : FLOAT) return FLOAT is
begin
   return (F - 32.0) * 5.0/9.0;
end TEMP_CONVERT;
```

could be used in a statement:

```
C := TEMP_CONVERT(READING);
```

Parameter associations can again be shown by position or name but are restricted to **in** transfers. However, a function may still alter its calling environment by changing visible variables in outer scopes.

8.6 Default Parameters

For **in** parameters only, default values may be assigned to parameters in the subprogram declaration. When the subprogram is called the formal parameters take the default value if no actual parameter is specified. The actual parameters are specified either by position or by named association.

For example, consider the following declarations:

```
-- an enumeration type for temperature scale used
type TEMPERATURE_SCALE is (CENTIGRADE, FARENHEIT);

-- a procedure to update a record of temperature readings
-- with input that may represent a °C or°F, °C being the default.
procedure UPDATE_TEMP (READING : in FLOAT;
                       SCALE : TEMPERATURE_SCALE := CENTIGRADE) is
begin
   ................
end UPDATE_TEMP;
```

This procedure may be called by:

```
UPDATE_TEMP (X); -- reading taken to be centigrade
```

or

```
UPDATE_TEMP (X, FARENHEIT);  -- for a Farenheit reading.
```

A second example concerns a procedure that makes airline reservations. Given the following declarations:

```
type DESTINATION is (NEW_YORK, PARIS, HONG_KONG);
type AIRLINE is (BRITISH_AIRWAYS, AIR_FRANCE, PAN_AM);
type CLASS is (FIRST, CLUB, ECONOMY);
procedure BOOK_FLIGHT (TO : DESTINATION := NEW_YORK;
                       BY : AIRLINE := BRITISH_AIRWAYS;
                       COMFORT : CLASS := FIRST) is ....
```

then, using all the defaults, a call of

```
BOOK_FLIGHT;
```

will reserve a first class seat on a flight by British Airways to New York.

Some alternative booking calls are:

```
BOOK_FLIGHT(HONG_KONG); -- first class by British airways
BOOK_FLIGHT(PARIS, AIR_FRANCE); -- still first class
BOOK_FLIGHT(BY => PAN_AM, COMFORT => ECONOMY); -- to New York.
```

8.7 Recursion

Ada allows both procedures and functions to call themselves recursively, either directly or indirectly. For example, a recursive version of a function to compute the factorial can be defined as:

```
function FACTORIAL (N : NATURAL) return FLOAT is
begin
   if N = 0 then return 1.0;
   else return FLOAT(N)*FACTORIAL(N-1);
   end if;
end FACTORIAL;
```

This function provides an opportunity to illustrate one of the benefits of using **separate** stubs in constructing a program. Recursive solutions are often easier to write and to make work correctly than an equivalent non-recursive version. During the construction of a program which needs factorials, no decision need be made. The declaration of the function can be limited to the specification, with a stub for the body:

```
function FACTORIAL (N : NATURAL) return FLOAT is separate;
```

The body can now be composed and compiled separately. For a first version, to get a quick working solution a recursive version can be used. Should the recursive version prove inefficient in execution it can be replaced by an iterative version:

```
separate (PROGRAM_NAME)
function FACTORIAL (N : NATURAL) return FLOAT is
   FACT : FLOAT := 1.0;
begin
     for I in 2..N loop
          FACT := FLOAT(I)*FACT;
     end loop;
    return FACT;
end FACTORIAL;
```

without recompilation of the whole program.

For both bodies the specification is the same and the function would be called in the same way.

Mutually recursive procedures present a problem since the declaration of the specification of each must be elaborated before the other so that they are in scope when called. This is overcome by allowing the incomplete declaration of a procedure which is re-declared later in the text.

```
procedure FIRST(A : in out ITEM);  --  incomplete declaration
procedure SECOND(B : in out ITEM) is
   ...............
begin
   ..............
   FIRST(THIS);  -- call of FIRST
   ..............
end SECOND;
```

```
procedure FIRST(A : in out ITEM) is
   -- full declaration must match incomplete declaration given earlier
   ...............
begin
   ...............
   SECOND(THAT);  -- call of SECOND
   ...............
end FIRST;
```

8.8 Overloading

The same identifier can be used to name different subprograms declared in the same scope if each declaration can be identified by a unique signature. This facility is called 'overloading' since the meaning of the identifier has been overloaded with more than one meaning.

For example, recall the procedure that exchanges the values of two INTEGER variables, as given on page 128. Similar code could be used to provide an overloaded SWAP for reals:

```
procedure SWAP (X, Y : FLOAT) is
   T : FLOAT := X;
begin
   X := Y;
   Y := X;
end SWAP;
```

Calls on SWAP can be distinguished by the types of the actual parameters given.

```
declare
   P, Q : INTEGER;  N, M : FLOAT;
begin
   .......
   SWAP(P,Q);  -- integer version used
   SWAP(N,M);  -- float version used
   .......
end;
```

Overloaded subprograms present one of the rare cases in Ada where an overloaded enumeration literal may lead to an ambiguity, and so have to be explicitly qualified.

Recall the overloaded literals SUN and STAR in the types NEWSPAPER and HEAVENLY_BODY; suppose an overloaded function F is defined, with the specifications:

```
function F(X: NEWSPAPER)      return BOOLEAN;
function F(X: HEAVENLY_BODY) return BOOLEAN;
```

Now a call F(SUN) does not enable the compiler to determine which of the alternative meanings should be taken for F, since the type of SUN is ambiguous. The call must now be written F(NEWSPAPER'(SUN)) if that was intended.

Chapter 11 will show how generics can be used to facilitate the declaration of overloaded program units.

In the case study a function FIND_PATIENT is overloaded as follows:

```
    function FIND_PATIENT(N: NAME_TYPE) return SEARCH_RESULT;
and function FIND_PATIENT(NO: HOSPITAL_PATIENT_NUMBER)
                                     return SEARCH_RESULT;
```

so that the patient directory can be searched on a name or number key.

Overloading is not really a new concept to readers familiar with other high level languages. The standard operator symbols are usually overloaded; for example, * can be used to indicate multiplication between integers or between real numbers. Ada allows the programmer to extend this overloading to user defined types.

Given the declarations:

```
type MASS is new FLOAT;
type DENSITY is new FLOAT;
type VOLUME is new FLOAT;
```

then the function

```
function "*" (V : VOLUME; D : DENSITY) return MASS is
begin
   return MASS(FLOAT(V)*FLOAT(D));
end;
```

overloads * with the expected actions for multiplying volumes by density to deliver a mass. The variables M, V and RHO can now be used in the assignment statement which preserves the physical dimensions:

The declared values:

```
M : MASS; V : VOLUME; RHO : DENSITY;
```

can be used in the statement:

```
M := V*RHO;
```

However, the multiplication RHO*V is not defined since the order of the function's parameters is significant. Another overloading of the operator for this combination could be declared.

Only the existing operators of Ada may be overloaded in this way but there is no obligation, other than the exercise of good taste, to preserve their intrinsic meaning.

References

[8.1] "Ada-Europe Guidelines for the portability of Ada programs"; J C D Nissen et al; NPL Report DNACS 52/81, November 1981.

Exercise 8

8.1 Write a function with the signature:

```
function VALID_DATE (D:DATE) return BOOLEAN;
```

that checks that the value in the date record is valid, (eg. not 31st February).

8.2 Give a recursive definition of a body for the specification:

```
function HCF(M,N : INTEGER) return INTEGER;
```

which finds the highest common factor of the values of the parameters.

8.3 Given the type declarations:

```
subtype INDEX_RANGE is INTEGER range 1..N;
type INT_VECTOR  is array (INDEX_RANGE) of INTEGER;
type REAL_VECTOR is array (INDEX_RANGE) of FLOAT;
```

write a procedure:

```
procedure CDF(OBSERVATIONS : in INT_VECTOR;
                      DISTRIBUTION : out REAL_VECTOR);
```

which takes in a vector of frequency observations and produces a normalized cumulative distribution in the **out** parameter.

8.4 Using the type INT_VECTOR and an enumeration type:

```
type SORT_ORDER is (UP, DOWN);
```

write a procedure that may take two parameters, an INT_VECTOR of elements to be sorted and a SORT_ORDER used to determine whether the array is to be sorted into ascending or descending order. If the SORT_ORDER parameter is omitted on call then the procedure is to sort into ascending order.

8.5 Define a type MEASURE to represent a measurement in yards, feet and inches. Overload the operators "+" and "_" to have the correct effect when applied to values of type MEASURE.

CHAPTER 9

PARALLELISM

9.1 Introduction

One of the requirements for embedded systems, identified in chapter 3, is the ability to exercise concurrent control of separate system components. In Ada the **task** is provided as the program unit that may be used to specify parallel execution. Tasks are used to represent logically parallel sub-processes of the main program process.

Ada tasks can be completely independently executing, parallel processes, whose pseudo-concurrency is handled by a run-time kernel supplied by the Ada language system. However, most applications call for tasks to be able to communicate either asynchronously, to pass information, or synchronously, to coordinate their activities. Ada tasks can communicate by two different methods: by the 'rendezvous' of an **entry** call in one task with an **accept** statement in another task, during which data may be transferred between the units, or by using shared variables declared in a scope global to both tasks. The latter of these methods has dangers and must be used with caution. Both methods will be described in detail in section 9.2.

A task cannot be a stand-alone unit in an Ada program but must be declared within another program unit. The enclosing subprogram of a task will be referred to as the 'parent' of the task and a task is said to be 'dependent' on its parent. The code of a task is made up of two sections - the specification and the body - and these must both appear in the declarative part of the parent. The specification may just identify the task name:

```
task TASK_NAME;
```

or may contain the declarations of entries that are used in communication with the task. Figure 9.1 shows the outline of a task.

Figure 9.1 - Structure of a Task

```
-- The task specification:
task TASK_NAME is
     -- This declares the entries  accepted by the task.
     entry ENTRY_NAME(<parameter list>);
end TASK_NAME;

-- The body of the task must be declared in the same declarative part
-- but need not immediately follow the specification.

task body TASK_NAME is
     -- The declarative part of the task,
     -- all objects declared here are private to the task
     -- and not visible to other program units.
begin
     -- The imperative part of the task,
     -- this will contain statements that accept calls
     -- on the entries declared in the specification.
     accept ENTRY_NAME(<parameter list>) do ...
end TASK_NAME;
```

The elaboration of the task specification makes its name, and those of the entries that it contains, visible throughout the rest of the enclosing unit, according to the normal Ada scope rules. The code of the body of the task is automatically activated when control reaches the imperative part of the parent, and this is called the 'initiation' of the task. At this point the elaboration of the body of the task makes its local declarations available within the scope of the task body. These declarations are private to the task and are not accessible from outside the task. After initiation a task is active in parallel with its parent and siblings.

Normal termination of a task will occur when its thread of control reaches the final **end**, where a parent will wait for the termination of any tasks initiated in its body and still active. There are other mechanisms that may be used to force termination and these are described in section 9.4.

The single task describes a unique process within the system. Ada also allows the declaration of named **task types**. These enable the program designer to define a template for a frequently required process which may subsequently be used to create instances of tasks. These mechanisms are described in detail in section 9.5.

9.2 Task Communication

Figure 9.2 shows the outline of a tasking solution to the problem of cooking a dinner of roast meat, boiled potatoes and salad. Three tasks are declared to control the cooking of the three components of the dinner. Each of these has a specification limited to the declaration of its name since there is to be no communication between the tasks. The bodies of the tasks will become active at the start of the imperative part of the procedure COOK_DINNER. In parallel with the tasks will be executed the code of this parent procedure which will control the laying of the table.

The procedure will terminate when the execution of all the imperative code of the three tasks and the procedure have all been completed. However, without communication between the tasks, it is unlikely that the dinner will be a success. By the time that the roasting of the meat is completed the potatoes will be a mush! What is required is a signal from the ROAST_MEAT task to the BOIL_POTATOES task indicating that it is now time to start the potatoes cooking.

This is an example of a case where communication is required only to achieve synchronization. This is effected by the simplest use of the rendezvous. The rendezvous is made possible by the task to be called providing an entry declaration in its specification:

```
entry ENTRY_NAME;
```

which is then accepted in the body of the task by the statement:

```
accept ENTRY_NAME;
```

A calling task then sends its signal by the entry call:

```
CALLED_TASK_NAME.ENTRY_NAME;
```

figure 9.2 - Outline Tasking Example

```
procedure COOK_DINNER is
        task BOIL_POTATOES;    -- specification
        task ROAST_MEAT;       -- specification
        task PREPARE_SALAD;    -- specification
        task body BOIL_POTATOES is
        begin
                ..........
        end BOIL_POTATOES;
        task body ROAST_MEAT is
        begin
                ..........
        end ROAST_MEAT;
        task body PREPARE_SALAD is
        begin
                ..........
        end PREPARE SALAD;
        procedure LAY_THE_TABLE is separate;
begin
        -- imperative part of the main procedure,
        -- the three tasks are now active.
        LAY THE TABLE;
end COOK_DINNER;
```

This technique is shown in figure 9.3 for the COOK_DINNER procedure.

Here, the BOIL_POTATOES task has an entry named TURN_ON_HEAT which is visible to the body of the task ROAST_MEAT. Each of these tasks will execute asynchronously until the BOIL_POTATOES task reaches the **accept** of the entry. Execution of this task will then be suspended until it receives a call from ROAST_MEAT in the form of an entry call, which will act as a signal that will allow resumption of the BOIL_POTATOES task. (Alternatively, the call may be reached before the accept, in which case the ROAST_MEAT task will be suspended until the signal is accepted). Figure 9.3 also shows how a task may contain its own local program units, in this case a procedure MAKE_GRAVY which is seen as a sequential activity in ROAST_MEAT and not a parallel process.

Figure 9.3 - Tasking with a Rendezvous Signal

```
procedure COOK_DINNER is
          task BOIL_POTATOES is
               -- specification of entry
               entry TURN_ON_HEAT;
          end BOIL_POTATOES;
          task ROAST_MEAT;
          task PREPARE_SALAD;
          task body BOIL_POTATOES is
          begin
               -- prepare potatoes ready for cooking;
               accept TURN_ON_HEAT;    -- accepts entry call
               -- cook potatoes
          end BOIL_POTATOES;
          task body ROAST_MEAT is
                    -- local procedure
                    procedure MAKE_GRAVY is
                         .......
                    end MAKE-GRAVY;
          begin
               -- start roast
               -- when there is 30mins left:
               BOIL_POTATOES.TURN_ON_HEAT;  -- entry call
               -- continue cooking when heat is turned on
               MAKE_GRAVY; -- call of local procedure
               -- carve the meat
          end ROAST_MEAT;
          task body PREPARE_SALAD is
          begin
               ......
          end PREPARE SALAD;

          procedure LAY_THE_TABLE is separate;
begin
          -- imperative part of the main procedure,
          -- the three tasks are now active.
          LAY THE TABLE;
end COOK_DINNER;
```

The full form of the rendezvous allows a sequence of statements to be defined in the accept statement, and these statements may be given in terms of formal parameters which are defined in the entry specification. These parameters may take the same forms as those allowed for a procedure.

```
entry ENTRY_NAME(<formal parameter list>);
```

The code in the body of the called task must contain an accept statement of the form:

```
accept  ENTRY_NAME(<formal parameter list>) do
    -- code of the rendezvous;
end ENTRY_NAME;
```

Any task body declared in the scope of the called task may call this entry with the statement:

```
CALLED_TASK_NAME.ENTRY_NAME(<actual parameters>);
```

The effect of the rendezvous is to cause the code between the **do** and **end** of the accept in the called task to be executed on behalf of the calling task as a remote procedure. On making an entry call the calling task may have to wait until the called task reaches its accept statement and is ready to service the call; alternatively, the called task may find that there is no task waiting to be accepted and suspend its execution until it receives a call. Thus, synchronization is achieved. When the rendezvous takes place the parameters will be exchanged using the same rules as those for procedures, as described in chapter 8. The calling task halts while the called task executes the **accept** code at the end of which any **out** parameters are returned to the calling task. The two tasks then resume the execution of their independent code concurrently.

If several tasks call the same entry they form a first-come-first-served entry queue. In a later example it will be shown how the called task may use the 'COUNT attribute of an entry to see how many tasks are currently waiting for a rendezvous.

It should be noted that the full dot notation must be used to name an entry and there is no tasking equivalent to the **use** facility of packages. However, a procedure may be declared to rename an entry. Given the entry:

```
entry DETACH_PATIENT (B :in BED);
```

in a task called DATA_PROTECTION then the renaming declaration:

```
procedure DETACH_PATIENT (B : in BED) renames
                DATA_PROTECTION.DETACH_PATIENT (B : in BED);
```

allows the entry to be called as:

```
DETACH_PATIENT(X);
```

Tasks may also communicate by using a variable that is visible to the bodies of both tasks. Consider an example where one task is responsible for providing the latest value of a externally monitored parameter which is read by another task. The tasks could communicate asynchronously as shown in figure 9.4 below.

Figure 9.4 - Access to a Common Data Area

```
procedure SHARE_DATA is
    type READING is ......
    COMMON : READING;

    task PROVIDE_VALUE;
    task READ_VALUE;

    task body PROVIDE_VALUE is
        T : READING;
        .......
    begin
        loop
            .....-- obtain latest reading;
            COMMON := T;  -- transferred to COMMON
        end loop;
    end PROVIDE_VALUE;
    task body READ_VALUE is
        .......
    begin
        loop
            -- use latest reading in COMMON when required;
        end loop;
    end READ_VALUE;
end SHARE_DATA;
```

However, with this program there is a danger that there will be contention over access to COMMON. If the shared data area were a composite data object it may be only partly updated by PROVIDE_VALUE when that task is suspended by the run-time kernel and the READ_VALUE task activated. A preferred solution to this problem is shown in section 9.3 below.

9.3 Selecting a Rendezvous

The called task must be free to exercise control over which of several possible waiting tasks are accepted for a rendezvous. Tasks calling the same entry will wait for service in a first-come-first-served queue on the entry. There may be several different points in the called task where the entry is accepted and, as each of these is executed, the first task is removed from the entry queue.

The **select** statement enables a called task to select one of several alternative entry calls. A simple form of the select statement is shown below:

```
select
     accept ENTRY_ONE do
          ......
     end ENTRY_ONE;
          ......
or
     accept ENTRY_TWO do
          ......
     end ENTRY_TWO;
          ......
or
     accept ENTRY_THREE do
          ......
     end ENTRY_THREE;
          ......
end select;
```

When execution reaches this statement the queues for all the entries named in the branches are inspected. If there are no waiting tasks then execution is suspended at the select. Subsequently, the first call to be received on any of the entries is accepted, the branch of the statement headed by the corresponding accept is taken, the rendezvous is executed and any code that may follow the end of the accept; control then passes to the statement immediately following the select statement. If there are waiting tasks on only one of the entry queues then the first of these is accepted immediately. If there are tasks waiting on more than one of the entries then the underlying run-time scheduler will select one of the entries for acceptance. The programmer is not allowed to make any assumptions about the behaviour of this scheduler but there is the assurance that there will be no starvation of acceptance of a particular entry.

The select statement can be used to provide a protected data-area to overcome the problem of the shared data-area of figure 9.4. The solution, shown in figure 9.5, introduces a task that encapsulates the common data area and entries that allow mutually exclusive read or write access to the data.

It should be noted that the called task (the server) may wait indefinitely at a select statement for a call on one of the entries. Such a wait could hold up the main processing work of the task unnecessarily. In the extreme case the call may never come due to the erroneous behaviour of other tasks (the customers). The **else** alternative in a select statement allows the server to execute alternative code rather than wait for a customer:

```
select
     accept ENTRY_NAME do
          -- rendezvous actions,
     end ENTRY_NAME;
or
     -- any number of other accept branches,
else
     -- do something else at once if all entry queues are empty;
end select;
```

The else code will be executed if there are no calls waiting on the named entries and execution will then continue with the statement following the select.

Figure 9.5 - Protected Data_Area

```
procedure SHARE_DATA is

     type READING is -- global type declaration for common data;

     task COMMON is
               entry READ(OUT_VALUE : out READING);
               entry WRITE(IN_VALUE : in READING);
               --task takes in a value on call of WRITE
               --the latest value is given on call of READ
     end COMMON;
     task PROVIDE_VALUE;
     task READ_VALUE;

     task body COMMON is
          VALUE : READING := --initial value;
     begin
          loop
                select
                          accept READ(OUT_VALUE : out READING)do
                                   OUT_VALUE := VALUE;
                          end READ;
                or
                          accept WRITE(IN_VALUE : in READING)do
                                   VALUE := IN_VALUE;
                          end WRITE;
                end select;
          end loop;
     end COMMON;

     task body PROVIDE_VALUE is separate;
     task body READ_VALUE    is separate;

end SHARE_DATA;
```

```
separate(SHARE_DATA)
task body PROVIDE_VALUE is
     T : READING;
     .......
begin
     loop
          ....-- obtain latest reading from hardware and store it in T;
          COMMON.WRITE(T);  -- reading put into protected data area;
     end loop;
end PROVIDE_VALUE;

separate(SHARE_DATA)
task body READ_VALUE is
     T : READING;
     .......
begin
     loop
          -- obtain latest reading when required;
          COMMON.READ(T);  -- reading obtained from protected data area;
          ....-- use the reading in T;
     end loop;
end READ_VALUE;
```

A similar problem can occur if a customer task is suspended awaiting the acceptance of its call on the server task. The select statement can also be used in this case to prevent a wait. The statement can only have a single call and an else-part.

```
select
     CUSTOMER_TASK_NAME.ENTRY_NAME(PARAMETERS);
else
     -- do something else at once if call not accepted;
end select;
```

9.3.1 Guarded Selection

It is often the case that a programmer may wish to place conditions on the acceptance of alternative branches in a select statement of a server task. Boolean conditions may be inserted after the key-word **when** and a branch of the select statement is said to be 'open' if the condition guarding it is true. On reaching the select statement all the guard conditions are evaluated and the rendezvous chosen non-deterministically from the open alternatives. If all the guards are closed, and there is no else clause, then a SELECT_ERROR exception is raised.

When there is the danger of all the guards being closed in a select statement then the **else** option can be used to cause some alternative action, so avoiding the SELECT_ERROR exception. A select statement may contain an unlimited number of open or guarded accept alternatives but only one else alternative.

```
select
      when CONDITION_1 =>
            accept ENTRY_1 do
            ......

or
      when CONDITION_2 =>
            accept ENTRY_2 do
            ......
or
      when CONDITION_3 =>
            accept ENTRY_3 do
            .....
else
      -- alternative actions;
end select;
```

The example of a common data area shown in figure 9.5 only ensures that access to the data is an indivisible action from which other tasks are excluded. It does not ensure that any value written is read before it is overwritten; thus, only the latest reading is provided. If a data buffer between producer and consumer tasks is required this can be implemented using guards to ensure that no data is lost. Figure 9.6 shows an Ada implementation of the bounded buffer with a task called BUFFERING.

Figure 9.6 - A Bounded Buffer

```
procedure PRODUCER_CONSUMER is
     -- global declaration of type for buffered items
     type ITEM is record ......... end record;

     -- task specifications
     task BUFFERING is
        entry READ_ITEM  (X : out ITEM);
        entry WRITE_ITEM (X : in ITEM);
     end BUFFERING;
     task PRODUCER;
     task CONSUMER;
     -- task bodies
     task body BUFFERING is separate
     task body PRODUCER  is separete
     task body CONSUMER  is separate
begin
     -- null body of enclosing procedure
     null;
end PRODUCER_CONSUMER;


separate(PRODUCER_CONSUMER)
task body BUFFERING is

   -- maximum buffer size
   MAXBUF : constant INTEGER:=80;
   -- buffer space to hold items
   BUFFER : array(1..MAXBUF) of ITEM;
   -- BUFFER is used as a circular buffer, INPOINT and OUTPOINT are used
   -- respectively to index the next free slot and the next slot to be read,
   subtype BUFFER_POINTER is INTEGER range 1..MAXBUF;
   INPOINT, OUTPOINT : BUFFER_POINTER := 1;
   subtype FREE_SLOTS is INTEGER range 0..MAXBUF;
   COUNT : FREE_SLOTS := MAXBUF; -- a count of empty buffer slots
```

```
begin
   loop
     select
         when COUNT>0 => -- stop when buffer is full
              accept WRITE_ITEM (X : in ITEM) do
                 -- insert an item in the circular buffer
                 BUFFER(INPOINT):=X;
              end WRITE_ITEM;
              -- update pointer and count
              INPOINT := INPOINT mod MAXBUF + 1;
              COUNT := COUNT - 1;
              end if;
      or
        when COUNT<MAXBUF => -- stop when buffer is empty
              accept READ_ITEM (X : out ITEM) do
                 -- remove an item from the buffer
                 X:= BUFFER(OUTPOINT);
              end READ_ITEM;
              -- update pointer and count
              OUTPOINT := OUTPOINT mod MAXBUF + 1;
              COUNT := COUNT + 1;
      end select;
   end loop;
end BUFFERING;


separate (PRODUCER_CONSUMER)
task body PRODUCER is
   function GENERATE_ITEM (........) return ITEM is
      -- local declarations
   begin
      -- generation of next data item,
   end GENERATE_ITEM;
   NEXT:ITEM;
   .
begin
   loop
      ......
      NEXT := GENERATE ITEM(......);
```

```
      -- write new item into the buffer
      BUFFERING.WRITE_ITEM(NEXT);
   end loop;
end PRODUCER;

separate (PRODUCER_CONSUMER)
task body CONSUMER is
   TEMP:ITEM;
   ......
   procedure CONSUME_ITEM is
      -- local declarations
   begin
      -- consumes next data item,
   end CONSUME_ITEM;
begin
   loop
      -- reads next item from the buffer
      BUFFERING.READ_ITEM(TEMP);
      CONSUME_ITEM;
   end loop;
end CONSUMER;
```

In this example the guards are both based on the variable COUNT which is used to record the number of empty slots in the buffer. The read guard is closed when the buffer is empty, thus suspending the CONSUMER task until there is data to consume, and the write guard is closed when the buffer is full, thus suspending the PRODUCER until space has been freed. In this way the the producer and consumer tasks are allowed to execute at their own rates within the capacity, MAXBUF, of the buffer.

At several points in the patient monitoring system transaction records, each recording some information about a patient, are written to a patient's disc file. The transactions are generated by tasks that are responsible for controlling some aspect of the patient's care and such tasks must not be allowed to become suspended awaiting disc transfers. To avoid any delay, a bounded buffer is used to receive transaction records as they are generated and then provide them for a task that is solely concerned with writing to files on disc. This part of the case study code will be found in the package FILE_HANDLING.

9.3.2 Time-out on the Rendezvous

When a rendezvous is expected either of the two tasks envolved may wait. However, an indefinite wait may occur due to failure in one of the tasks. In embedded computer systems this would be unacceptable because the tasks will also be responsible for time-critical interactions with the external world. The **delay** statement can be used to give a time limit to the wait, either of the server or the customer, at the end of which alternative actions are taken.

The delay statement takes the form of the reserved word **delay** followed by a value of an intrinsic type DURATION which gives time in decimal seconds. Thus

```
      delay 0.1;
```

would cause execution of the current process to be delayed for at least one-tenth of a second. Conceptually, the task waits for a rendezvous with the clock. Full details of the timing facilities of Ada will be found in chapter 13.

A select statement with a time-out alternative can be used in a server task as follows:

```
select
      accept ENTRY_CALL(....) do
      -- Rendezvous if a task is waiting or if an entry call
      -- is made before the time-out rendezvous with the clock.
      end ENTRY_CALL;
or
      delay 10.0;
      -- Alternative actions to be taken
      -- if no entry call occurs within at least 10 seconds;
end select;
```

The delay statement may be used as one of the select alternatives in place of an accept, but the select statement cannot use both delay and else.

A select statement may also be used to time-out the wait for an entry call to be accepted in the customer task, or to make a call conditional on immediate acceptance. These are the only uses that can be made of select in a calling task.

```
select
      PROVIDER.READ(.....);
      --only one call allowed
or
      delay 1.0;
      --alternative actions
end select;
```

```
select
      PROVIDER.READ(.....);
      -- also only one call
else
      -- do something else
      -- if call not accepted
end select;
```

It should be noted that Ada does not provide any means by which a calling task can time-out the completion of a rendezvous. Erroneous behaviour of the server task during the rendezvous could have drastic consequences for the calling task. It is up to the program designer to be aware of this possibility and, where possible, design the customer-server interactions so that the customer makes a request in a rendezvous and then waits on a time controlled acceptance of a reply.

9.3.3 Families of Entries

The underlying scheduling algorithm that will be used at run time to select between open alternatives guarantees fair treatment of each entry queue. In cases where there is to be priority treatment of some tasks with respect to others, limited user controlled scheduling can be achieved by setting up families of entries.

For example, consider a task that is responsible for displaying messages on a VDU screen. These messages are sent from other tasks and would normally be displayed in the order in which they are received. A classification of messages can be introduced with three classes - URGENT, NORMAL, BACKGROUND. Most messages will be in the normal class but, occasionally, urgent messages are to be displayed ahead of any waiting normal messages. When there are no other waiting messages a background message will be displayed.

The type declarations

```
type MESSAGE is.......;
type MESSAGE_CLASS is (URGENT, NORMAL, BACKGROUND);
```

are declared in a scope visible to both the message displaying task and any task that may call it.

The specification of the message displaying task will contain:

```
entry REQUEST (MESSAGE_CLASS)(M : MESSAGE);
```

which declares a family of three entries, each taking the same parameter.

Calling tasks must specify which of the entry family is being called. The call of the NORMAL entry can be made by

```
MESSAGE_DISPLAY.REQUEST(NORMAL)(MY_MESSAGE);
```

The server task can exercise control over which entry to accept by using guards:

```
select
   when REQUEST(URGENT)'COUNT=0 and REQUEST(NORMAL)'COUNT=0 =>
      accept REQUEST(BACKGROUND)(M : MESSAGE) do
      LOCAL_MESSAGE := M;
      end;
or
   when REQUEST(URGENT)'COUNT=0 =>
      accept REQUEST(NORMAL)(M : MESSAGE) do
      LOCAL_MESSAGE := M;
      end;
or
    accept REQUEST(URGENT)(M : MESSAGE)do
     LOCAL_MESSAGE := M;
    end;
end select;
 DISPLAY_ON_SCREEN(LOCAL_MESSAGE);
```

Here, the urgent request is always accepted. The normal request is accepted only if there are no urgent requests, determined by the attribute enquiry on the length of an entry queue ENTRY_NAME'COUNT. Background messages are accepted only if both the other entry queues are empty.

9.4 Task Termination

Tasks terminate automatically at the end of their code sequence, where parent tasks or subprograms may wait for the completion of any active children. However, it is often necessary to cause the explicit termination of a task. This can be done in one of two ways - from inside the task using the **terminate** statement or from outside the task by abortion.

Many of the processes in an embedded computer system are essentially infinite control loops with some provision for system start-up and close-down. The logic of such processes can be modelled by an uncontrolled **loop** statement.

Within such a loop the option for termination of the task can be given using **terminate**, as shown below:

```
loop
   select
      when CONDITION_1 =>
         accept ENTRY_1 do
          ......
         end;
   or
      when CONDITION_2 =>
         accept ENTRY_2
          ......
         end;
   or
         terminate;
   end select;
end loop;
```

A task which has reached a terminate option in a select statement is said to be 'potentially terminated'. The terminate option may also be guarded and an open alternative to terminate will be selected only if the parent of the task, all siblings of the task, and any children of the task are either terminated or potentially terminated. (It should be noted that the **terminate** alternative will not be selected in a task that is declared in an independently compiled library package, for reasons that will be explained in chapter 14.)

A select statement may only contain one of the **terminate, delay** or **else** options.

On some occasions one task may wish to explicitly terminate another. Firstly, the attribute enquiry:

```
TASK_NAME'TERMINATED;
```

may be used to discover whether or not another task has already terminated.

If not, it may be aborted with the statement:

```
abort TASK_NAME;
```

which will cause the abnormal termination of the named task and all its children.

An attempt to rendezvous with a terminated task will cause a TASKING_ERROR exception.

9.5 Task Types

The task examples considered so far have all been single processes. Many concurrent problems require a programming mechanism which allows for the creation of several processes of the same type. This is provided in Ada by Task Types.

The following task type defines the template for the standard semaphore:

```
task type SEMAPHORE is
      entry SEIZE;
      entry RELEASE;
end;

task body SEMAPHORE is
      ACQUIRED : BOOLEAN := FALSE;
begin
    loop
```

```
        select
              when not ACQUIRED =>
                    accept SEIZE;
                    ACQUIRED := TRUE;
        or
              accept RELEASE;
              ACQUIRED := FALSE;
        or
              terminate;
        end select;
    end loop;
end SEMAPHORE;
```

These declarations do not create a semaphore, only a template. Task types are limited private (see chapter 10) and can only be created by the declaration of objects of the task type or by using the allocator **new**.

Objects of type semaphore can be declared directly

```
        S : SEMAPHORE;
```

or in arrays

```
        PROTECTOR : array (1..BED) of SEMAPHORE;
```

and in each case they are initiated at the start of the imperative part of the unit containing the declarations.

Task types can also be created with access types in which case the parent of any such tasks is the unit in which the access type is declared. A full description of this use of task types will be found in chapter 12.

The entries of the task type are named by using the dot notation, S.SEIZE or PROTECTOR(J).SEIZE.

The code below shows the use of a semaphore task type in a data record where it is used to protect access to a common data pool.

```
    type DATA_NODE is
       record
          INFO : DATA_POOL;
```

```
        LOCK : SEMAPHORE;
      end record;
    COMMON : DATA_NODE;

begin
    -- imperative part of program unit using common;
    -- SEMAPHORE task in COMMON now initiated.
```

Tasks declared in the scope of COMMON can access the data area with the following select statement in a loop:

```
    loop
      select
        COMMON.LOCK.SEIZE;
        exit; -- success in gaining access rights;
      else
        -- do something else while the data area is not free;
      end select;
    end loop;
    -- access the data area then release it
    COMMON.LOCK.RELEASE;
```

9.6 Using Tasks

Tasks should be used freely in modelling an embedded system to reflect the truly concurrent nature of processes. Their use will greatly help in the system design processes of understanding and decomposition.

Considerable use of tasks will be found in the case study. The main procedure of the program is concerned with responding to requests input at the central control nurse station, and this represents one thread of control in the system. There are several other independent sequences of execution, controlled by tasks. Bedside monitoring functions are given by three tasks and, since these functions are replicated at each bedside, task types are used. MONITOR is a task type responsible for monitoring the patient's life signs, TREATMENT is a task type for recording and displaying treatment schedules, and COMMAND_CONTROL is a task type that processes all commands input at the bedside terminal. Arrays of these task types are declared and instances of the tasks take control of each bed. At the central nurse station there is a task NURSE_STATION_MONITOR that responds to alarm signals from the bedside monitors. There is also a task which acts as the DETACHED_PATIENT_MONITOR.

As well as tasks directly concerned with the functions of the system, there are tasks that are used to protect access to data areas, to buffer data records and provide time signals for certain actions.

A full rationale for the use of each task will be found in chapter 15.

The run-time efficiency of the kernel that supports the execution of the tasks may have a profound effect on the overall efficiency of the final system. Some methods of optimizating the rendezvous have already been demonstrated [9.1] but the quality of production compilers is, as yet, an unknown factor.

All task interactions must be designed with failure in mind and comprehensive use made of time outs.

References

[9.1] "Efficient Implementation of Ada Tasks"; N Habermann and I R Nassi; Computer Science Carnegie-Mellon University report, 1979.

Exercise 9

9.1 Using a pre-defined type MESSAGE, write a task that repeatedly accepts input messages and then passes them on to another task called RECEIVER by calling an entry with the specification:

```
entry INPUT(M : MESSAGE);
```

9.2 Provide a MAILBOX task for a multitasking program in which there are N other tasks. Any task may put a MESSAGE in the mailbox and this message may not be overwritten until all the other tasks have read it from the mailbox. Tasks identify themselves by a unique integer in the range 1 to N.

9.3 The code for a semaphore given in section 9.5 is not secure. There is no check that the task that calls RELEASE was the task that first called SEIZE and nothing to stop a task calling RELEASE before SEIZE and thus obtaining illegal access. Design an improved semaphore task. Show how your semaphore task would be used.

9.4 Design an N-ary semaphore that will allow up to N tasks access to a protected resource.

9.5 Write a program that contains three tasks, called IN_CHAR, MAKE_LINE and OUT_LINE. IN_CHAR reads characters from an input stream by calling a procedure specified as:

```
procedure GET(C : out CHARACTER);
```

The characters are assembled into words, separated by a space or punctuation mark. Each complete word is passed on to MAKE_LINE by calling an entry. MAKE_LINE assembles the words into lines conforming to:

```
subtype LINE is STRING(1..120);
```

When a line is full, that is when the next word cannot be included in the line, it is passed on to OUT_LINE through an entry call. OUT_LINE writes lines on a printer by calling a procedure with the specification:

```
procedure PUT(L : in LINE);
```

The input is terminated by an exclamation mark.

CHAPTER 10

PACKAGES

10.1 The Package: a Unit of Modularity

In earlier chapters two approaches to the design and construction of a complex program were described, the use of modular decomposition, on the one hand, and the construction of components to implement abstract models of objects in the world, on the other. Ada supports these two approaches, paradoxically, by the same programming device, the package. This provides the encapsulation of program parts behind a 'fence', forming a well defined unit of modularity and a separate specification of its external properties, its interface to other program parts. This separation of the specification from the implementation encourages an abstract view of the module's behaviour.

The benefits of modular programming were discussed in chapter 2, with emphasis on the need for controlling precisely the interface between modules, to prevent malfunction when separate units are assembled to form a complete program or system. The need was also noted for the provision of a degree of encapsulation of program units, to hide information about their data resources and operations from the rest of the program. These are the features provided in Ada by the package.

Conceptually a package may be viewed as in figure 10.1. There is a visible or specification part, which forms a window to the rest of the program, and a body, or hidden part which encloses the details of the implementation behind a secure fence, protecting it from access by other parts of the program.

In the program the package is presented with the following syntax, which is the outline of a package called PACKAGE_NAME.

```
package PACKAGE_NAME is

            -- declarations defining the visible part

end PACKAGE_NAME;

package body PACKAGE_NAME is

            -- definition of the hidden part.  Includes
            -- declarative and possible imperative parts.

end PACKAGE_NAME;
```

The name of the package is shown here repeated at the end of each part. This is good practice, but not essential; it may be omitted from either or both places. If, however, a name is associated with the **end** of any unit it must match exactly the name of the unit.

The declaration of a package may occur in the normal declarative part of a program unit, in which case its scope follows the usual rules for scope of declared objects. However, the direct visibility obtained consists only of the name of the package itself. Items within the visible part are not automatically visible, except from within the package body. Elsewhere in the scope of the package they may be accessed by the dot notation, as for the elements of a record. Alternatively, they may be made directly visible by introducing a **use** clause. Within the scope of the package declaration, either in the same declarative part or in the declarative part of an inner nested unit, the items in the visible part can be made directly visible by introducing a statement:

```
use PACKAGE_NAME;
```

This makes all the names in the package specification available for use by the program as if they were declared in the ordinary way at that point. The effect of the **use** extends over the normal scope from the appearance of the **use** clause in the program, exactly as described for variable declarations in chapter 8.

figure 10.1 The Package

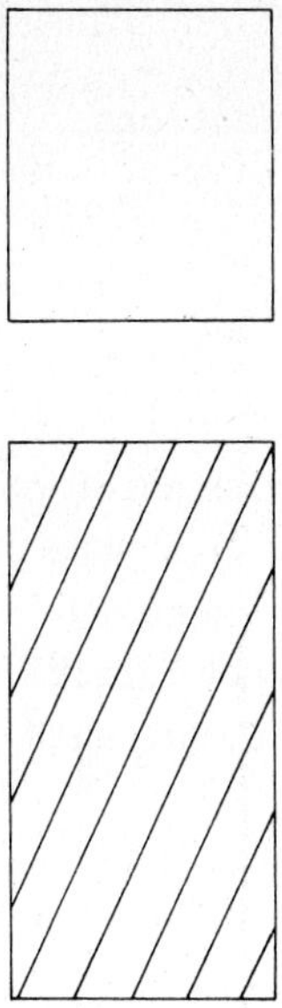

The visible part of the package forms a window to the rest of the program.

The package body contains details of the implementation of programs specified in the visible part, and program parts which are of no relevance to the rest of the program.

If the package specification part appears in the declarative part of some unit, then the declaration of the package body, which constitutes the scope for direct visibility of the declarations in the visible part, must appear after the definition of the visible part, and in the same declarative part. The specification and body may, however, be textually separated by other declarations.

More often a package is treated as a separate compilation unit. In that case it is visible only to program parts which name it in a **with** clause. If it is so named, it becomes visible within that unit as if it were included in the standard library; items within it are then accessible by the dot notation or through a **use** clause, in the usual way. This introduces a new dimension to the overall design of programs, providing greater control of visibility, hiding data and operations from units which do not request them while making them accessible to those that do. More details of the use of the **with** clause and of separate compilation of Ada program units will be given in chapter 14.

There are several styles of package. In the following sections their properties are discussed under the headings:

Named collections of declarations
Collections of logically related data and operations
Generalised data types
Protected data
Hiding low level details
Packages containing encapsulated tasks.

Unfortunately, although it is useful to understand the roles of the package construct in these terms, realistic examples tend to mix the different classes, and examples in the case study do not fall cleanly into this classification. In the following, where it seems helpful to the presentation, some of the concepts will be illustrated first with idealised 'paradigm' examples.

10.2 Named Collection of Declarations

In this simplest case the package is degenerate, having no hidden part. The visible part contains only a collection of constants, variables and types, associated by some logical relationship. Enclosing them in a package ensures that all their names are visible in the program unit which requests them, or none are. An example is:

```
package PRINTER_FORMAT is
    type SPACING is (SINGLE, DOUBLE, TRIPLE);
    type CHANNEL is (PRINTER, SCREEN);
    subtype WIDTH is INTEGER range 0 ..  132;
    subtype PAGE  is INTEGER range 0 ..  100;

    MARGIN: WIDTH:= 0;                 -- assignment
    COLUMNS: WIDTH:= 60;               -- of default
    LINES: PAGE:= 30;                  -- initial values
    LINE_SPACE: SPACING:= SINGLE;      -- at declaration

end PRINTER_FORMAT;
```

Within the scope of this declaration, the types and variables declared may be accessed by the dot notation:

```
LINE_HEIGHT: PRINTER_FORMAT.SPACING := DOUBLE;
```

which defines a variable of the type SPACING taken from the package, and initialises it to a value from the type.

Alternatively, the contents can be accessed through the use clause as in the following example.

```
declare
   use PRINTER_FORMAT;          ⎫
                                ⎪
begin                           ⎪ scope of the
                                ⎬ use clause
     -- access values from package directly
                                ⎪
end;                            ⎭
```

In this style the package is a kind of 'common block', a unit of useful data which can be made available in exactly those program parts which request it.

Many systems are constructed with one or more packages containing nothing but types and constants defining a vocabulary of concepts prevalent in the problem area. Such is the package SYSTEM_TYPES, which is the first item declared in the patient monitor system given in chapter 16, and defines the model of a patient and some other objects in a hospital environment. Another example from the patient monitor is the package INTERFACE_DATA which defines types and variables forming the interface to the external instruments, with their representation specifications. This is also used as an example in chapter 13.

10.3 Logically related data and operations

Commonly, the related items are also subject to operations and it is convenient to enclose the data and the relevant operations together in a single unit. This is achieved by enclosing the data with the specification parts of the relevant procedures and functions in a package. The bodies of the procedures and functions are given in the body of the package, since they form part of the implementation.

Typically, such a package has the following structure:

```
package EXAMPLE is

        ...-- type definitions
        type T is -- etc.

        ...-- data definitions
        V: T;                -- etc

        ...-- specifications of procedures and functions
        procedure PROC (X: in T, Y: out T);
        function  F(X: in T) return T;
                             -- etc
end EXAMPLE;
```

The package body then contains the definitions of the bodies of the procedures and functions.

```
package body EXAMPLE is

        procedure PROC (X: in T; Y: out T) is
              ...
              ...  -- details of procedure
        end PROC;

        function F (X: in T) return T is
              ...
              ...
        end F;

end F;
```

All operations specified in the package specification part must be provided with full definitions in the body of the package. The signatures of the functions and procedures must agree exactly with those in the visible part of the package.

The following example shows how the data structure in the patient monitor modelling the collection of patients associated with their beds is provided as a package. This uses access types, which are the subject of chapter 12, and this package will be described more fully there.

```
package PATIENT_DIRECTORY is
                -- a type for information about patients
    type PATIENT_DATA is
        record
            HOSPITAL_NUMBER: HOSPITAL_PATIENT_NUMBER;
            PERSONAL_DATA  : PERSONAL_INFO;
            TRANSACTION_RECORD: TRANSACTION_FILE;
        end record;
    type PATIENT_DETAILS is access PATIENT_DATA;

                -- a variant record giving patient status information
    type PATIENT_STATUS is (IN_BED, DETACHED, NONE);
    type SEARCH_RESULT(STATUS: PATIENT_STATUS := NONE) is
        record
            PATIENT: PATIENT_DETAILS;
            case STATUS is
                when    IN_BED  =>
                   BED_NO: BED;
                when    DETACHED=>
                   null;
                when    NONE    =>
                   null;
            end case;
        end record;

            -- reference list of attached patients
    BED_ALLOCATION: array (BED) of PATIENT_DETAILS;
            -- list  management for detached patients.  The list  follows
            -- the first in first out discipline of a queue.

            -- transfer patient currently in bed B to detached list.
            -- patients are automatically deleted after 48 hours
```

```
    procedure DETACH(B: in BED);

              -- search in both lists to find patient by name or by number
    function  FIND_PATIENT (NAME  : NAME_TYPE)  return SEARCH_RESULT;
    function  FIND_PATIENT (NUMBER: HOSPITAL_PATIENT_NUMBER)
                                                    return SEARCH_RESULT;
              -- procedure to print and archive all remaining detached
              -- patients, then delete them from the list
    procedure PURGE;
end PATIENT_DIRECTORY;
```

The body of this package is not given here, since it uses features of Ada which have not yet been described. The reader should, however, be able to appreciate how this package specifies the properties of the package which are of importance to other program parts, defining the external interface, those functions and procedures which define the services provided by the package to the rest of the program, and which may be called from those other program parts. The fact that a reader can appreciate the package behaviour without having details of its body, illustrates the way in which the specification displays the abstract properties of the package.

This specification part contains all the information required by other parts of the program in order to use the data and types made available. The operation of the procedure and functions it contains is not of concern to the rest of the system. The specification part defines the interface presented to the the rest of the program by the package, and separates the concerns of the programmer and the reader for what the program does and how it does it.

Declared as separate compilation unit, such a package makes the data items and the operations available to all parts of the program which may require such access. For example, a procedure requiring access to its facilities might be written:

```
with PATIENT_DIRECTORY; use PATIENT_DIRECTORY;
procedure ..... is...
```

Care must be exercised if a package containing data is made accessible to a number of tasks which can execute in parallel. Data shared between such programs may be a cause of erroneous program operation. A program may be part way through an updating action, writing new values into the shared variables, and be interrupted by another which reads the data. Operations to read or write to a data structure must be 'indivisible'. To avoid errors it is good practice to protect shared resources by a 'lock' preventing simultaneous access by more than one task. Data which is not so protected should normally only be accessed by a single task. Often, therefore, packages containing visible variables are used only in a single procedure or task.

Section 10.7 describes how packages may be created which are protected by synchronization against such erroneous operation, and so can be made accessible to many concurrent tasks.

Such protection is in the nature of an implementation detail. That the data is not a single indivisible element does not concern the programmer using it. In fact package PATIENT_DIRECTORY does have such protection, in a way which is described later.

10.4 Generalised Data Types

As explained in chapter 5, the full concept of a type includes the set of operations valid on objects of the type. These operations model the behaviours of the objects whose states are represented by the value sets specified in the type declaration. To capture the full abstract behaviour of the objects being modelled, the operations must be associated with the type declarations. A package provides the means by which this can be accomplished.

Predefined types have their standard predefined sets of operations. Many are hardware supported on most machines, but that is of no concern to the user. Since the operations on user defined types depend on the problem area, the system can do nothing to create operations, though it can provide facilities permitting the programmer to create them. Types are defined in the visible part of a package, and the operations declared in the same visible part. Details of how the operations work are hidden from the rest of the program by encapsulating those details in the package body. The programmer is thus able to create a situation in which, so far as the rest of the program is concerned, the types and their operations are available as if they were standard types with their defined behaviours.

As a simple paradigm, consider the type DAY. The true concept of a day involves, of course, the ordered set of values given in the enumeration, but should include some other operations. The type should certainly capture the cyclic nature of the week. Perhaps it should also permit an operation to find the day N days ahead, where N is an integer. That operation can be represented by an overloading of the addition operator, so that it can add integers to days. These operations can be encapsulated in a package definition:

```
package DAYS is

    type DAY is (MONDAY, TUESDAY, WEDNESDAY, THURSDAY,
                                  FRIDAY, SATURDAY, SUNDAY);
    function NEXT_DAY(D: DAY) return DAY;
    function PREVIOUS_DAY(D: DAY) return DAY;
    function "+" (D: DAY; I: INTEGER) return DAY;

end DAYS;
```

This specifies the operations suitable for days. Of course, some problem areas might need more special operations on days, but this will suffice as a simple example. The package specification has captured the properties of days in the week at an abstract level. The package body must now define how the operations work, thus:

```
package body DAYS is

    function NEXT_DAY (D: DAY) return DAY is
    begin
        if D = DAY'LAST then return DAY'FIRST;
        else return DAY'SUCC(D);
        end if;
    end NEXT_DAY;
```

```
        function PREVIOUS_DAY (D: DAY) return DAY is
        begin
             if D = DAY'FIRST then return DAY'LAST;
             else return DAY'PRED(D);
             end if;
        end PREVIOUS_DAY;

        function "+" (D: DAY; N:INTEGER) return DAY is
        begin
             return DAY'VAL((DAY'POS(D) + N) mod 7);
        end;  --integer addition not a recursive call on "+"

    end DAYS;
```

In this illustration attribute enquiries have been used in writing the program. This made it unnecessary to remember that DAY'FIRST is MONDAY. If, instead, the week was redefined so that the first day was SUNDAY the programs would still be correct. Indeed, while writing this section type DAY was changed, having first been defined with abbreviated day names MON, TUE etc. This change involved no change in the package body.

Within the scope of this package declaration the program could contain the following block:

```
    declare
        use DAYS;
        MAY_DAY, INDEPENDENCE: DAY;
    begin
        MAY_DAY := FRI; -- in some year
        INDEPENDENCE := MAY_DAY + 64;
        ...
        ...             -- then a year later
        ...
        MAY_DAY := MAY_DAY + 365;
        ...
        ...             -- and further operations

    end;
```

Note that the overloaded definition of "+" provides only for the addition in the order MAY_DAY + 365. The expression 365 + MAY_DAY would be an error, unless a second overloading was explicitly included in the package definition to provide for that too.

The predefined package CALENDAR to be found in the system library of every Ada system, and which is described in full on page 225 in chapter 13, is an excellent example of such a package, where the type TIME, defined as a record:

```
type TIME is
    record
        YEAR: INTEGER range 1901 .. 2099;
        MONTH: INTEGER range 1 .. 12;
        DAY: INTEGER range 1 .. 31;
        SECOND: DURATION;
    end record;
```

is associated with a collection of appropriate operations.

Consider, now, a more significant example. This is a package to provide the users with a facility to declare and use stacks. A stack is a 'push down' store, in which data items can be inserted and removed on a last in first out basis.

There are many ways of implementing a stack, but a simple one is illustrated in fig 10.2. The data items are stored in order of entry in an array, and there is a pointer to indicate which item is the 'top' of the stack, the most recently inserted.

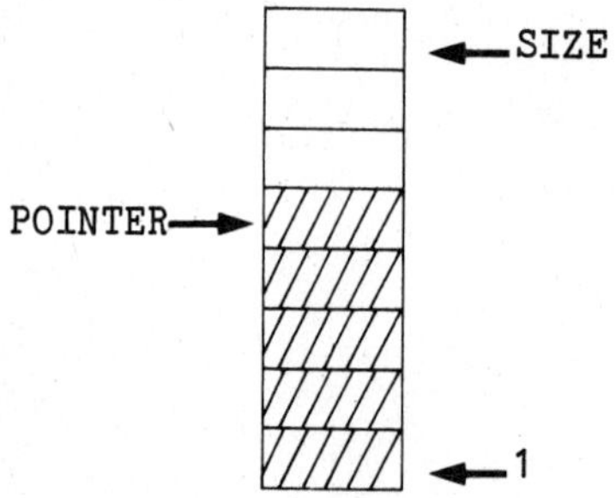

figure 10.2

The array STORE(1 .. SIZE)

Operations on a stack are conventionally:

push: adds a new item to the top of the stack
pop: removes the most recently inserted item
top: inspects the value of the topmost item, leaving it unchanged
isempty: inspects to see if the stack is empty

Using an array to implement the stack type implies some maximum number of entries. A possible way to handle this is to provide an operation isfull, complementary to isempty, which users may invoke to check that there is room to add an item. In the following example, the stack is defined as a record type collecting together the declaration of the array and the associated pointer. By making the size of the array a discriminant, stacks may be created of whatever size is required by the user.

```
package STACKS is
        MAX: constant INTEGER := 100;
                -- defines biggest permitted stack

        subtype STACK_INDEX is INTEGER range 1 ..  MAX;
        subtype POINTER_VALUE is INTEGER range 0 ..  MAX;
        type STACK(SIZE: STACK_INDEX) is
            record
                STORE: array (1 ..  SIZE) of INTEGER;
                POINTER: POINTER_VALUE := 0;
                                -- each new stack is initially empty
            end record;

        procedure PUSH(S: in out STACK; ITEM: in INTEGER);
        procedure POP (S: in out STACK);
        function  TOP     (S: STACK) return INTEGER;
        function  IS_EMPTY(S: STACK) return BOOLEAN;
        function  IS_FULL (S: STACK) return BOOLEAN;

 end STACKS;
```

Within the scope of this package definition a programmer can introduce as many new stacks as are required, and operate on them with the approved set of operations, supplied to implement the behaviour of a stack. Within this package definition is enshrined an abstract view of the properties of a stack, while the way in which the procedures and functions actually operate is hidden from the rest of the program, appearing only in the package body.

Within the scope of this declaration, the user can declare and use stack variables:

```
declare
     use STACKS;
     MY_STACK: STACK(SIZE => 40);
            -- a stack of 40 elements
     DATUM, TEMP: INTEGER;
begin
     ...     -- generate new DATUM;

     PUSH(MY_STACK, DATUM);

     ...

     if not IS_EMPTY(MY_STACK) then
          TEMP := TOP(MY_STACK);
          POP(MY_STACK);
     end if;

          ... etc.

end;
```

The following is an outline of the body as it might appear in the program:

```
package body STACKS is

     procedure PUSH(S: in out STACK; ITEM: in INTEGER) is
     begin
          if S.POINTER < S.SIZE then
               S.POINTER := S.POINTER + 1;
               S.STORE(S.POINTER) := ITEM;
          end if; --new items are ignored if no space
     end PUSH;
     function IS_EMPTY(S: STACK) return BOOLEAN is
```

```
        begin
             return S.POINTER = 0;
        end IS_EMPTY;
             ...etc.
    end STACKS;
```

It is important to appreciate that this package provides no storage for stacks; it contains no variable definitions, only the definition of the type and the operations. Storage is allocated dynamically on the stack of the using program by the declaration of variables of type stack in that program.

10.4.1 Private Data Types

Using only the defined operations ensures a high level of quality assurance for the program: users of stacks are provided with the appropriate tools for their use, and the code to provide the stack operations will have been very well tested. However, in the circumstances of this example, the user of type STACK is not constrained to use the operations provided. Possibly to achieve some short cut to solving some special problem, it is possible that a programmer might use his knowledge of the structure of a stack, and access the contents of the record directly, writing, say:

```
    I := MY_STACK.STORE(MY_STACK.POINTER - 2);
```

to obtain the element two below the top. There is a risk of a program error, for example, when the stack is nearly empty. The definition of the stack type is not fully abstract, since its substructure is accessible to the users.

Such use by a using program of the internal structure of the stack variables also increases the interdependence of the modules, since a decision to change the details of the package STACKS may make the user's program invalid. The definition of the type STACK is not fully abstract.

It is possible to hide even this structure from users by declaring the STACK type to be a 'private data type'. This is done as follows:

```
package PRIVATE_STACKS is
        MAX: constant INTEGER := 40;
        type STACK(SIZE: INTEGER range 1 ..  MAX) is private;
                -- defines the name of the type and its discriminant
        procedure PUSH(S: in out STACK; I: INTEGER);
           -- etc all as before

  private type STACK(SIZE: INTEGER range 1 ..  MAX) is
       record
           STORE: array (1 ..  SIZE) of INTEGER;
           POINTER: INTEGER range 0 ..  MAX:= 0;
       end record;
 end PRIVATE_STACKS;
```

Like the body of the package the contents of the part of the package specification between **private** and **end** is hidden from the users. The program statement accessing the record structure by the dot notation given above is now illegal. Indeed, the storage for a stack could be redefined as a linked list, and the push and pop operations suitably recoded for the alternative representation, with no danger that any other program part could be affected. The rest of the program depends only on the abstract properties of a stack, and not at all on the details of how the program provides them. With the earlier definition, users could have avoided using features which increase unnecessarily the interdependence of the components. By choosing to make the type private, the system designer can ensure that they do not.

Objects of a type which is defined as a private data type may be assigned to each other, and compared for equality, but no other operations are legal, except those provided by the package. Still stronger protection is afforded by making the type **limited private**. In that case the items cannot be assigned to each other, either. In general, copying of a complete stack to another, or comparing two stacks for equality, are not useful operations, so a stack type would sensibly be declared:

```
type STACK is limited private;
```

Private and limited private data types have not been used in the case study.

Private types behave to the programmer like the primitive types of the language; the programmer can know their axiomatic properties and their operations, but is totally unaware of their representation. It has been pointed out that, to this extent, type TIME discussed above is over specified in the language definition. It is not appropriate to allow programmers to access the internal structure of the TIME records. A more consistent definition would use:

```
type TIME is private;
```

A change in the language definition to introduce this more logical form is likely. It will not change the use of the CALENDAR by disciplined programmers, but will prevent its misuse.

10.4.2 **Extending Operations to More General Types**

In the stack example, the type of the objects stored was INTEGER. A programmer needing to store some other type of objects on a stack would, on the face of it, have to write a separate package, almost the same, except for the replacement of the name INTEGER with the name of the new type. There would have to be a new definition for every type of object for which a stack was required. This may appear to be a shortcoming of the strongly typed language, where objects of different type cannot be assigned to the same storage. In fact, however, by the use of generic packages, a single definition may be given from which stacks for any type of object may be derived. This will be covered fully in chapter 12.

10.5 Protected Data

In the previous section, the package bodies contained only definitions of procedures and functions which operated on data supplied as parameters by other program components, or on data items declared in the package specification part, and so publically accessible to users of the package. Of course, there could be local variables declared in the subprograms to provide them with temporary working space, but such variables, being stored on the stack, are destroyed after the subprogram has completed its operation.

An important new dimension is obtained when data objects, and possibly types, are declared in the declarative part of a package body. In that case the items in question are invisible in any other part of the program, and may be accessed only from the code in the bodies of the subprograms within the package, and, as will become apparent, in the imperative part of the package itself. The structure of the package is now:

```
package body X is

    --declarations of hidden data

    --declarations of local procedures and functions

    --definitions of visible procedures and functions

begin

    --imperative part. Initialization code

end X;
```

The program contained in the imperative part of the package body is entered once during the elaboration of the package declaration. If the package is declared in the declarative part of some subunit this implies that it is executed when the subunit is invoked, and the local declarations are elaborated. If, on the other hand, the package is a separately compiled library unit, forming a stand-alone item, accessed by other program parts by a **with** clause, then the initialization code is executed once before the main program is first entered. Its purpose is to initialise the locally defined data.

In general the use of such a package is to provide a shared data structure, available for use from many parts of the program, while enforcing discipline on the users in the manner in which they use it. The difference between this and a private data type lies in the fact that there is only one data structure per package, whereas the data structures involved in a private data type are owned by the using programs, which can create as many instances of the type as they need.

An example of a shared data structure of this kind can be found in the case of a queue of items, to represent jobs to be done in some computer system. These are to be stored in the order of arrival, and handled in a first in first out order.

```
package JOB_QUEUE is
    procedure JOIN (in JOB);
    procedure DELETE;
    function  HEAD return JOB;
    function  IS_EMPTY return BOOLEAN;

end PATIENT_DATA;
```

This package specification can be valid only within the scope of the declaration of a type JOB which is not further defined here. It announces the existence of storage for a queue of JOB's accessible to the rest of the program through the use of the procedures to insert or delete jobs and the function to find the job currently at the head of the queue.

The program to define the operation of the queue is contained in the package body, which has the form outlined above. There are, of course, many different ways in which the queue could be implemented. The procedures JOIN and DELETE could provide accesses to a disc file, so that individual jobs are stored on disc and recovered into memory as and when they are required. Alternatively, the data may be contained in the store, in which case it can be represented as an Ada data structure. Even so the structure could take one of many forms. Possible methods of storing such a queue of data for convenient access include circular array buffer and a linked list. In the following, a package body is given in implementing the queue as a circular buffer.

```
package body JOB_QUEUE is
                -- first the data structure
    BUFFER_SIZE: constant := 30;
    type JOB_COUNT is INTEGER range 0 ..  BUFFER_SIZE;
    type POINTER   is INTEGER range 1 ..  BUFFER_SIZE;
    STORE: array(1 ..  BUFFER_SIZE) of JOB;
    COUNT: JOB_COUNT;
    HEAD, TAIL: POINTER;
```

```
            -- next the operations
      procedure JOIN(X: in JOB) is
      begin
           TAIL := TAIL mod BUFFER_SIZE +1;
           STORE(TAIL) := (DATA => X, T => CALENDAR.CLOCK);
           COUNT := COUNT +1;
      end INSERT;

      procedure DELETE is
      begin
           HEAD  := HEAD  + 1;
           COUNT := COUNT - 1;
      end DELETE;

      function IS_EMPTY return BOOLEAN is
      begin
           return COUNT = 0;
      end
 begin      -- initialize the queue to be empty
      COUNT := 0;
      HEAD  := 1;
      TAIL  := 1;
 end JOB_QUEUE;
```

The initialization has been done this time in the imperative part of the package, as an illustration, but could again as well been done in the declaration.

There is another class of situation in which a package can be used, whose structure is exactly the same, but whose use is conceptually somewhat different. In this class of problems the hidden structure is not a store to contain data for some external problem, but rather a finite state machine in its own right. The only thing it represents is itself. An example can be based on a popular puzzle known as Rubik's Cube. This is a cube of six coloured faces, each composed of nine coloured squares. These squares are themselves the surfaces of 27 smaller cubes from which the whole cube is constructed. Any surface of the main cube, consisting of 9 of the small cubes may be rotated about its centre, so that after a few moves the small squares become almost irretrievably muddled. A computer model of such a cube will consist of a data structure representing its current state, with operations to rotate the surfaces. Externally, the details of the structure and the operations to produce the rotations are irrelevant:

```
package RUBIK is
    type COLOUR is (RED, BLUE, GREEN, WHITE, ORANGE, YELLOW);
    subtype ROTATION is INTEGER range 1 .. 3; --in quadrants
    procedure ROTATE(R: in ROTATION; SIDE: in COLOUR);
    procedure DISPLAY;
end RUBIK;
```

The package body contains the representation of the cube and of the operations. Solving this problem is left as an exercise, though a possible solution is given with the collection of specimen answers in the appendix.

10.6 Hiding Low Level Details

A further role of a package is to hide from the rest of a program those details which are inevitably machine dependent, presenting a uniform high level view of the interface to external hardware, while the body is written in low level terms using representation specifications to handle the particular mechanisms of the implementation. In this way, the abstract view of the system is machine independent, and the parts of the system which must be rewritten if the program is moved to a different machine are localised in a small number of well defined places.

So, for example, in the patient monitoring system, access to the hardware interfaces of the instruments measuring the vital signs of the patient is obtained by a package whose specification, in a slightly simplified form is:

```
package INTERFACE_DETAILS is

    function INTERFACE(B: BED) return FACTORS;

end INTERFACE_DETAILS;
```

The body of this innocent looking package involves the mechanisms of the physical interface and encapsulates details of a highly machine dependent nature concerning addresses, representations and the handling of interrupts. It is discussed in chapter 13, which deals with low level features of this kind.

10.7 Packages Containing Tasks

Packages may contain tasks for two reasons. On the one hand they may encapsulate program units which model coexisting elements of the problem domain. On the other hand tasks may also serve to coordinate access to shared resources by concurrent program units, providing the locks to prevent simultaneous access by readers and writers, as described in the previous chapter. In this case the package behaves as a 'monitor'.

Consider first the first category. It will be recalled that a task cannot be a stand-alone program unit: to model a subsystem which forms a permanent part of the application, it must be enclosed in a package. It is then necessary for the designer of the system to consider whether the task in question is to make its 'entries' visible to other units external to the package. In most cases, since such units comprise a system, communication between tasks is required. In that case the specification of the task is made visible also to the rest of the program by declaring it in the visible part of the package. The structure of such a package is of the form:

```
package TASK_UNIT is

    type ....-- declare types for entry parameters
                  -- if not globally known
    task HIDDEN_TASK is
                  -- declare entries to the hidden task
    end  HIDDEN_TASK;

end TASK_UNIT;
```

```
package body TASK_UNIT is

        -- declare local resources for package

    task body HIDDEN_TASK is
        -- declare task resources
    begin

        -- imperative part of task body

    end HIDDEN_TASK;

        -- other packaged units

begin
    -- initialization code
end TASK_UNIT;
```

The embodied task becomes active at the time when the package declaration is elaborated, concurrently with the initialization code. In practice that means that they become active in an undefined order. It is important, therefore, that the task should not depend on any initialization of the package resouces, for which it is not itself responsible. A package may contain several tasks, in which case the same remark applies concerning the order of initiation of those tasks. A common case involves a rendezvous consisting of an entry call to the task by the initialization code to initialize the task itself.

Note also that if the task is one member of an array of tasks derived from a task type definition, it does not spontaneously know its own identity; it may have to be passed it as data in a rendezvous. This will be found in the patient monitor, where the package BEDSIDE_MONITORING_SYSTEM contains an array of MONITOR tasks, which are given their bed numbers in a rendezvous with the initializing code.

Task entries need not be made visible to the rest of the program in the way illustrated above. The visible part of the packaged task may itself be internal to the package body, accessible only to the code of other units internal to the task body. Procedure bodies may contain entry calls to tasks visible to them. This may be used to permit access by other program parts to certain of the task entries, while keeping others hidden.

A task in a package body may also be used to ensure the coordination of access to shared data resources by concurrent tasks, providing the security against error from simultaneous access, as explained in section 10.2.

```
package SHARED_RESOURCE is

    procedure P1.....  ;
    procedure P2.....  ;

end SHARED_RESOURCE;
```

This package can be made available to other program parts in the usual way by the **with** and **use** clauses. If the package contains hidden shared data, and the procedures are called by several concurrent programs then the body must contain a task to control the accesses.

```
package body SHARED_RESOURCE is

    -- declare the shared resource

    task CONTROL is
        entry START;        --task entries visible
        entry STOP;         --only within the package
    end CONTROL;

    task body CONTROL is
    begin
        loop
            select
                accept START;
                accept STOP;
            or
                terminate;
            end select;
        end loop;
    end CONTROL;
```

```
        procedure P1....  is
        begin
              CONTROL.START;
                -- actions of the procedure P1
              CONTROL.STOP;
        end;

        procedure P2....  is
        begin
              CONTROL.START;
                -- actions of the procedure P2
              CONTROL.STOP;
        end P2;

    end SHARED_RESOURCE;
```

In this simplest form of coordination of access, only one call on one procedure can advance beyond the call on the START entry of the controlling task at a time. The task will only admit another call on START after the active task has signed off by calling STOP. This ensures that the actions of the procedure bodies can be completed in the assurance that those actions are indivisible. Even if, for example, the actions of P1 constitute a complex algorithm, an external program calling the procedure P1 may consider its action to be atomic. It may utilise the resource in ignorance of its possible concurrent use by other program parts. Of course, should a call be made while another program is active, the caller may be delayed in the completion of the procedure call. If there is a danger that an intolerable delay could arise, it is possible to use a timed entry call, as explained in chapter 9.

10.8 Summary of Packages

This completes the account of the use of Ada packages for structuring programs. It should be clear that correct use of these facilities permit programs to be written with great clarity and elegance, whose behaviour can be guaranteed to other program parts. The visible part may be regarded as a specification, a contract with the users of the package. The package body defines the implementation of the contract.

Exercise 10

10.1 Write a package to provide a new type COMPLEX enabling users to perform arithmetic on complex numbers. Objects of type COMPLEX should be capable of participating in the normal operations of arithmetic, as defined for complex numbers. Multiplication is also to be defined between INTEGER and COMPLEX.

Users of type COMPLEX should not be aware of the representation used.

10.2 Write a body for package RUBIK specified in section 10.5. Since the necessary information to write procedure DISPLAY is not available, it should be deferred by writing a null procedure, or by defining it as **separate** (see Chapter 14).

10.3 Make the type MEASURE from Exercise 8.5 into a private data type. Discuss possible representations of the values of the type.

10.4 Write a package to simulate a game of noughts and crosses (Tic Tac Toe). This should associate the representation of the board and the operations for placing a mark on a square, and checking to see if someone has won.

Incorporate the package in a program containing tasks to represent the players. Give the task bodies in outline only, showing, however, the passing of control between the players.

Is it necessary to protect the board from simultaneous access by the players?

CHAPTER 11

GENERICS

11.1 Program Units for a Class of Problem

It commonly happens that there exists a class of problems for which the solutions are logically related, giving rise to programs with the same schematic form, but differing in respect of certain details. In a strongly typed language the commonest case is that in which the same operations are required on objects of different type. However, that is not the only case to be considered: another is the situation in which the same algorithm is used at an outer level, but some of the subprograms used differ in different instances. A simple example would be a program to tabulate some arbitrary function. Generic program units are used in Ada to enable programs to be written in general form, and converted to meet the needs of the particular instance at the time of compilation.

Though the mechanisms are different, there is a strong analogy with the definition of a type. In declaring a type for a complex structure, the programmer defines a template, a pattern against which variables conforming to the type can be later constructed. By using discriminants, certain details of the structure can be left undefined in the template, to be specified at a later stage, when variables of the type are declared. It is the variable declarations which create actual storage to represent the objects defined.

So it is with generic program units. When a program component is defined as generic, it does not form part of any program. It defines only a template for the construction of one or more such units by the compiler at a later stage, the generic instantiation. With the definition are given formal parameters in terms of which the program is defined; these are substituted by actual parameters at the later stage.

The parameters are not restricted, however, as are parameters of subprograms, to data objects, but may be identifiers for types or subprograms, used to generalize the program unit.

In the simplest case of generics, the parameter list is empty. In that case each instance of the unit created is identical, and there is then considerable similarity to a record.

```
generic
package PATIENT_DATA is
     SENSOR_DATA: FACTORS;
     ..
end PATIENT_DATA;
```

This does not create any instance of the package in question. Rather it specifies the pattern for the subsequent 'instantiation' at some point in the program. Within the scope of the generic declaration, and in some declarative part, a package declaration may appear, in the form:

```
package DATA_FOR_CURRENT_PATIENT is new PATIENT_DATA;
```

which creates a package declaration, at that point, identical to the body of the declared generic unit.

The declarations of the generic unit are now accessed in the usual way, as selected components:

eg. DATA_FOR_CURRENT_PATIENT.SENSOR_FACTORS

or the declaration may be followed by a **use** clause in the usual way, and the objects can then be accessed directly.

There is, of course, some similarity to a macro expansion. However, there are two differences. First, there is no separate expansion into source code: the compiler deals with the generic units in the course of the translation of the program. Secondly, it is free to the compiler to arrange optimization, in which any program actions declared in the generic unit can be implemented as reentrant code shared between the various instances.

11.2 Generic Parameters

The parameters for a generic unit may be types, procedure of functions, or normal parameters. As a first example consider the typical procedure to exchange the values of a pair of variables. Suppose that both variables are of type T; then the program would be of the form:

```
procedure EXCHANGE (A,B: in out T) is
    TEMP: T := A;
begin
    A    := B;
    B    := TEMP;
end EXCHANGE;
```

Within its scope, this procedure can be called to exchange the values of any pair of variables of type T. However, strong typing prevents its being used to exchange values of other items, even those derived from T. Since exchanging of values is an important action in many algorithms, such as sorts, it would be tedious if a separate, and differently named, procedure had to be written for each type of variable; the essential steps are the same whatever the type.

This example is a paradigm for cases in which a type is supplied as a parameter to a generic program unit. In a program where the use of exchanges is needed, a library unit could be constructed defined as follows:

```
generic
type ITEM is private;
procedure EXCHANGE (A,B: in out ITEM) is
    TEMP: ITEM := A;
begin
    A    := B;
    B    := TEMP;
end EXCHANGE;
```

This definition gives the form of the exchange algorithm for any data type. The name of the formal type ITEM is introduced following the **generic** specification, and is given here as **private.** That is not to be interpreted as implying that the actual type is a private data type. Since this unit defines the form of an exchange algorithm for an arbitrary type, the program can make no assumptions about the structure of the type. The only operations which can safely be assumed to be meaningful on objects of type ITEM are, therefore, assignment, and testing for equality. These are the same restrictions as those which apply to private data types. The specification of ITEM as a **private** enables the compiler to enforce their application.

As already explained, such a definition does not create a program unit, but only defines the shape of any unit conforming to the definition.

The usual rules apply to the scope of a generic definition. If this is a separately compiled library unit, then any program component requiring access to it will be prefixed by a clause **with** EXCHANGE;. Within the scope,instances of the algorithm can be created for different types of data by the use of the **new** allocator.

```
declare
     procedure SWAP_COLOUR  is new EXCHANGE(ITEM => COLOUR);
     procedure SWAP_INTEGER is new EXCHANGE(ITEM => INTEGER);
     M, N: INTEGER;
     BODY_COLOUR, SEAT_COLOUR: COLOUR;
begin
     ....
     ....

     SWAP_COLOUR(BODY_COLOUR, SEAT_COLOUR);
     SWAP_INTEGER(M, N);
     ....
     ....

end;
```

The declarations in the declarative part of this block define procedures for exchanging, respectively, colours and integer values. These behave in exactly the same way as if two normal procedures had been defined at that place, using the same algorithm as in the generic outline, but with ITEM replaced explicitly by COLOUR and INTEGER.

Since Ada permits the overloading of procedure names, it was not in fact necessary to use different names for the two instantiations of the procedure. They might as well both have been called SWAP and the compiler left to distinguish according to the types of the actual parameters.

When the type is given as **private** the restrictions on the operations which are possible on the variables of the type in the algorithm make the range of possible generic functions and procedures very restricted indeed. However, it is also possible to specify some limitations on the class of types which may be supplied as actual parameters at the generic instantiation. Some properties of objects of the actual type may then be assumed. Consider first scalar types; the possibilities are the following:

```
type ITEM is (<>);        -- specifies that ITEM is an discrete type
type ITEM is range  <>;   -- specifies that ITEM is an integer  type
type ITEM is digits <>;   -- specifies that ITEM is floating point type
type ITEM is delta  <>;   -- specifies that ITEM is fixed point type
```

In each of these cases the information provided permits the programmer to use special operations and attributes relevant to the case in question.

If, for example, the type is specified to be one of the numeric types then operations of arithmetic are valid. If the formal type is specified to be one of the discrete types, the attributes 'FIRST and 'LAST may be used to find the first and last values in the ordered set implied by the definition of the actual type. It is thus possible to write algorithms which are general in their application to variables of any type belonging to the restricted class, but which allow more powerful operations than those permitted to completely general types, specified as **private.**

In illustrating packages in chapter 10, a program was given specifying the algorithm to make the week cyclic, by using attributes of the type DAY. This can be written as a generic unit, and used to make any enumeration type cyclic. Thus:

```
generic
type ANY is (<>); -- any discrete type
function NEXT (A: ANY) return ANY is
begin
     if A = ANY'LAST then
          return ANY'FIRST;
     else return ANY'SUCC(A);
     end if;
end NEXT;
```

This generic function utilises the attributes of enumeration types to permit the operation to be specified for an arbitrary enumeration type. The compiler will ensure that the programmer does not attempt to instantiate this function to operate on items of other types.

Functions to find the next value in a cyclic sense for DAYS and for SEASONS may now be created in the same way as before:

```
function NEXT_DAY is new NEXT (ANY => DAY);
function NEXT_SEASON is new NEXT (ANY => SEASON);
```

It may also be desirable to provide for the corresponding cyclic operations in reverse order. It will be good sense to provide these as a generic package:

```
generic
type ANY is (<>);
package CYCLIC is
     function NEXT (A: ANY) return ANY ;
     function PREVIOUS (A: ANY) return ANY;
end CYCLIC;

package body CYCLIC is
     function NEXT ....
     function PREVIOUS .....
               -- definitions of the function operations in terms
               -- of the attributes as in the above example
end CYCLIC;
```

11.2.1 Structured Types as Generic Parameters

Structured types may also be supplied as generic parameters. This usually requires the definition also of scalar generic parameters. Thus, for example, consider the following procedure which can be instantiated to form a program to sum the elements of any array with elements of fixed point type. The index is any discrete type:

```
generic
type ELEM is digits <>;
type INDEX is (<>);
type VECTOR is array (INDEX) of ELEM;
procedure SUMARRAY(V: vector) return ELEM is
     TOTAL: ELEM := V(INDEX'FIRST);
begin
     for I in INDEX range INDEX'SUCC(INDEX'FIRST) ..  INDEX'LAST loop
                         TOTAL := TOTAL + V(I);
     end loop;
     return TOTAL;
return;
```

This example requires several comments. First, since ELEM is a floating point type, addition is defined, the sum of values of type ELEM yielding a result of the same type. However, the range of ELEM is not guaranteed to include zero. Thus, the temporary variable TOTAL cannot be initialised to zero. Instead it is given the first element of the array. That in turn complicates the **for** loop, which is not over the whole of the range of INDEX, but omits the first element.

In fact the program as given is not fully adequate, since it fails if presented with an array of a single element. In that case INDEX'SUCC(INDEX'FIRST) does not exist, and attempting to evaluate it would cause a constraint error exception. This inadequacy can be corrected by testing whether ELEM'FIRST = ELEM'LAST before entering the loop:

```
if INDEX'FIRST /= INDEX'LAST then
     for I in INDEX range INDEX'SUCC(INDEX'FIRST) ..  INDEX'LAST loop
          ...etc.
     end loop;
end if;
```

Recalling the example in chapter 6 (page 90), using an array of rainfall data, indexed by month:

```
type WEATHER_DATA is array (MONTH) of RAINFALL;
```

a procedure to sum the rain for the year can be defined:

```
procedure ANNUAL_TOTAL is new SUMARRAY(VECTOR=> WEATHER_DATA;
                         ELEM=> RAINFALL; INDEX=> MONTH);
```

This can be invoked in the scope of a declaration:

```
NEW_YORK_RAIN_DATA: WEATHER_DATA;
TOTAL_RAIN: HOURS;
```

by the statement

```
TOTAL_RAIN := ANNUAL_TOTAL(NEW_YORK_RAIN_DATA);
```

11.3 Generic Operations

Most languages derived from Algol permit the definition of procedures and functions, in which one or more of the formal parameters is defined as a function or procedure, whose name is supplied as an actual parameter in the calling statement. This permits the definition of algorithms written in general terms, which call on a procedures or functions supplied by the calling program. It was, however, a requirement of the STEELMAN specification that Ada should not permit this. In practice, an almost equivalent effect can be obtained by the use of formal function or procedure parameters to generic units.

Generic program units may be defined which use formal names for function or procedure subprograms. Actual program objects may be derived from these by by the compiler, using generic instantiation. The generic definition specifies the formal function or procedure by giving its full declaration with the specification of its parameters and the type of its result. These types may also be generic. Consider, for example, a function to integrate some arbitrary function. The latter will take a floating point type as its argument and return floating point result. The integration will be between limits given by values which are also of that type. Thus:

```
generic
type FORMAL is digits;
function  F(X:  FORMAL) return FORMAL;
function INTEGRATE(UPPER, LOWER: FORMAL) return FORMAL is
begin
    ...
    ...  -- program to integrate function F
    ...  -- between limits LOWER and UPPER
    ...  -- and return the result.
    ...

end INTEGRATE;
```

This definition can be instantiated to provide appropriate integration routines for functions already defined in the program. For example, to integrate the sin function

```
declare

    function INTEGRATE_SIN is new INTEGRATE(FORMAL= > FLOAT;
                                            F=> SIN);
    PI: constant:= 3.14158;
begin
    ...
    ...
    Y := INTEGRATE_SIN (0.0, PI / 2.0);              ...
    ...
end;
```

The use of generic units with formal function or procedure parameters does not seem likely to figure strongly in the field of embedded systems. This short section is included here to give the flavour of the concept. Readers are referred to the reference manual for further details including the specification of defaults for formal functions.

Generic units of great generality are difficult to write correctly, and they will figure mostly in libraries of programs provided by systems programmers for the use of application programmers. They are usually not difficult to use. Some understanding of their use is necessary to handle input and output in Ada.

11.4 Generic Units in the Standard Environment

Several of the library packages in the standard environment contain generic definitions from which programmers may generate units of their own. These relate particularly to input and output.

11.4.1 Text Input and Output

Package TEXT_IO provides for input and output of character strings to the printer. Facilities to convert numeric types to strings for printing, and to generate string representations of the literals associated with enumeration types are obtained by instantiating the appropriate package from TEXT_IO for the types required. Note that it is necessary to instantiate I/O even for the predefined types.

```
with TEXT_IO; use TEXT_IO;
procedure ......is
    package INT_IO is new INTEGER_IO (INTEGER);
    use INT_IO
    I, J: INTEGER;
begin
   ...
   ...
   GET(I); PUT(J); -- GET and PUT from the package INT_IO
   ...
   ...
end;
```

The function GET will expect to find a value on the input stream conforming to a literal of type INTEGER. PUT will generate output in the default format, though a field width and base may be defined. Full details are given in chapter 14 of the reference manual.

Similarly:

```
with TEXT_IO; use TEXT_IO;
procedure ...... is
     package FLUID_IO is new ENUMERATION_IO(FLUID);
     use FLUID_IO;
     GAIN, LOSS: FLUID;
begin
    ...
    ...
    PUT(LOSS);  GET(GAIN); -- PUT and GET from FLUID_IO
    ...
    ...
 end;
```

In this case GET will expect to find in the input stream a string corresponding to a literal from the type FLUID.

Since all I/O in the patient monitoring system is handled at terminals driven by special interface software, these packages are not used in the case study, though the body of the report generator might well use them.

11.4.2 File Input and Output

Facilities are provided to create files on an external medium consisting of collections of records of common type. Suppose it is required to create a disc file of items of type T. The programmer creates a package for the purpose containing the definitions of a set of file types

```
type IN_FILE;
type OUT_FILE;
type INOUT_FILE;
```

and a set of operations to create files of the type, to write to them and to read from them.

A new file for type T will be created by first defining a variable of the appropriate file type, and then calling the procedure CREATE with parameters defining the logical name of the file, as defined in the declaration, and the name to be given to the physical file on the external medium, in the form of a character string. The file may now be opened by calling the procedure OPEN, written to or read from, reset, closed etc. by calling appropriate procedures. All these features are provided by a generic package INPUT_OUTPUT, defined in terms of an element type ELEMENT, in outline as follows:

```
generic
type ELEMENT_TYPE is private;
package INPUT_OUTPUT is

      type IN_FILE    is limited private;
      type OUT_FILE   is limited private;
      type INOUT_FILE is limited private;

      procedure CREATE(FILE: INOUT_FILE; NAME: STRING);
            -- etc.  other procedures to provide operations on files
            -- of elements of type ELEMENT_TYPE.  Operations are
            -- overloaded for the classes of file type read only,
            -- read/write, and write only as required.
      private
            -- implementation dependent definitions of the files

end INPUT_OUTPUT;
```

The user of file I/O creates a package in the usual way, by instantiating this package for his particular type.

```
package FILE_OF_T is new INPUT_OUTPUT (ELEMENT_TYPE => T);
```

so creating the facilities needed to declare types for files of T items.

```
declare
     NEW_FILE: FILE_OF_T.INOUT_FILE;
     NEXT_T  : T;
begin
     FILE_OF_T.CREATE(NEW_FILE, "MY DATA FILE");
     ...
     ...  -- get next value for NEXT_T for filing
     ...
     FILE_OF_T.WRITE(NEW_FILE, NEXT_T);
     ...
     etc
end;
```

This gives the flavour of the facilities provided by Ada, and used in the patient monitoring system in the packages FILE_HANDLING and in those program units which use it to write to the patient's transaction record. There is reason to believe that an early language revision will introduce some changes in the details of these facilities, though not the basic concept. For this reason the packages are not defined in full detail in this book. Readers intending to write programs using file operations are advised to consult their language reference manual.

Exercise 11

11.1 A bounded buffer for ITEMs was given in chapter 9, page 151. Write a generic package to provide a buffer store for an arbitrary type, giving both the specification and the body. Instantiate it to provide a buffer for objects of type UNIT_RECORD.

11.2 Write a generic procedure to tabulate an arbitrary array, as a table with the index and the component value. Instantiate the procedure for WEATHER_DATA as in section 11.2.

11.3 Write a generic procedure to tabulate a function to be provided as a parameter.

CHAPTER 12

BUILDING DATA STRUCTURES

12.1 Introduction

Advanced program design techniques often call for the implementation of data structures that can represent complex logical relationships between their components. In an operating system, for example, the module responsible for the allocation of resources to processes may dynamically build an ordered list of requests. A compiler concerned with the analysis of the syntax of statements may require the facilities for the construction of trees.

Construction of such data structures not only requires the ability to show relational linkages, but also statement control over storage allocation and deallocation. As a new resource is requested the storage for a request notice must be allocated, given appropriate values, and linked into the list. After a request has been dealt with the corresponding notice is no longer required and can be returned to free storage.

The building of linked lists, queues, stacks and trees can be achieved using nothing more than array facilities with integers linking the indices of related elements [12.1]. However, such an approach has two fundamental drawbacks: firstly, it compels the implementor to be aware of the 'how' of the implementation and, secondly, it does not solve the problems of storage allocation. The first of these drawbacks is against the philosophy of Ada. The program designer should always think at the most abstract level and should not run the risk of confusing the problems of the application of the data structures with the problems of their implementation. The second drawback concerns the artifical provision of statement level storage allocation. In fact, all the storage that may be required for each complex structure must be allocated in advance of its use. The programmer then has the responsibility of constructing a further structure of linked free space from which elements are taken as required, and to which they are returned. Such techniques are tedious and error prone.

A language that aims to allow the programmer to directly express the application requirements of building structures must provide the following facilities:

A data type for variables that can represent pointers to other data objects.

Statements that will allow the programmer to allocate and release storage independently of the block-structured environment.

Ada provides these facilites with **access** types and the **new** allocator.

12.2 Access Types

A named type declaration defines a template for objects of that type, it does not create any objects. Thus, the declaration:

```
type PERSONAL_INFO is
     record
          NAME             : NAME_TYPE;
          DATE_OF_BIRTH    : DATE;
          ADDRESS          : ADDRESS_TYPE;
          GENDER           : SEX;
          TELEPHONE_NUMBER: PHONE_NO;
          NEXT_OF_KIN      : KIN;
          BELIEF           : RELIGION;
     end record;
```

specifies a pattern for objects of type PERSONAL_INFO. Subsequent declaration of the variables:

```
FRED, JIM : PERSONAL_INFO;
```

uses this pattern as a template for storage allocation. This declaration will cause two objects to be allocated, each conforming to the PERSONAL_INFO structure. The name FRED will be associated with the first such object and the name JIM with the second. These naming associations are immutable and exist throughout the scope of the storage allocation (although the identifiers FRED and JIM may be reused within this scope, such an action only causes the original meaning to be hidden).

The declaration:

```
type NAME_PERSONAL_INFO is access PERSONAL_INFO;
```

defines a template for a variable whose value may be the name of an object of type PERSONAL_INFO. The subsequent declarations:

```
NEXT_PATIENT : NAME_PERSONAL_INFO;
```

will cause the allocation of a storage locations which is capable of holding the name of a PERSONAL_INFO object. However, no PERSONAL_INFO object is actually generated and the access variable has the value **null**, where **null** is a reserved word used to indicate the value of an empty access variable.

To create instances of objects of type PERSONAL_INFO the allocator **new** is used:

```
NEXT_PATIENT := new PERSONAL_INFO;
```

In general, **new** DATA_TYPE is used as an expresion that will allocate new storage of the specified type and deliver the name of that storage; this may then be assigned to an access variable. Such storage must be free of the normal block-structure scope rules and is referred to as 'heap storage'. The implication is that each language implementation must provide for a spare heap of storage, separate from the stack, where space for dynamically created objects can be allocated on demand. There will also be a 'garbage collector' provided to identify storage that is no longer capable of being accessed and return it to the heap.

The **new** allocator may also be followed by a bracketed expression that gives an initial assignment of a value to the object generated, except when the object is of a **type** that is private.

Consider the following example:

```
declare
       type NAME_INTEGER is access INTEGER;
       NJ, NK, NL : NAME_INTEGER;
  -- three objects of type access to INTEGER are created,
  -- they have the scope of this declare block,
  -- they have the values null which indicates that
  -- they do not name any storage
begin
       NJ := new INTEGER(4);
  -- an object of type INTEGER is created
  -- this object is named by the access variable NJ
  -- the initial value 4 is assigned to the object
       NK := new INTEGER(6);
  -- another object of type INTEGER is created
  -- named by NK, initial value 6
       NL := NK;
  -- NL now names the same object as NK
       NJ := NK;
  -- NJ also names the same object as NK
  -- the object previously named by NJ still exists but
  -- can no longer be accessed
       NL := new INTEGER;
  -- NL now names a newly allocated INTEGER object
  -- this object has an undefined value
       NL.all := NJ.all;
  -- this causes the contents of the object named by NJ
  -- to be copied into the object named by NL
end;
```

After the end of this block the identifiers NJ, NK, and NL are out of scope and the INTEGER objects named by them are no longer accessible. The space occupied by these objects can be reclaimed by a garbage collector.

Allocated objects may be assigned to access variables declared in a scope external to that in which they are allocated, and thus continue to exist beyond the end of that scope.

```
declare
   N_OUTER : NAME_INTEGER;
begin
   -- do something;
   declare
      N_INNER : NAME_INTEGER;
   begin
      N_INNER := new INTEGER(34);
      -- an INTEGER object is allocated from the heap
      -- it is named by N_INNER
      -- and assigned the value 34
      N_OUTER := N_INNER;
      -- N_OUTER now names the same object as N_INNER
   end;
   -- N_INNER is now out of scope and no longer exists
   -- but the INTEGER allocated from the heap still exists
   -- and is now named by N_OUTER
end;
```

12.3 Building a list

Access types can be used in the construction of linked lists and this will be demonstrated by means of an example. Consider a real-time system where there is a single console used to display messages from several concurrent processes. A program module is responsible for handling display requests from the processes. Each request is noted in a display request block (DRB) and then dealt with in a first come first served order. The implementor of the display handler wishes to construct a queue of DRBs in response to requests from processes and to extract the first request from the queue when the console is ready to receive a message.

To implement such a queue as a list the following facilities will be required:

- a template for an DRB,
- an identifier for the start of the list,
- a procedure that adds new request blocks to end of the list,
- a function that delivers the first DRB from the list,
- a function that tests to see if the list is empty.

The exact detail of the DRB will depend on the peculiarities of the system. At the very least it will contain values giving:

the identification of the requesting process,
the text of the message.

This can be provided by an Ada record type declaration.

```
type REQUEST is record
    REQUESTER : PROCESS_NAME;
    MESSAGE   : STRING(1..50);
end record;
```

Objects of this type are to be presented by the requesting process and used to generate a linked list. To implement this list each DRB must contain the name of the next block in the list, this name being of type **access** DRB. This type is to be identified by NAME_DRB. However, if the declaration of the DRB is to contain the use of NAME_DRB then this identifier must have been predeclared. But it cannot be declared until DRB is declared! This is a recursive problem that is overcome by allowing the incomplete declaration of a type identifier which is later redeclared in full.

Thus, the declarations required to provide a pattern for the DRBs and their links are:

```
type NAME_DRB;
type DRB is record
     DATUM : REQUEST:
     LINK  : NAME_DRB;
end record;
type NAME_DRB is access DRB;
```

The head of the list can be identified by an access variable which is either **null**, indicating an empty list, or names the first request block. However, initially there will be no member of the list. This situation can be represented by a NAME_DRB variable that is initially **null.**

Thus, the following declaration will initialize the list.

```
LIST : NAME_DRB; -- all access variables are set to null initially
```

To add a new request block to the list new storage has first to be created, the details of the request then copied into this storage which is linked into the list.

Since the list is representing a queue the addition of the new DRB must be at the end of the list, So an additional:

```
TAIL : NAME_DRB;
```

is useful for accessing the tail of the list. The new item can then be added by the following statements:

```
TAIL.LINK := new DRB(INFO,null);
TAIL := TAIL.LINK;
```

However, this does not account for the initial condition when the list is empty. The full code of a procedure ADD_TO_LIST, that can be called whenever a new request is to be inserted, is shown below. It assumes the initial declarations of LIST and TAIL in a scope global to the procedure, within a package that will be used to encapsulate the queue.

```
procedure ADD_TO_LIST(INFO : in REQUEST) is
begin
   if TAIL = null
   then TAIL := new DRB(INFO,null);
        LIST := TAIL;
   else TAIL.LINK := new DRB(INFO,null);
        TAIL := TAIL.LINK;
   end if;
end;
```

The first request block can be removed from the list by a function HEAD with the code:

```
function HEAD return REQUEST is
   Q : NAME_DRB;
begin
   Q := LIST;
   LIST := LIST.LINK;
   return Q.DATUM;
end;
```

However, this function will not work if the list is already empty. A function to check for this condition would be:

```
function IS_EMPTY return BOOLEAN is
begin
   return LIST = null;
end IS_EMPTY;
```

The display handler would contain these subprograms organized together in a package with the specification:

```
package REQUEST_QUEUE is
   procedure ADD_TO_LIST(INFO : in REQUEST);
   function IS_EMPTY return BOOLEAN;
   function HEAD return REQUEST;
end;
```

and a body:

```
package body REQUEST_QUEUE is
   type NAME_DRB;
   type DRB is -- as above
   type NAME_DRB is access DRB;
   LIST, TAIL : NAME_DRB;
   -- bodies of the subprograms as above;
end REQUEST_QUEUE;
```

Assuming that the type REQUEST is declared in a scope global to the package.

Within the imperative part of the code of the display handler the facilities of this package will be used to encapsulate the queue of request blocks. When a call is received from a process for a display to be made there will be a call of ADD_TO_LIST by the display handler. When the console is ready to receive the next message the code:

```
if IS_EMPTY
then -- display "no message";
else -- display message of HEAD();
end if;
```

will be executed.

A more complex list is used in the case study to handle the details of patients who have been discharged from the intensive care unit but whose data must remain accessible for a further 48 hours. The details of each patient are given by an access to a value of type PATIENT_DATA, by using the following declarations:

```
type PATIENT_DATA is
     record
          HOSPITAL_NUMBER: HOSPITAL_PATIENT_NUMBER;
          PERSONAL_DATA   : PERSONAL_INFO;
          TRANSACTION_RECORD: TRANSACTION_FILE;
     end record;
type PATIENT_DETAILS is access PATIENT_DATA;
```

An access type is used so that a pointer to a patient's data records may be passed between processes in the intensive care control system.

Details of patients in beds are held in an array:

```
BED_ALLOCATION: array (BED) of PATIENT_DETAILS;
```

and a **null** value for any of the elements in the array indicates an empty bed. When a patient leaves a bed the pointer to his data is inserted in a list by calling the procedure:

```
procedure DETACH (B : in BED);
```

This procedure also puts a value in the list node that gives the time for the deletion of the patient's data in 48 hours. Because patients are deleted in order, all additions will be to the tail of the list and the next patient to be deleted will be on the front of the list.

The representation of patient data and its associated list handling is encapsulated in a package called PATIENT_DIRECTORY, the full specification of which is given in chapter 16. This specification contains the declarations given above, plus types and functions that allow a search to be made for particular patients, identified either by name or by hospital number.

```
type PATIENT_STATUS is  (IN_BED, DETACHED, NONE);
type SEARCH_RESULT(STATUS: PATIENT_STATUS := NONE) is
     record
          PATIENT : PATIENT_DETAILS;
          case STATUS is
               when    IN_BED      => BED_NO: BED;
```

```
                when     DETACHED    => null;
                when     NONE        => null;
            end case;
        end record;
    function  FIND_PATIENT(NAME  : NAME_TYPE) return SEARCH_RESULT;
    function  FIND_PATIENT (NUMBER: HOSPITAL_PATIENT_NUMBER)
                                                  return SEARCH_RESULT;
```

The rest of the list handling mechanisms are hidden within the package body. Because access to the list may come from different tasks in the program there is a risk of contention; one task may be attempting to detach a patient while another is searching for the same patient. To avoid any contention all the list handling is done by separate rendezvous with a task called DATA_PROTECTION, with the specification:

```
    task DATA_PROTECTION is
        entry DETACH_PATIENT             ( B: in BED);
        entry DELETE;
        entry GET_NEXT_TIME             ( T: out CALENDAR.TIME);
        entry FIND_PATIENT_BY_NAME      ( N: in NAME_TYPE;
                                          X: out SEARCH_RESULT);
        entry FIND_PATIENT_BY_NUMBER(NO:in HOSPITAL_PATIENT_NUMBER;
                                          X: out SEARCH_RESULT);
    end DATA_PROTECTION;
```

This task ensures that only one process may access the list at a time.

There is a task, called DETACHED_PATIENT_MONITOR, which calls the entry GET_NEXT_TIME to find the time for the next deletion, delays until the specified time and then calls DELETE. (A full description of timing facilities in Ada will be found in chapter 13.) The other entries are used by the search functions:

```
    function FIND_PATIENT(N: NAME_TYPE) return SEARCH_RESULT is
        X: SEARCH_RESULT;
    begin
        DATA_PROTECTION.FIND_PATIENT_BY_NAME(N, X);
        return X;
    end FIND_PATIENT;
```

```
function FIND_PATIENT(NO:HOSPITAL_PATIENT_NUMBER)
                              return SEARCH_RESULT is
     X: SEARCH_RESULT;
begin
     DATA_PROTECTION.FIND_PATIENT_BY_NUMBER (NO, X);
     return X;
end FIND_PATIENT;
```

The code of the body of DATA_PROTECTION, which manages the linked list, is as follows:

```
task body DATA_PROTECTION is
     type LINK;
     type NODE is
          record
               PATIENT: PATIENT_DETAILS;  -- access to patient record
               T      : CALENDAR.TIME;    -- time detached
               NEXT   : LINK;             -- next list item
          end record;
     type LINK is access NODE;
     HEAD, TAIL, TEMP: LINK; -- for list management

begin
   loop
       select
           accept DETACH_PATIENT (B: in BED) do
                TEMP := new NODE(BED_ALLOCATION(B),
                                 CALENDAR.CLOCK, null);
                if HEAD = null then
                     HEAD := TEMP;  -- add new item as head
                     TAIL := TEMP;  -- of the list
                else
                     TAIL.NEXT := TEMP;  -- add new item
                     TAIL := TAIL.NEXT;  -- to end of list
                end if;
                BED_ALLOCATION(B) := null;  -- empty bed
           end DETACH_PATIENT;
       or
```

```
    when HEAD /= null =>
      accept DELETE do -- remove from list
           PATIENT_IO.CLOSE  (HEAD.PATIENT.TRANSACTION_RECORD);
           PRINT_FINAL_REPORT(HEAD.PATIENT);
           SAVE_TO_ARCHIVE   (HEAD.PATIENT);
           if HEAD = TAIL then
                HEAD := null; -- remove only item
                TAIL := null; -- in list
           else
                HEAD := HEAD.NEXT; -- move down list
           end if;
      end DELETE;
or
    when HEAD /= null =>
      accept GET_NEXT_TIME ( T: out CALENDAR.TIME) do
                 T:= HEAD.T; -- time to delete next patient
      end GET_NEXT_TIME;
or
    accept FIND_PATIENT_BY_NAME(N:inNAME_TYPE;
           X: out SEARCH_RESULT) do
         declare
              FOUND: BOOLEAN := FALSE;
         begin
              for B in BED loop
                   if N = BED_ALLOCATION(B).PATIENT.NAME then
                        X := (IN_BED, BED_ALLOCATION(B), B);
                        FOUND := TRUE;
                        exit;
                   end if;
              end loop;
              if not FOUND then
                   TEMP := HEAD;
                   while  TEMP /= null and not FOUND loop
                        if N = TEMP.PATIENT.NAME then
                             X := (DETACHED, TEMP.PATIENT);
                             FOUND := TRUE;
                        else
                             TEMP := TEMP.NEXT;
                        end if;
```

```
                    end loop;
                end if;
                if not FOUND then
                    X := (NONE);
                end if;
            end;
        end FIND_PATIENT_BY_NAME;
    or
        accept FIND_PATIENT_BY_NUMBER (NO:inPATIENT_NO;
                                X: out SEARCH_RESULT) do
            -- similar logic to above search for name;
        end FIND_PATIENT_BY_NUMBER;
    end select;
  end loop;
end DATA_PROTECTION;
```

12.4 Building Trees

Another frequent usé of linked data structures is the construction of binary trees in which each node of the tree contains some information and links to its right and left subtrees.

To illustrate the way in which Ada can provide facilities for trees a more abstract approach will be taken than was taken in the case of the example on linked lists. Ada is designed to encourage the construction of general purpose software components that can be incorporated into particular applications. One such component could be a generic package for tree structures. The Ada philosophy of component design requires that the specification of what facilities are needed should be separated from the detail of how these facilities are implemented.

For constructing trees the requirement is for a generic package TREE_STRUCTURES which can be instantiated in terms of the type of information to be stored in the nodes. Let this type be identified by DATUM, then the specification of the package could be as follows:

```
generic
type DATUM is private;
-- data type for information in tree nodes
package TREE_STRUCTURES is

-- visible type declaration for TREE
   type TREE is private;

   -- subprograms for manipulating trees of nodes
   function EMPTY(T : TREE)return BOOLEAN;
      -- tests for T naming an empty tree
   function VALUE(T : TREE)return DATUM;
      -- gives the value of the item in the node named by T
   function RIGHT(T : TREE)return TREE;
      -- gives the right sub-tree of T
   function LEFT(T : TREE)return TREE;
      -- gives the left sub-tree of T
   function MATCH(KEY : DATUM;T : TREE)return BOOLEAN;
      -- tests key against the item in the named node
   function BUILD_TREE(X : DATUM; L,R : TREE)return TREE;
      -- forms a tree from the given subtrees and datum
private
   -- private type declarations to represent tree-nodes
   type NODE is record
      ITEM : DATUM;
      LEFT_TREE, RIGHT_TREE : TREE;
   end record;
   type TREE is access NODE;

end TREE_STRUCTURES;
```

Any programmer with access to the library containing the TREE_STRUCTURES package can now instantiate it in a program that requires tree building capabilities. To do this a knowledge of how the trees are implemented in the body of the package is not required, in fact it is hidden from the user by the use of private data types.

The example program below uses an instantiation of this package to implement an algorithm for sorting four letter words into alphabetical order. However, before this program could be written the library file must already contain a body for the generic package TREE_STRUCTURES. This body will contain the code for the implementation of the functions specified in the visible part of the package.

```
procedure WORD_SORT is
   -- a type is declared for the four-letter words
   subtype WORD is STRING(1..4);

   -- generic package instantiated to provide for trees of words
   package TREE_WORD is new TREE_STRUCTURES(WORD);
   use TREE_WORD;

   -- new words will be read into NEW_WORD
   -- the data will start with a copy of its terminating LAST_WORD
   NEW_WORD, LAST_WORD : WORD;
   SORT_TREE : TREE;

   procedure ADD_TO_TREE (T : in out TREE; W : WORD) is
   -- procedure used to build the tree
   begin
      if T = null  then
           T := BUILD_TREE (W,null,null);
      elsif W < VALUE(T) then
           ADD_TO_TREE(LEFT(T),W);
      else ADD_TO_TREE(RIGHT(T),W);
      end if;
   end ADD_TO_TREE;

   procedure SCAN_TREE (T : TREE) is
   -- procedure that scans the tree and prints ordered words
   begin
      if not EMPTY(LEFT(T)) then
           SCAN_TREE(LEFT(T));
      end if;
      PUT(VALUE(T));
      if not EMPTY(RIGHT(T)) then
           SCAN_TREE(RIGHT(T));
      end if;
   end SCAN_TREE;
```

```
-- imperative part of WORD_SORT
begin
   GET(LAST_WORD);
   loop
      GET(NEW_WORD);
      exit when NEW_WORD = LAST_WORD;
      ADD_TO_TREE(SORT_TREE,NEW_WORD);
   end loop;
   SCAN_TREE(SORT_TREE);
end WORD_SORT;
```

Internal to the body of TREE_STRUCTURES the body of the function LEFT could be implemented as:

```
function LEFT(T : TREE)return TREE is
begin
   return T.LEFT_TREE;
end;
```

a very simple process. However, coding this function requires knowledge of how the trees are represented. Separating this knowledge from the user of the package means that the method of representation can be changed, by recompiling a new version of the body of TREE_STRUCTURES, without any of the programs using the package having to be altered.

12.5 Multilinked Structures

Data structures more complex that simple lists and trees often require that the nodes of the structures be mutually dependent, as in the case of a doubly linked list. The Ada access type facilities can be used to build such structures provided that care is taken over the order of declaration of the node types and their links.

Consider the representation of two generations of a family. Two basic data types are required - one to represent the parents and the other to represent children. Objects representing parents are to have two access links, one to their spouse and the other to their first born child. Objects representing children are required to have three access links, one to each parent and one to their next eldest sibling.

Using the declarations:

```
subtype NAME_TYPE is STRING(1..10);
subtype AGE_RANGE is INTEGER range 0..120;
type GENDER is (MALE, FEMALE);
```

a suitable type for a parent could be:

```
type PARENT_RECORD is record
     NAME : NAME_TYPE;
     AGE : AGE_RANGE;
     SEX : GENDER;
     FIRST_BORN : CHILD;
     SPOUSE : PARENT;
end record;
```

and a suitable type for a child could be:

```
type CHILD_RECORD is record
     NAME : NAME_TYPE;
     AGE : AGE_RANGE;
     SEX : GENDER;
     FATHER : PARENT;
     MOTHER : PARENT;
     SIBLING : CHILD;
end record;
```

Each of these types contain variables of type PARENT amd CHILD which will be names of a PARENT_RECORD and CHILD_RECORD respectively. The sequential order of declaration call for CHILD and PARENT to be declared before their use. However, they cannot be declared before the types to which they give access! This impasse is overcome by using the incomplete declaration again and the full ordering of required declaration is:

```
type CHILD;
type PARENT_RECORD;
type PARENT is access PARENT_RECORD;
type PARENT_RECORD is -- as above;
type CHILD_RECORD is -- as above;
type CHILD is access CHILD_RECORD;
```

by the end of which all the type templates have been declared. These types can then be used to represent the data on a family:

```
declare
   FATHER, MOTHER : PARENT;

   procedure BIRTH_OF(BABY : CHILD) is
      P : CHILD := FATHER.FIRST_BORN;
   begin
      if P = null
      then FATHER.FIRST_BORN := BABY;
           MOTHER.FIRST_BORN := FATHER.FIRST_BORN;
      else
         while P.SIBLING /= null loop
            P := P.SIBLING;
         end loop;
         P.SIBLING := BABY;
      end if;
   end BIRTH_OF;

begin
   FATHER := new PARENT_RECORD("CHARLES    ",34,MALE,null,null);
   MOTHER := new PARENT_RECORD("DIANA      ",20,FEMALE,null,FATHER);
   FATHER.SPOUSE := MOTHER;
   delay 9*MONTHS;
   BIRTH_OF(BABY =>
       new CHILD_RECORD("WILLIAM   ",0,MALE,FATHER,MOTHER,null);
   delay 12*MONTHS;
   BIRTH_OF(BABY =>
       new CHILD_RECORD("GEORGE    ",0,MALE,FATHER,MOTHER,null);
   -- and so the family is established

end;
```

12.6 Access to Task Types

Chapter 9 section 5 described task types and gave the definition of a SEMAPHORE. Instances of task types can be allocated with the **new** allocator, in which case they are initiated at the point of allocation. Any tasks created in this way are dependent on the program unit in which the access type is declared. Given the declarations:

```
type NAME_SEMAPHORE is access SEMAPHORE;
MUTEX : NAME_SEMPHORE;
```

then a semaphore task may be created with the statement:

```
MUTEX := new SEMAPHORE; -- initiation happens now
```

and its entries called as MUTEX.SEIZE and MUTEX.RELEASE.

12.7 Summary

The access type facility of Ada provides an adequate mechanism from which complex data structures can be built and relieves the programmer of the mechanical details of storage allocation. However, the implied heap storage, with its garbage management, will mean that extensive use of access types could lead to high run-time overheads. The programmer should be aware of these overheads, especially in embedded applications where loss of performance can be critical.

The section on low-level features in chapter 13 will show how greater control can be exercised over the allocation and freeing of storage.

Ada has avoided the problem of dangling references encountered in the pointer variables of some other languages by not allowing access objects to name stack locations.

References

[12.1] "The Art of Computer Programming: Volume 2/ Seminumerical Algorithms"; Donald E Knuth, Addison-Wesley, 1969.

Exercise 12

12.1 The example given in section 12.3 is to be changed so that the requests are no longer dealt with in the order that they are received but in a priority order. The priority is given with the request as an integer between 1 and 99.

Re-define the REQUEST data type to allow this change.

Write a revised version of ADD_TO_LIST that will add requests in their correct priority position in the LIST.

12.2 Define a data structure to represent a stack of integer values.

12.3 Give the full coding of a body for the package TREE_STRUCTURES.

12.4 A package EVENT_LIST is required that will provide the mechanism for scheduling events in a discrete event simulation program. It has the following specification:

```
package EVENT_LIST is
    type SIM_TIME -- a numeric type to represent simulated time;
    type EVENT    -- an enumeration type naming the events
                  -- in the program;
    CLOCK:SIM_TIME -- a variable to hold the present time;
    procedure SCHEDULE (WHEN : SIM_TIME; WHAT : EVENT);
            -- adds notice of an event to the list, given the
            -- type of the event and the time at which it is
            -- to occur;
    function NEXT_EVENT return EVENT;
            -- finds the next event in the list,
            -- updates the system clock to the time of this event,
            -- removes the event from the list,
            -- returns the name of the event;
    function IS_EMPTY return BOOLEAN;
            -- checks to see if the list is empty;
end EVENT_LIST;
```

Write a body for this package. (Note that there may be several instances of the same event type in the list.)

12.5 In a multitasking program several different tasks require a particular service that may be provided, in a rendezvous, by one of a number of identical server tasks. Write an outline program that implements service requests as a single queue from which each customer is served in turn by the first free server task.

CHAPTER 13

LOW LEVEL AND REAL TIME FEATURES

13.1 Timing and Delays

Embedded applications of Ada are concerned with controlling the behaviour of an external system with which the computer interacts. In consequence, special language features are required to express these interactions, and to specify how they are handled by the interface hardware. Moreover, time will appear in many of the requirements specifications.

Simulations involving time usually have a variable to represent it, incremented to represent the advance of the clock. The time taken to run the program has nothing to do with the simulated time in the model. Such a simulation is often intended to run much faster than the simulated time since, if it does not do so, the solution will come too late for it to be useful. The prediction of tomorrow's weather based on today's observations would be useless if the computation took two days. Problems in which there is a need to compute fast enough to obtain a result before the elapse of time on the clock has made the result useless are often referred to as real-time problems.

Clearly, programs for embedded systems are real-time programs. Decisions concerning the control of external parts of the system must occur fast enough that the observations of the environment on which the decisions are based are still valid. Moreover, many systems require that actions should be initiated at defined times, or repeated at defined intervals. It follows that every computer running such programs must have access to a clock enabling the programs to take account of the elapse of time. The language in which the programs are written must then permit the programmer to express the interactions with this clock.

Each Ada system has a predefined fixed point type called DURATION declared in the package STANDARD. Objects of type DURATION are used to represent time intervals, measured in seconds. The precision depends on the hardware implementation, and so is not fixed by the language definition. The range, however, is always sufficient to store a time interval of at least one day, a minimum of 86,400.0 seconds.

Within the library of predefined program units there is a package CALENDAR, a typical example of a package containing a type with its operations.

```
package CALENDAR is
   type TIME is
      record
         YEAR: INTEGER range 1901 ..  2099;
         MONTH: INTEGER range 1 ..  12;
         DAY:    INTEGER range 1 ..   31;
         SECOND: DURATION;
       end record;

   function CLOCK return TIME;
   function "+"(A:TIME;B: DURATION) returnTIME;
   function "+"(A: DURATION; B:TIME) return TIME;
   function "-"(A: TIME;     B: DURATION)  return TIME;
   function "-"(A: TIME;     B: TIME)      return DURATION
end CALENDAR;
```

Program units requiring the use of the calendar are prefixed:

```
with CALENDAR;
```

and optionally

```
use CALENDAR;
```

and may then declare items of type TIME and set them to represent the current time using the function CLOCK whose value is the current time. It is perhaps worth noting that the range used for the YEAR is considered adequate, and avoids the complication of leap years at the start of new centuries which are missing unless the century divides by 400. With this constraint every fourth year is a leap year.

13.2 Delaying Actions by Specified Times

The control of actions which must occur after some prescribed delay is obtained by the use of a **delay** statement. This is written:

```
delay simple-expression;
```

The simple expression must return a value of type DURATION. The task obeying this statement will temporarily cease execution, resuming it after the prescribed delay.

To cause an action at a prescribed time, the programmer can write:

```
declare
   NEXT: TIME; -- the desired time for the action
begin
   ...
   ...   -- give a value to NEXT;
   ...
   delay NEXT - CALENDAR.CLOCK;
   ...
   ...   -- the delayed action
   ...
end;
```

It is never possible to guarantee that the delay will be precisely that specified, since, in a multi-task system, it may not be possible to release a processor for immediate use by the program having just completed a delay. For this reason it is prescribed that the delay will be at least equal to the specified duration.

It follows that, on the average, every delay is actually longer than that specified. This is often acceptable. However, in a cyclic program intended to execute at a prescribed frequency, every repetition comes a little late: there is a cumulative drift in the time of execution, as well as jitter in the actual intervals. The drift may be eliminated by checking against the clock at each cycle. An example from the case study is the following.

In the patient monitor, a task is required to read a patient's vital factors at fixed intervals defined by a variable, INTERVAL, of type DURATION. This is provided by a task POLLING, whose outline contains the following:

```
task body POLLING is
     NEXT: CALENDAR.TIME;
begin
     ...
     NEXT := CALENDAR.CLOCK;
     loop
          NEXT := NEXT + INTERVAL;
          delay NEXT - CALENDAR.CLOCK;
          ...
          ...          -- read the sensors and
          ...          -- take appropriate action
          ...
      end loop
 end PULSE_MONITOR;
```

This program will poll the interface to read the data at times separated by an average of INTERVAL, provided the delay in resumption of the program after each delay statement does not approach INTERVAL seconds. If it does, then the system is failing to achieve its commitments in real time.

13.3 Priorities

It commonly happens that tasks executing in parallel are not all equally urgent. System behaviour will then be better if the more urgent task can be given higher priority for the use of the processor. It may then be possible to satisfy the requirements of the urgent, time-critical tasks, without having large amounts of time when the processor is idle.

Such priority can be assigned to a task by a pragma PRIORITY. The pragma may appear in the specification part of a task as for example:

```
pragma PRIORITY(5);
```

Such a pragma will assign the appropriate priority to the task in question. The possible priorities are implementation dependent, and the value given may be a static expression of subtype PRIORITY, a predefined (but system dependent) subtype of INTEGER.

The scheduler must arrange that no task is using a processor which is of lower priority than one which is waiting and able to run. Scheduling is therefore 'pre-emptive', the processor being released by a running task, if a task of higher priority which has been waiting for some event, becomes able to run.

Note, however, that priorities influence only the scheduling of the processor among ready tasks. Tasks waiting on a common entry form a queue in strict first come first served basis.

13.4 Address Specifications

Address specifications may be used to define the position in store of a data object, variable or constant, or the start address of a program unit. In the latter case the unit may be a subprogram, package or task, the address being the start address of the unit named in the specification. The form of an address specification is:

for object-name **use at** static-simple-expression.

The syntax of the representation specification:

for ... **use** ...;

is the typical form in which such specifications are presented, and will be encountered again in the next sections.

The address of a task entry may also be specified, as explained in the next section.

13.5 Interrupt Handling

An interrupt is regarded as a rendezvous with an external task. The interrupt handler is a task containing an **accept** statement for the entry which is associated with the interrupt in question. The association of an entry with an interrupt is obtained by including in the task specification an address specification for the entry, as shown in the following example:

```
task HANDLER is
     entry INTERRUPT;
     for INTERRUPT use at 16 #2000# ;
end HANDLER;

task body HANDLER is
begin
     loop
          accept INTERRUPT;
          ...
          ...       --handle interrupt
          ...
          end;
     end loop;
end;
```

The address given in the **use** part of an entry specification, given here in base 16 (often called HEX), specifies the address to which the interrupt in question 'traps', i.e. transfers control. It is, however, inevitable that the exact interpretation of the address may be machine dependent; the simple model of an interrupt implied by this statement may not always apply. In each case where the hardware requires special interpretations of the address, this will be documented in APPENDIX F of the user manual for the implementation.

To ensure that an interrupt is handled with the requisite urgency, the task associated with an interrupt specification is given the highest possible priority. In other respects it is a normal task, and the interrupt entry may also be called by software. Since an interrupt task is given such high priority, it will lock out any other activities during its execution. The programmer must be aware of this when writing the program, and include in the task body only those actions which must have immediate treatment. Control should be transferred to a normal task as soon as possible after the occurrence of an interrupt.

An interrupt can be masked by including appropriate additional entries in the interrupt task, and organizing the task body to control whether the entry will be accepted or not. A simple version of such a handler might be as follows:

```
task HANDLER is
     entry MASK;
     entry UNMASK;
     entry INTERRUPT;
     for INTERRUPT use 16 #2000# ;
end HANDLER;
```

The calls on MASK and UNMASK by software are to determine whether the INTERRUPT entry is immediately accepted or not. This might be achieved by the following task body:

```
task body HANDLER is
begin
     loop

          select
               accept INTERRUPT do
                    ...
                    ...          --handle interrupt
                    ...
               end INTERRUPT;
          or
               accept MASK;
               accept UNMASK;
          end select;

     end loop;
end HANDLER;
```

If the hardware queues interrupts the behaviour of the interrupt is that of a normal entry call; if, however, an interrupt is lost when not immediately serviced, it is equivalent to a conditional entry call.

An effect similar to this is obtained in the patient monitor system, where the instrument interface is shared between the patients in different beds. The interface is handled by an interrupt task which manages a handshake with the external instruments. The assignment of the bed number to a variable representing the output channel leads to an output which switches a multiplexor to the appropriate bed. The task then waits for an interrupt signalling that the data is ready. When it in turn has safely completed its action to transfer the data to its destination, it informs the calling task by accepting the rendezvous with the entry FINISH. This arrangement ensures that only one bed can use the interface at a time.

```
task body INTERRUPT_HANDLER is
begin
     loop
          select
               accept CALL(B: in BED) do
                    CHANNEL := SELECTOR(BED);
               end;
          or
               terminate;
          end select;

          select
               accept DATAREADY;
          or
               delay 1.0;
               ....       --handle timeout
          end select;
          ....            --transfer data

          accept FINISH;
     end loop;
end INTERRUPT_HANDLER;
```

13.6 Representation Specifications

An embedded system frequently interacts with its external environment through hardware interfaces which are specially constructed for the purpose, and provide data in formats which are not necessarily of the same structure as normally used to represent data in the machine. In these circumstances it is necessary to provide means by which named variables in the program can be related to items of non standard structure.

In the normal way, use of a high level language relieves programmers of the responsibility for selecting the representation of data in the store of the computer. The declaration of a data type determines the logical properties of objects of the type, while the declaration of variables allocates storage. Mappings between data types and the internal bit patterns used to encode them, and between variable names and memory locations used to store them, are the responsibility of the compiler. There is a proper separation of concerns for the abstract properties of the data and the implementation details, for which the programmer is not responsible.

In almost every circumstance this is to be desired; the same program can be compiled unchanged to run on different machines, and the compiler is in a position to select the representations which will be most efficiently implemented on the machine in use. Though Ada does permit the specification of internal representations in ways to be described in the following sections, it must be realised that the use of these features will normally lead to a less efficient program than would be generated by the compiler without them. Having said that, there remain circumstances when the implementation of interface routines cannot be done without them. Traditionally, systems programmers write such routines in machine code.

In Ada provision is made for the control of the representations of data types, and of the storage addresses. In each case the program contains normal definitions of the logical properties of the objects in question, and separate statements defining the low level representations. The separation of concerns for abstract properties and implementation details is still preserved.

The following facilities are provided:

Length specifications permit the programmer to specify the space to be used in store for representing objects,

Address specifications permit control of storage locations used,

Enumeration type representations can be specified,

Record structures can be mapped to the underlying bit patterns.

In the following sections these cases are described separately.

13.7 Length Specifications

'Length specifications' enable the program to control the space allocated for objects to be represented in store. The name is loosely given to a collection of facilities provided by the language. The space occupied by an object is one of the attributes for which attribute enquiries are possible. Length specifications work by enabling the programmer to override the values otherwise chosen by the system. The value of the attribute is declared in the program in a statement, called a representation specification; this must appear in the same declarative part as the type in question, but after all other declarations. An attribute which is controlled in this way cannot be used in other declarations before its definition is encountered in the usual linear elaboration of declarations. The syntax of a representation specification is of the form:

for attribute **use** simple expression;

A length specification may be given for any of the following attributes:

T'SIZE

The storage occupied by an object of type is written T'SIZE. This specifies the size in bits of the storage occupied by such an object.

T'STORAGE_SIZE for access types.

The storage available for the collection of items associated with an access type T, and generated dynamically by the program. The attribute gives the size in storage units(words) of the space allocated.

T'STORAGE_SIZE for task types.

If T is a task or a task type, then space is allocated for the activation of the task, or for each task of the type. This is given in storage units by the attribute T'STORAGE_SIZE and may be controlled by a length specification.

T'ACTUAL_DELTA.

For a fixed point type T, the value of **delta** given in the type definition defines only the biggest value which may be used by the compiler. The actual value used may be controlled by the programmer using a length specification for T'ACTUAL_DELTA.

The following pakage specification appears in the patient monitor system, as part of the specification of the interface to the instruments monitoring the patient's vital signs. This includes size specifications for the types for the SELECTOR and the INTERFACE_VALUE, and address specifications for the variables CHANNEL and X. Additionally, the layout of the record of type SENSOR_VALUES is specified in a way explained in section 13.9 below.

```
package INTERFACE_DATA is
     WORD : constant := 16;
     type SELECTOR is new BED;
     type INTERFACE_VALUE is range 0 ..  65535;
     type SENSOR_VALUES is
          record
               BODY_TEMP,
               RIGHT_ATRIAL,
               LEFT_ATRIAL,
               DIASTOLIC,
               SYSTOLIC,
               PULSE_RATE: INTERFACE_VALUE;
          end record;
     CHANNEL: SELECTOR;
     X: SENSOR_VALUES;
               -- and now the representation specs
     for SENSOR_VALUES'SIZE use 6*WORD;
     for INTERFACE_VALUE'SIZE use WORD;
```

```
        for SENSOR_VALUES use
            record
                BODY_TEMP         at 0*WORD range  0 ..  15;
                RIGHT_ATRIAL      at 1*WORD range  0 ..  15;
                LEFT_ATRIAL       at 2*WORD range  0 ..  15;
                DIASTOLIC         at 3*WORD range  0 ..  15;
                SYSTOLIC          at 4*WORD range  0 ..  15;
                PULSE_RATE        at 5*WORD range  0 ..  15;
            end record;
        for SELECTOR'SIZE use 8;
        for CHANNEL use at 16 #8000# ;-- an 8 bit output PIA
        for X use at 16 #8002# ;
    end INTERFACE_DATA;
```

13.7.1 Length Specifications for Access Types

As remarked above, the attribute T'STORAGE_SIZE determines the total space available for objects of access type T. Thus, for example, the records of type PATIENT_DATA in the case study are referenced by variables of type PATIENT_DETAILS. To aid the compiler in allocating space on the heap for records of type PATIENT_DATA, the programmer can introduce a representation spec:

```
        for PATIENT_DETAILS'STORAGE_SIZE use
                    50 * ((PATIENT_DATA'SIZE/SYSTEM.STORAGE_UNIT)+ 1);
```

This enables the compiler to allocate space in store for approximately 50 patient records. An odd design detail in the language involves the use of a size in bits for an ordinary type, but a size in storage units(words) for an objects referenced through an access type. The word size for the machine in use can be accessed by referencing SYSTEM.STORAGE_UNIT.

Since the compiler can now allocate a definite amount of store to these objects, it may be able to do so in a static way, and release the space when the program leaves the scope of the type definition.

There is some ambiguity here as to which machine words are involved in SYSTEM.STORAGE_UNIT. In most cases the host will be different from the target. In that case, the portable form of the program may not work, and it may be necessary to use an explicit word size.

13.8 Enumeration Type Representations

Consider an enumeration type T. This may be given a length specification determining the size of the storage unit allocated for a variable of the type. It may be necessary also to specify the representation used for the constant values whose names are the enumeration literals in the high level language. This may be done using an array aggregate of type:

```
array (T) of INTEGER
```

to define a table giving the mapping between the literals of the type and a set of integers. The integers are the values (in decimal code) corresponding to the stored bit patterns, interpreted as binary numbers.

The notation used for the specification is:

```
for T use aggregate;
```

To give an actual example, suppose that a set of 5 commands,derived from single button depressions on a control panel are coded onto a parallel interface of 4 wires. The codes to be used are as follows:

0001	START
0010	STOP
0100	REPEAT
1000	HOLD
1010	RESUME

The interface is store mapped so that the state of the wires is available to be read from the address 16 #8001# in the less significant half byte, the rest of the byte being wired to zeros. The representation specifications would be as follows:

```
type COMMAND is (START, STOP, REPEAT, HOLD, RESUME);
ORDER: COMMAND;
for COMMAND'SIZE use 8;
for ORDER use at 16 #8001# ;
for COMMAND use (START=> 1, STOP=> 2, REPEAT=> 4,
                              HOLD=> 8, RESUME=> 10);
```

The order in which the enumeration literals are given must be such that the specified representation values are given in the order which satisfies the order relation implicit in the type declaration. In that case, all the attribute enquiries which would apply to a variable of the enumeration type are still valid; COMMAND'SUCC(STOP) has the value REPEAT whether specifications are given or not. The values need not be contiguous, and consequently there may be efficiency penalties in evaluating an attribute, if a representation specification is given.

A simple device for displaying data for human inspection is the seven-segment display. This is illustrated in figure 13.1 with the representations used for the HEX characters 0 .. F.

figure 13.1

A Seven Segment Display

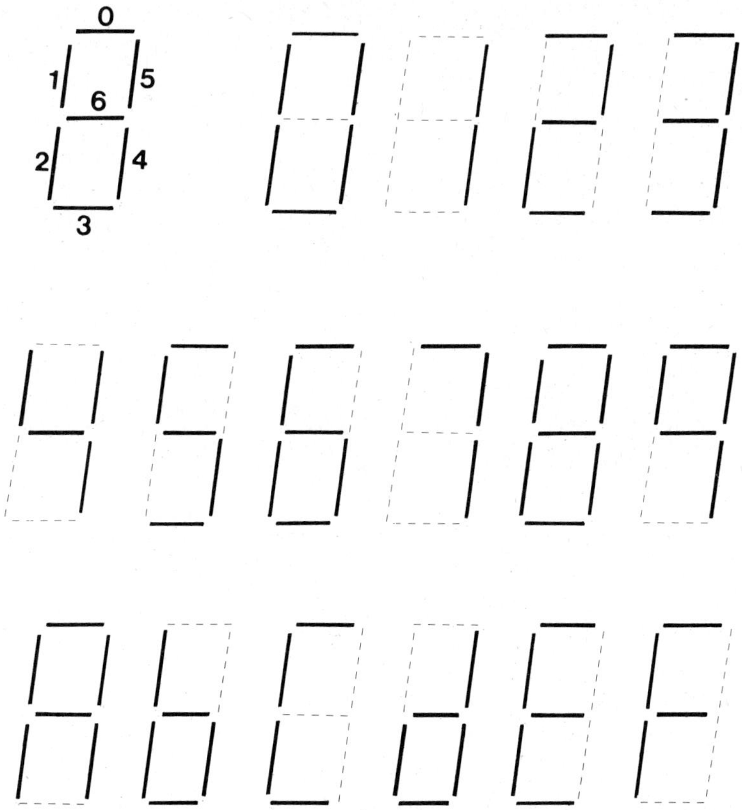

The codes representing the characters are then as follows:

	0	1	2	3	4	5	6	DECIMAL VALUE
0	1	1	1	1	1	1	0	63
1	0	0	0	0	1	1	0	48
2	1	0	1	1	0	1	1	109
3	1	0	0	1	1	1	1	121
4	0	1	0	0	1	1	1	114
5	1	1	0	1	1	0	1	91
6	1	1	1	1	1	0	1	95
7	1	0	0	0	1	1	0	49
8	1	1	1	1	1	1	1	127
9	1	1	0	0	1	1	1	115
A	1	1	1	0	1	1	1	119
B	1	1	1	1	1	0	1	94
C	1	1	1	1	0	0	0	15
D	0	0	1	1	1	1	1	124
E	1	1	1	1	0	0	1	79
F	1	1	1	0	0	0	1	71

This mapping can be obtained between character literals used as enumeration type values, and a variable linked by hardware to the display, by the following declarations.

```
type DIGIT_DISPLAY is
('C','1','7','0','F','E','5','B','6','2','4','9','A','3','D','8');

for  DIGIT_DISPLAY use

        ('C'=>  15, '1'=>  48, '7'=>  49, '0'=>  63,
         'F'=>  71, 'E'=>  79, '5'=>  91, 'B'=>  94,
         '6'=>  95, '2'=> 109, '4'=> 114, '9'=> 115,
         'A'=> 119, '3'=> 121, 'D'=> 124, '8'=> 127);
```

A variable of type DIGIT_DISPLAY will now be declared, and associated with an interface, by some address specification. If the variable is called SEVEN_SEGMENT then the assignment:

SEVEN_SEGMENT := 'B'

Will cause the display of the character B.

13.9 Record Type Representation

The total space allocated for an object of type record, say R_TYPE may be controlled by the use of a length specification, defining R_TYPE'SIZE. The address at which a variable of record type is to be stored is also accessible. Such specifications do not, however, affect the representations of the fields within the record, which have been declared to be of normal types. The length specification can affect only the unused space between the fields. To control the layout of the fields, how the bits are allocated to the objects within the record, is the role of a record type representation specification. The use of bits within the fields of the record is controlled by location clauses associated with the fields, as follows. As in other cases the logical properties of the type are given first, followed by a separate representation specification, containing so called location clauses, describing the lay out of the fields within the total record.

Suppose that some messages arrive over a network in the form of bit strings of length 32 bits. The network software deposits these strings into a fixed buffer of 32 contiguous bits starting at a 16 bit word boundary an even byte address Into these strings are packed informations of several kinds. Figure 13.2 shows the layout of a message frame.

figure 13.2

The Message Frame

SOURCE	PRIORITY	CLASS	SEQUENCE NO	SPARE	DATA
0 3	4 5	6 7	8 12	13 15	16 31

This structure can be related to a record structure as follows:

```
type NODE is (HEADQUARTERS, BRANCH1, BRANCH2);
type INFORMATION is range -32_768 ..  32_767;
type MESSAGE_CLASS is (REPLY, REQUEST, ALARM);
type MESSAGE_FRAME is
                          --a normal record declaration
    record
        SOURCE:       NODE;
        CLASS:        MESSAGE_CLASS;
        PRIORITY:     INTEGER range 1 ..  4;
        SEQUENCE_NO:  INTEGER range o ..  31;
        DATA:         INFORMATION;
    end record;
```

Representation specifications can now be given:

```
for MESSAGE_FRAME use
    record
        SOURCE        at 0*BYTE range 0 ..  3;
        CLASS         at 0*BYTE range 4 ..  5;
        PRIORITY      at 0*BYTE range 6 ..  7;
        SEQUENCE_NO   at 1*BYTE range 0 ..  4;
                                  -- bits 5..7 are spare
        DATA          at 2*BYTE range 0 ..  15;
    end record;

for MESSAGE_CLASS use (REPLY=> 1, REQUEST=> 2, ALARM=> 4);
                                       --bit strings 01, 10, 11
for MESSAGE_FRAME use 4*BYTE;
```

13.10 Machine Code Insertions

It goes beyond the scope of this book to describe in detail how machine code insertions may be written. The matter is covered in section 13.8 of the reference manual.

Machine instruction words are composed as records in a way very similar to the above example, and planted in-line as statements in the imperative part of a procedure.

13.11 Unchecked Programming

Every Ada system provides two generic units in the library to enable certain low level operations to be carried out which it is not possible to check by software. The programmer uses these features at his own risk, and so they are given suitable names to emphasise their dangerous nature. They are described briefly in the following sections.

13.11.1 Unchecked Deallocation

When an object referenced by a variable of access type is no longer required, then the program will often reassign the access variable to another object. When there are no longer any variables accessing a given object, then the system may recover the space by the operation of a garbage collector. However, the overheads of a garbage collector are considerable, and there is no guarantee that one will be provided. The efficiency of the system may be increasd if the programmer can signal to the system that an object is no longer required. This is done by calling a procedure, derived from a generic procedure in the standard environment, called UNCHECKED_DEALLOCATION. If O_TYPE is the name of the object type, and A_TYPE is that of the access variables, then the programmer defines an instance of this procedure by writing, for example,

```
    procedure RELEASE is new UNCHECKED_DEALLOCATION (O_TYPE,A_TYPE);
```

In the case of the patients in the case study, the objects are of type PATIENT_DATA, while the access types are PATIENT_DETAILS. The programmer could write:

```
    procedure RELEASE is new UNCHECKED_DEALLOCATION
                                     (PATIENT_DATA, PATIENT_DETAILS);
```

When the patient in bed N is released, then the program could include the statement

```
        RELEASE (INTENSIVE_CARE(N));
```

The compiler is unable to ensure that there is not a second variable naming the same item, so it is entirely up to the programmer to ensure that there will not be a subsequent access to the same item by another access variable, which would have dangerous and unpredictable results.

13.11.2 Unchecked Type Conversions

In the last resort it may be necessary to break the strong typing and bring about a type conversion between variables of unrelated type. This is a question of reinterpreting the bit pattern representing one logical type in terms of another. Possibly the main use is for finding the integer address corresponding to the value of an access variable.

Such conversion can be achieved by creating an instance of a generic function supplied in the environment called UNCHECKED_CONVERSION. This returns a value of the target type corresponding to the parameter of the source type.

13.12 Exceptions

As pointed out in chapter 3, an essential feature of real-time programs concerns the effects of failures of hardware or software on the rest of the system. A computer system controlling a nuclear reactor, for example, cannot abandon control because some error condition has been detected in the system. Rather, actions to recover from the failure should be invoked, and an attempt made to 'contain' the failure, preventing its effects from being felt more widely than need be.

If a program component creates or detects an error, it is usually necessary to invoke some alternative action. If an erroneous subprogram unit has already performed some actions it can be expected to round off or undo what it has done and possibly report the failure to the calling program. In most languages this can only be achieved by including a status flag among the parameters of the invocation, to be tested by the calling program on return. Ada exception handling provides a special mechanism for managing such situations.

Exceptional conditions caused by failure in some part of a system are referred to as **exceptions.** Reacting to an error situation is called raising an exception; reporting the problem to a higher authority(the calling program) is called propagating the exception while taking appropriate corrective actions is referred to as handling it. A special program segment to manage the error condition is called an exception handler.

A programmer may associate a potential error situation with a named exception, by declaring in a declarative part of the program, for example:

```
ERROR : exception;
```

The declared object may be thought of as a status flag, visible within the normal scope of the declaration.

Within that scope the program may contain a statement to raise the exception, thus:

```
raise ERROR;
```

If the program control reaches this point, the program discontinues its current activity and seeks a handler for the exception. If a handler has been provided in the current program unit, then that will be used. Such a handler is written at the end of the block which it protects, thus:

```
begin  --the start of the imperative part of a procedure,
       --function, task, package or declare block
    ...
    raise ERROR;
    ...
    ...
exception
    when ERROR =>
        ...          --text of handler
end;
```

It is also possible to include in the handler section of the block a 'catch all' handler by writing:

```
when others =>
        ...        --text of handler
```

which can serve as a handler for any exception raised in the block which it protects, and which is not explicitly named in the handler.

After executing the handler, the program exits from the current program unit procedure. There is no attempt to return to complete the action which has been abandoned: the **raise** has produced a transfer of control to the handler which is executed instead of the normal code. The error is now considered to have been handled successfully, the calling unit being unaware that any error has occurred; the exception was reset ('disabled') on entering the handler. If it is necessary to pass the problem up to the calling program a further raise statement may be included in the handler body.

If no handler has been provided, or if the handler has reraised the exception, then, when control is returned to the unit which invoked the current one, it will behave as if the same exception had been raised at the point where the call on the subprogram occurred, or at the point following a faulty declare block. This unit will therefore in turn seek a handler for the exception, and in due course may pass the control up again. It is possible for this sequence of events to be repeated until control leaves the scope of the name of the exception. In that case it can only be handled by a catch-all handler.

If the process of propagating an exception continues to the level of the main program without finding a suitable handler, then the program will be aborted. If, however, an exception is raised in a task, and no handler is found, then the task is aborted, but the exception is not propagated further.

It is perhaps helpful to illustrate by an example from real life the behaviour of the Ada exception facility, and to show the circumstances in which it seems appropriate. Suppose a cook is preparing a meal using an electric oven. In the normal way the oven is switched on, cooking is completed and then the oven is switched off again. If, however, the cooking is started and shortly afterwards the electric oven fails, it is necessary for the cook to decide how to proceed. It is certainly not appropriate for the oven to decide to light the hot plate and continue cooking on that. The procedure for oven cooking must not, however, be abandoned without first switching off the oven. When that has been done control can be transferred to the cook who will decide how to procede.

```
procedure COOK_DISH is
     OVEN_FAILURE: exception;        -- declares the exception in whole
                                     -- procedure scope.
     procedure COOK_IN_OVEN is
     begin
          LIGHT_OVEN;
          ...
          if OVEN_FAILS then
               raise OVEN_FAILURE;
          end if;
          ...
          SWITCH_OFF_OVEN;                -- normal completion
     exception
          when OVEN_FAILURE =>
               SWITCH_OFF_OVEN;           -- an essential step
               raise OVEN_FAILURE; -- sends the problem up to caller
     end COOK_IN_OVEN;

     procedure COOK_ON_HOTPLATE is
          -- an alternative method
     end COOK_ON_HOTPLATE;

begin      -- body of COOK_DISH
     COOK_IN_OVEN;
exception
     when OVEN_FAILURE =>
          COOK_ON_HOTPLATE;
end COOK_DISH;
```

This analogy is to emphasize two things. First, the need for a local handler to tidy up first, even though the exception is being reraised, and secondly the need to refer to higher authority in order to proceed.

13.12.1 Handling Standard Exceptions

Certain exceptions are standard, built in exceptions, and raising them is automatic, requiring no program action. Such for example, is NUMERIC_ERROR, raised when numeric underflow or overflow is detected by the hardware. CONSTRAINT_ERROR is raised if variable is assigned a value outside its range constraints. Similarly, the SELECT_ERROR is raised when the guards of a select statement are all false. Arrangements for the handling of these are just like programmer named exceptions.

As an example, consider the following function:

```
function FACTORIAL(N: in INTEGER) return FLOAT is
    FACT:FLOAT := 1.0;
begin
    for I in 2 .. N loop
        FACT:=FACT*FLOAT(I);
    end loop;
    return FACT;
exception
    when NUMERIC_ERROR =>
        return FLOAT'LAST;
end FACTORIAL;
```

On raising the exception, control is transferred to the exception handler, which in this case is present, and capable of dealing with NUMERIC_ERROR in a reasonable way, returning the largest possible value belonging to type FLOAT. The exception code is executed, and the program unit is considered to have completed its work, so control is returned to the program which called it.

In the example given here, the solution works well. This is because the unit is a well-behaved function which does not change any global data. In many situations, however, the program which has abandoned its actions may have left a computation in some undetermined intermediate state when it abandoned control and passed it to the handler. The mechanism has great power and can be an invaluable aid to programming error conditions. They must, however, be well understood by the programmer, dangerous unpredictable actions are liable to happen. If the same exception can arise at several points in a part of a program protected by a handler, the handler cannot discover which was responsible. Nor can control be returned to the point where the error occurred. There is no doubt that these mechanisms must be treated with the greatest caution.

13.12.2 **Some General Guide Lines**

The following rules should be observed by programmers introducing exceptions into their programs.

They should be kept for truly exceptional error situations, and not be used to handle an event which is sure to occur from time to time, albeit rarely. For example, an end of file is not an exception.

There should usually be a handler in the block immediately surrounding a raise statement. This must tidy up, completing the normal actions as far as possible. Careful attention must be given to any partially updated data structure to restore its integrity. The handler should, if at all possible, ensure the preservation of any data invariants which would be maintained by the normal code. If it is then necessary to invoke the help of the calling procedure to decide how to continue, this may be done by including a further **raise** statement in the handler body.

Never let an exception propagate beyond the scope of its name.

A package may have an exception declared in its visible part, to enable users of the package to include handlers for exceptions raised in the package body. In this case users must under no circumstances issue raise statements for that exception.

Since an unhandled exception in a task will abort the task, it is wise to ensure that every important task is protected by a 'catch all' handler.

13.12.3 **Exceptions Raised in the Declarative Part of a Unit**

Exceptions may be raised during the elaboration of declarations in the declarative part of a unit. For example, an initialization might be given for a variable, the declaration being:

```
COUNT: INDEX := N + M;
```

the type INDEX being that used in earlier chapters, constrained to the range 0 .. 100. In that case the arithmetic value of the expression used in the initialisation could exceed the constraint for the type and raise a CONSTRAINT_ERROR exception. Even if a handler is provided at the end of the current block, there may be declarations in the present declarative part which are not yet elaborated. Since the handler will exist within the scope of those declarations, it is unsafe to transfer control to a local handler. In this case the exception is immediately referred to the calling program.

In a similar way, any exception raised by the program of a handler is also referred immediately to the calling unit.

13.12.4 Exceptions During Task Communication

If a task calls an entry in some other task which has terminated, or which terminates before the entry call is accepted, then the TASKING_ERROR exception is raised at the point of the call in the calling task. This may be handled in the normal way by that task.

A more difficult case arises if an exception is raised during the execution of a rendezvous code. This could be handled locally within the accept statement, but if it is not, then the exception is propagated in both the tasks involved in the rendezvous.

Further special cases arise if one or other task is terminated prematurely by abortion by some third task during a rendezvous. In the case that it is the task containing the accept statement which is aborted, the TASKING_ERROR exception is raised in the calling task at the point of the entry call. If the calling task is aborted during the rendezvous, the code in the accept statement is allowed to run to completion, and the called task is unaware of the death of its partner.

Exercise 13

13.1 Exercise 9.2 involved the construction of a MAILBOX in which messages were to be held available pending their acceptance by customer tasks. Extend the solution to that problem so that there is a time-out if the customers have not all examined the message within ten minutes.

13.2 As pointed out earlier, the CALENDAR package given on page 255 over-specifies the time, since it specifies its representation as well as its meaning. Give a package specification for time as a private data type, having the same properties as those provided by package Calendar.

13.3 Write a representation specification for a type DATE which will pack the date into a single sixteen bit word. Use that in a package to provide dates as a private type.

CHAPTER 14

VISIBILITY AND PROGRAM STRUCTURE

14.1 Visibility and the Use Clause

In the absence of a **use** clause, all items enclosed in a package are accessed as selected components, using the dot notation. A **use** clause opens up the scope of a package specification, enabling direct naming of items in the package named. Occasionally such a use clause will therefore make a name in the package clash with some other name in the program. There are two cases to consider.

> The other use of the name is in a declarative part directly visible to the program at the point where the **use** is introduced. In that case the local meaning of the name takes precedence, and the object in the package is not directly visible.
>
> Alternatively, the clashing names are from two packages for which use clauses are introduced in the same declarative part. In that case, neither object becomes directly visible.

Other items in the packages are not affected by the fact that a clash exists between objects alongside which they happen to have been declared. Of course, items which remain hidden in this way are still accessible by the dot notation.

Occasionally, if such failure to open the scope of a package with respect to the name of some element leads to cumbersome naming by dot notation, then a shortened alias can be introduced by renaming, as described in chapter 6.

14.2 Separate Compilation and the Library File

This chapter enlarges and clarifies some aspects of Ada which were outlined in the overview in chapter 5. It explains the way in which Ada permits the construction of programs in terms of components which are separately compilable, without sacrificing the security provided by compile time checks on the consistency of the interactions between the parts.

To enable checking of each component as it is written, the compiler maintains a 'library file'. In this file are stored the compiled modules, together with symbol tables and information concerning types of objects defined in the units. When some new unit is being compiled, consistency of its use of items from previously defined modules is checked, just as if the program was compiled as a single unit. This possibility has consequences for the order in which units may be compiled. Evidently, if a unit is dependent on some other, then the latter must have been compiled first. The rules are quite easy to understand in these terms.

Separate compilation is permitted in two ways. Internal details, describing the implementation of a program unit, contained in the body of the unit have no significance for the rest of the program, so such bodies may be separately defined and compiled. Thus, the programming of the construction of such a unit may be postponed until a later time. On the other hand, as previously described in chapter 10 for packages, complete units whose purpose is to provide a service for other program parts may be compiled first into the library, and introduced to the using program by a **with** clause. In this case, the specification part of the unit providing the service must be compiled first. The consequences of these two approaches are discussed in the following sections.

14.3 The Main Program

An Ada main program is a procedure. It has the normal procedure structure, consisting of declarative and imperative parts. Logically, it behaves like a task, but may be thought of as a procedure called once, at system start up from the underlying operating system.

As explained at length in Chapter 8, such a procedure may contain declarations; these may be of types and variables, but may also be of program units, further procedures, functions, tasks or packages. Within the imperative part there may also be **declare** blocks containing further declarative parts. Such structure has a natural relationship to problem solving by refinement, 'from the top-down'. A problem may be expressed in terms of subproblems, and those in terms of sub-subproblems and so on, to any depth. The nested problem structure may be reflected in the program, developed in terms of nested program units each providing the solution of some subproblem.

This style of hierarchic decomposition, encouraged and supported by the nested program structure, has for a long time been the recommended approach to program construction in languages derived from Algol. However, in those languages it was not usually possible to test any of the units until the whole set of nested blocks had been fully defined down to the level of detailed code. Compiling parts of such a program separately from the rest was not possible.

As explained in outline in chapter 5, the requirements for Ada, defined by the Steelman, included the capability for separate compilation of components of Ada programs. This capability was recognised as fundamental to the development of large programs. Components must be capable of being handled separately by the compiler, so that each can be tested as and when it is written. This was to be achieved without loss of security by the type checking at compile time.

The Ada design satisfies this requirement in two different ways, described in the following sections.

14.3.1 Separate Compilation of Nested Units

Each of the classes of sub units used in an Ada program, described in earlier chapters, shares one important feature. Each has a specification and a body. The body is logically hidden from the using program. There is therefore no reason why it should be physically visible either. The body can therefore be replaced by a 'body stub'. At any place in a program where a program unit may be declared, the full declaration may alternatively be represented by the specification part of the unit only, with the stub **is separate** to indicate that the body of the unit is being separately defined. Since the rest of the program knows nothing of the contents of such a body, the compiler is able to compile the incomplete program and check its consistency with respect to types and parameter names. Compilation of the bodies may be postponed to a later time. Since, however, the body of the subunit may use objects and names defined in the higher level, either as parameters or as global objects, it is essential that the body be compiled **after** the program of which it is logically a part, and not the reverse.

Of course an incomplete program cannot actually be run; testing at that level is only for syntactic and semantic correctness, and for consistency in the of the interface of the subunit by the body of the parent. Only after the body has been supplied can the complete program be assembled. Nevertheless, the approach does lend itself, to the testing of prototype programs with temporary dummy bodies for the subunits, if desired.

The following is the outline of a program with separately defined sub units. The program operates on a list of floating point numbers, stored as an array. It uses operations on such lists, to read them from input and to sort them. Details of these operations are postponed for later development. In the mean time, their existence is recognised by the appropriate body stubs.

```
procedure MAIN_PROGRAM is

    type LIST is array (INTEGER range <>) of FLOAT;
    procedure SORT      (L: in out  LIST) is separate;
    procedure READ_LIST (L: out LIST) is separate;
                                        -- separate body stubs
    CLASS_MARKS:  LIST(50);

begin

    READ_LIST(CLASS_MARKS);
    SORT(CLASS_MARKS);
    ...  etc.

end MAIN_PROGRAM;
```

Though this program can be compiled, it is not complete until the procedures SORT and READ_LIST have been fully defined. In the meantime the the compiled unit is entered into the library file, together with all the symbol tables and other necessary information to be used by the compiler when, at a later time, it is presented with the procedure specifications.

Eventually, in order to complete the program definition, a subprogram unit which has been named in a body stub is presented to the compiler. To enable the compiler to relate the definition to the corresponding body stub, the former is preceded by the word **separate** and the name of the program unit to which it logically belongs. Thus:

```
separate (MAIN_PROGRAM)
procedure SORT(L: in LIST) is

        procedure SWAP_INTEGER (A,B: INTEGER) is separate;

begin

        ...  --body of the sort algorithm

end SORT;
```

Items visible in the main program at the point where the body stub is given are visible to the separately declared body, exactly as if it had been written in the program at that place.

The separate subprogram defining the sort algorithm uses a procedure to exchange values of a pair of variables given as parameters. In this illustration the details of the swap algorithm have been further postponed by treating that in turn as a separate subunit. This must be presented to the compiler at a still later stage. Such separate definition of subprogram units may be carried to any depth. To avoid possible ambiguity, the **separate** clause must then use the dot notation to trace its ownership back to the first unit from which it has been extracted. Here, for example:

```
separate (MAIN_PROGRAM.SORT)
procedure SWAP_INTEGER(A,B: in out INTEGER) is

    ...--text of the SWAP program

end SWAP_INTEGER;
```

Separate bodies can be given in a similar way for functions, packages and tasks. Examples will be found in the case studies elsewhere in this book.

14.3.2 Library Modules

The nested structures of program units declared within program units, in a hierarchy starting with the main program, is ideal for the composition of programs of modest size, particularly a program to be written by one person. With the use of separate compilation as described in the previous section, programs can be defined in outline, and gradually refined by the specification of the details of the separate units.

Nevertheless, the approach is not without its problems. A large program introduces many names to represent variables and other objects used in the program. By the operation of the normal scope rules, these are visible as global objects within all the inner units. Names are known within such an inner program unit which have no relevance to the needs of the program. There is an invasion of the name space with hoards of unwanted items. Much of the time these do no harm, since declaration of a new item with the same name as some existing one introduces a new object of that name, distinct from the one automatically visible in that context. Nevertheless, errors can be caused. A declaration may be omitted, so that the program refers to the wrong item, but no compiler error is reported, or mis-spelling of an identifier may by accident cause it to coincide with an existing name, so that the compiler does not notice any error. The program compiles correctly, and malfunctions during execution. Such errors are extremely difficult to detect. In the spirit of 'information hiding' it is preferable to keep the set of identifiers known at any point in the program as small as possible; ideally, only items actually used by the program should be visible.

An alternative approach used in Ada is relevant to situations when a program unit provides a service to one or more other units, but does not itself depend on any local declarations in any of the using programs. In this case the unit providing the service may be compiled separately into the library file, as a complete library unit. (It may itself contain stubs for separately compiled subunits). Neither user nor server has any visibility of the other when items are compiled as independent library units in this way. In order to use the facilities offered by the server, the user must be prefixed by the **with** clause, as previously explained. The user program now sees the server exactly as if the latter had been predefined in the standard library. However, it is now essential that the specification of the server should have been compiled first. In contradistinction to the previous case, it is the subordinate components which must be first written and compiled.

Development of a large program in terms of separate library units in this way imposes a 'bottom-up' approach to the construction of programs. Program components are first written which will provide some facilities, operations required for the solution of problems in the application area. Such units then form bricks to be used in the building of still more powerful components. The choice of bricks is driven by the abstract concepts of the problem area.

As a simple example, consider the program designed 'from the top-down' in the previous section. The declarations in the main program might have been recognized as a generalized data type and packaged as follows:

```
procedure MAIN_PROGRAM is
     package LIST_HANDLING is
          type LIST is array (INTEGER range <>) of FLOAT;
          procedure SORT      (L: in out LIST);
          procedure READ_LIST (L: out    LIST);
     end LIST_HANDLING;
     package body LIST_HANDLING is
          procedure SORT      (L: in out LIST) is ..etc.
          procedure READ_LIST (L: out    LIST) is ..etc.
     end LIST_HANDLING;
     use LIST_HANDLING;
     CLASS_MARKS: LIST(50);                       -- continued
```

```
-- MAIN_PROGRAM continued

   begin
         READ_LIST(CLASS_MARKS);
         SORT(CLASS_MARKS);
             ...  etc.
    end MAIN_PROGRAM;
```

However, the package body can be declared **separate** and presented to the compiler later as a separate subunit.

```
    separate (MAIN_PROGRAM)
    package body LIST_HANDLING is
         ...  --body as before
    end LIST_HANDLING;
```

The main program would now read:

```
    procedure MAIN_PROGRAM is
         package LIST_HANDLING is
              ...  -- as before
         end LIST_HANDLING;
         package body LIST_HANDLING is separate;
         use LIST_HANDLING;
         CLASS_MARKS:  LIST(50);
   begin
         READ_LIST(CLASS_MARKS);
         SORT(CLASS_MARKS);
             ...  etc.
    end MAIN_PROGRAM;
```

However, in this program the package does not depend on anything else in the main program. It is declared where it is to make it visible to the body of the main program. It is, in fact, a utility which could first be compiled into the library.

The complete program would then be compiled in the order:

```
package LIST_HANDLING is
     type LIST is array (INTEGER range <>) of FLOAT;
     procedure SORT      (L: in out LIST);
     procedure READ_LIST (L: out    LIST);
end LIST_HANDLING;

procedure MAIN_PROGRAM is
     CLASS_MARKS: LIST(50);
begin
     READ_LIST(CLASS_MARKS);
     SORT(CLASS_MARKS);
         ...  etc.
end MAIN_PROGRAM;

package body LIST_HANDLING is
          procedure SORT      (L: in out LIST) is ..etc.
          procedure READ_LIST (L: out    LIST) is ..etc.
end LIST_HANDLING;
```

At this stage, however, the compilation units have no knowledge of each other. There is no visibility of LIST_HANDLING by the main program, and the compiler would record errors in compiling the latter, due to unknown types and procedures. To make the library unit visible, it must be named in a **with** clause at the start of MAIN_PROGRAM:

```
package LIST_HANDLING is
     ...  -- as before
end LIST_HANDLING;

with LIST_HANDLING;
procedure MAIN_PROGRAM is
     ...  -- as before
end MAIN_PROGRAM;

package body LIST_HANDLING is
     ...  -- as before
end LIST_HANDLING;
```

The effect of the **with** is to make the package LIST_HANDLING visible in the main program as if it was part of package STANDARD, which means, in this case, that the situation is back to what it was in the beginning, when it was declared first in the procedure.

It is, however, still necessary to introduce a **use** clause if the main program is to access the items in the package directly. It is immaterial whether it is associated with the with clause, or placed in the declarative part of the procedure.

Program construction has now gone 'bottom-up', the utility program unit for managing lists being the first object compiled, followed by the unit which uses it. However, the body of LIST_HANDLING can be provided at any convenient time, either before or after the MAIN_PROGRAM.

In the package body, the definition of the procedure SORT could still define SWAP as **separate,** so that the package body itself is developed 'top-down'. However, the procedure SWAP might also be considered to be a useful utility, rather than an essential part of SORT. It could also be extracted, and presented as a library procedure. Since it will be used by the body of the package, neither the main procedure nor the package specification need have knowledge of it. Thus the program now is in the form:

(A) **procedure** SWAP(X,Y: INTEGER) **is** ...

(B) **package** LIST_HANDLING **is** ...

(C) **with** LIST_HANDLING;
use LIST_HANDLING;
procedure MAIN_PROGRAM **is** ...

(D) **with** SWAP;
package body LIST_HANDLING **is** ...

The with clauses define a partial ordering on the order of compilation; no unit can be compiled before any other which it names in a with clause. Also, no body may be compiled before its specification. Any order consistent with these constraints is acceptable. Thus, in the above, the following orders would be acceptable:

```
(A) (B) (C) (D);
(B) (A) (C) (D);
(B) (C) (A) (D);
```

A further variant of this program would be to define SWAP as a library unit, but leaving the package as an inner unit of the main program, with the body **separate.** It would now read:

```
procedure SWAP (X,Y: INTEGER) is ...etc.

procedure MAIN_PROGRAM is
     package LIST_HANDLING is
          ...  -- as before
     end LIST_HANDLING;
     package body LIST_HANDLING is separate;
     use LIST_HANDLING;
     CLASS_MARKS: LIST(50);
begin
     READ_LIST(CLASS_MARKS);
     SORT(CLASS_MARKS);
        ... etc.
end MAIN_PROGRAM;

with SWAP;
separate (MAIN_PROGRAM)
package body LIST_HANDLING is
     ...  --body as before
end LIST_HANDLING;
```

SWAP is used only by the body of LIST_HANDLING. If the body had not been made separate, then visibility of SWAP could only be provided by prefixing the main program with the **with** SWAP, which would make it also visible to the body of the main program.

14.4 General Rules for Program Construction

Packages, procedures, functions and tasks may all be treated as separate subunits, and their definition deferred until a convenient future time.

Only packages, procedures and functions can be treated as library units, in the way illustrated in the above example. Tasks cannot be so treated: they must be declared in the declarative part of one of the other three program units. The specification of a task may be made visible to other units by declaring it in the visisble part of a package. Such compilation units may be presented to the compiler singly or in groups. In either case the rules for the order in which units may be compiled is the same. The specification part of a unit must precede its body, which may be presented at a later stage if preferred. The body of any unit automatically has access to its own visible part, but to nothing else.

Any unit may gain access to the visible part of another by naming it in a **with** clause, provided the specification part of the named unit has already been compiled. Mutual visibility of two units requires that one of them should have its body separated from its specification, as illustrated in the preceding section. To achieve this with procedures, the specification part may be repeated:

```
procedure X (....) ;

with X;
procedure Y (....) is
begin
    .....
end;

with Y;
procedure X (....) is
begin
    .....
end;
```

Apart from the requirement that compilation of a unit must be postponed until after the specification part of any unit which it uses, including, in the case of a body, its own specification part, bodies may be compiled at any convenient time. It will frequently be a sound methodology to postpone compilation of all bodies until the visible parts have all been compiled and checked for consistency. The visible parts constitute the interfaces between the units, and checking these before investing large amounts of effort in programming the bodies of the units, will avoid risk of wasted effort, creating incompatible modules. Visibility of a unit by another is obtained only by naming it in a **with.** Such with clauses, therefore, constitute a partial order on the compilation time.

Note that a unit need only name another if it uses it directly. If unit A uses unit B, while unit B uses unit C, A need only name C if it names items from C directly. If, as often happens, A depends on C only indirectly through its use of services of B, it is a mistake to include a with clause for C in A, since it only serves to make visible unwanted names. The with relationship is not transitive.

14.5 The Role of Tasks

Tasks model concurrent actions. Since they cannot be free standing library units, it may seem worth discussing the circumstances in which they should treated as internal to procedures, functions or packages.

If a task is packaged within a procedure, it starts operating when the procedure is called by the using program. The latter has no knowledge of the task, but the procedure cannot terminate until the task terminates. The procedure should model a collection of actions which can occur concurrently, but which together are regarded as a single composite action. If, however, the task is packaged in a package body, then its role is usually rather different. Now it serves to model some object with its own behaviour, coexisting with others in the program. It need not terminate spontaneously, and may last for the whole life of the embedded system.

The next chapter discusses the design of the programs for the case study, and most of the ideas introduced here will be seen in action.

Exercise 14

14.1 Consider the following sequence of definitions:

```
package A is
     type A_TYPE is ... ; -- whatever
     procedure A_PROC (X: in out A_TYPE);
end A;

with A; use A;
package B is
     B_VAR: A_TYPE;
     procedure B_PROC (X: in out A_TYPE);
end B;

with B; use B;
package C is
     ...  --declarative part of C
begin
     .... --program steps of C
end C;
```

What objects can package C see? Can it:

declare variables of type A_TYPE?
use the variable B_VAR?
call the procedure A_PROC?
call the procedure B_PROC?

CHAPTER 15

CASE STUDY - ENGINEERING A SOLUTION

15.1 The Design of an Ada Program

The preceding chapters have described the considerable armoury of tools which Ada provides to help programmers developing high quality programs for embedded systems. How best to use these facilities may still seem unclear. In particular, their use to compose complete programs requires further discussion. This chapter describes the approach which has been followed in order to pass from the requirements specification to the design and construction of the programs for the patient monitoring system.

There is no doubt about the value of using some appropriate methodology in order to construct well-designed programs according to the requirements. The use of CORE has permitted the careful analysis and documenting of those requirements, but says little or nothing about the design and implementation. In this work the programs have been described subsequently in terms of hierarchic structure charts, in a style which owes much to the school of Structured Design, as used, for example, by Yourdon and Constantine[15.1]. These are particularly helpful in explaining the design to others.

15.2 Design Details for the Patient Monitoring System

The discussion of chapter 4 concerning requirements was conducted at an abstract level, with no reference to considerations of implementation. Great care was exercised to ensure that the specification concerned what was required, not how those requirements would be met. In this way a specification is given which leaves options open about questions such as which language will be used, which computer, or which algorithms. Note that, even the details of the method of user interaction have been left undefined. To a large extent considerations of control have been left out of the requirements definition. Clearly, in a purely logical sense, methods of control are not system requirements, but details of implementation. To proceed further, however, it is necessary to introduce design decisions, freezing the system with respect to some of these details.

In fact some of the design decisions were listed among the requirements; it is common for a systems analyst to be given a list of 'requirements' which contain many details which constitute premature system design. Such requirements must eventually influence the design, though the analyst should carefully remove them from his abstract view. In this case, the hospital laid down that there would be a VDU at each bedside, and that the human interface is to be a menu driven command interpreter. This is good sense, so there is no reason not to follow it.

The present book is concerned with programming in Ada, so the use of that language is the first important design decision. Further decisions, using assumptions as to the computer architecture in use, will be required when consideration is given in due course to questions of interface mechanisms for external devices. In the meantime, however, the portability of Ada enables most of the program design to proceed in a machine independent manner. Properties of Ada will, however, influence many decisions.

At the outermost level the specification recognises the presence of a system into which data concerning a new patient enters, while reports of an unspecified nature are generated and records of the patient's life in the system are archived.

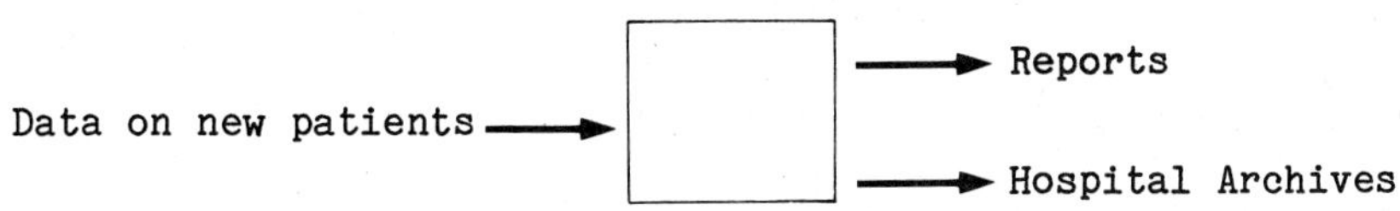

Input to the system consists of patient details obtained from the admissions interview, and from the letter sent by the doctor referring the patient for treatment.

Looking now into the first level of decomposition of the requirements analysis, as shown in figure 4.1, three subsystems are identified consisting of

> A fixed set of beds, each of which may or may not at any time contain a patient. Arrangements exist to attach a new patient when he is allocated to an empty bed.
>
> A set of 'detached patients' still known to the system, having left a bed within the previous 48 hours. The number of these is open-ended, since patients may stay any length of time in the system.
>
> A central nurse station.

Lines on the CORE diagram indicate the flow of data. Critical flows imply direct interaction between the parts, and will usually be implemented by either procedure or function calls, or by task entry calls, the parameters defining the flow of data. Where the timing of the data transfer is not critical, a buffer store may be provided, to uncouple the actions of producing and consuming data. This will usually be a bounded buffer, operating on a first in first out basis (i.e. a queue). Non-critical flow, on the other hand, implies shared access to intermediate storage. In most cases, such sharing of data must be subject to appropriate synchronization to ensure that access by any unit is 'indivisible', as explained in section 10.7.

A flow leading out of the system at the boundaries must involve facilities to drive some interface, be it a terminal, printer, or other hardware device. It follows that the lines joining boxes often imply the existence of program objects, in a way which is not obvious in the diagram.

The lines leaving the system are outputs and may be assumed to be directed onto external output devices connected to the computer system. They will be managed in the program system by packages, called:

```
                    package REPORT_GENERATOR;
                    package DISPLAY_GENERATOR;
    and             package FILE_ARCHIVE;
```

Some details of the facilities provided by these packages will be given later but, for the most part, they are considered to lie outside the boundary of the patient monitor under design. To write detailed programs would involve many assumptions about the computer system in use, and would make the size of the program excessive without adding to its pedagogic value.

Input data could be entered online from a remote terminal or terminals: such details were not given in the requirements. If it were so, then this would require further package to handle that interface. In the present work it is assumed that such information enters the system on paper, and is entered into the computer, via a bedside terminal, by the nurse responsible for the patient's care. In this case, though it is logically input information at the highest level, it appears in the programs at a lower level of detail, where it arises, along with keyboard commands and video output, as if derived from indirect viewpoints internal to the total system; it will not appear in the programs at the outermost level. It is important to recognize this as a design decision which was not imposed by the requirements, and which is typical of many more to be made during the construction of the total system. The primitives to handle the terminal interactions are contained in **package** TERMINAL_HANDLER.

Further progression from the requirements specification to the system design involves the definition of the structures of data involved in the data flows, and the data structures for static storage. These are discussed in the following section.

15.3 The Design of the System Data

The data to be defined consist of those items which form the patient database, and the data flows between the main program units and between those units and the database. Most of these data definitions are contained in the **package** SYSTEM_TYPES, which is the first unit compiled, and is accessible by all the other parts. The names it provides are the problem-specific vocabulary, forming the universe of discourse for the application. Note, however, that only the **types** are declared globally: the data items derived from these types are known only within the relevant scopes.

The database is to contain all the information on a patient throughout his stay in intensive care, including a record of every transaction envolving the patient. Some of this information will be be accessed repeatedly by modules of the system concerned with the monitoring of vital signs, and is held in main memory for quick access; the rest of the database has the form of a transaction file and is used to generate reports and archives, it is disc resident with each patient having his own file. These files are defined and accessed through a **package** FILE_HANDLING.

In the present design, the subsystems share access to the database, containing records of transactions concerning patients currently known to the system, during their time in its care. Consideration must, therefore, be given to the structure of the patient database. This is not the place to give an account of the theory of database structures, but the following design is driven by the concepts of data independence, used in database construction. The data is structured to conform to the third normal form.[15.2]

The data to be stored consists of the following:

The personal data of each patient. This is not accessed on a time-critical basis, and must be maintained in the system as long as the patients are in bed or in the detached state.

The accumulated history of all transactions involving each patient. This is to be held on secondary storage, a disc file. These files are maintained in the system until the patient leaves the detached state.

The set of data concerning the current medical state of the patient. The main component of this data is the set of readings from the sensors. The hospital requires measurements of temperature, pulse rate, and four readings of the blood-pressure. The current fluid balance is also maintained. Further, the current schedule of treatment is stored, updated from time to time, and accessible for consultation by the nursing staff.

The complete database contains a collection of data structures, corresponding to these parts. The first,

```
BED_ALLOCATION: array (BED) of PATIENT_DETAILS;
```

defines the association between bed and patient. Since this is a functional relation, it is stored in a separate logical file, and, being of fixed size, implemented as an array. The type PATIENT_DETAILS is an access type, providing a name for a record containing the unique hospital identifier for each patient, the corresponding personal information and the identifier which is the logical name of the transaction file. This arrangement allows the **null** value to be used to indicate an empty bed, and permits easy transfer of the data to the detached patient list in due course.

The second set of data is a list of identifiers for detached patients. This is an extension of the first, in which there is no association with a bed. Also, the number of such patients is undefined, so is implemented as a linked list. The union of the patients in these two lists constitutes the complete set of patients known to the system.

Next, associated with each patient currently in care, there is the collection of medical data, the medical factors, the safe ranges for these factors, the timings for polling of the sensors, and the doctor's instructions concerning treatment. This data is sensitive data, but can be changed by the doctor or nurse by commands from the keyboard. It is relevant to patients in beds, and is associated in the programs with the sensors, which are a function of the bed rather than the patient. Thus, could be represented by an array:

```
PATIENT_FACTORS: array (BED) of FACTORS;
```

However, since there is also an array of monitors, it seems preferable, for reasons of security, to place the data for each patient within the corresponding monitor which will use it. It is then hidden from other program parts. The array specified here is then logically present, but distributed in the various sections of the program.

Finally, for each patient in the system, there is a transaction file, in which record is kept of all transactions involving him, including the measured vital signs, obtained from the sensors, and all details of medical history. Each transaction will be registered, together with the time and date. There is a file of this type for each patient currently in the system. When a patient finally leaves the system, his record will be transferred to the archive. Unlike the other data sets, this one is of undefined size, both in respect of the number of entries for each patient, and the number of patients. To retain flexibility, a sequential file is maintained on disc, for each patient. The number of such files being indefinite, they are accessed through access variables stored with the patient identifier.

A further complication in the structuring of the file store for the patient record lies in the fact that the file must include also records of treatments given, and of the issue of presciptions by the doctor in charge. The records to be stored are therefore of several types. To provide for these circumstances, the package FILE_HANDLING defines an instance of the generic input output package INPUT_OUTPUT for a unit record which is declared as a variant record type, covering all possible transactions.

At any time an enquiry may be made from the nurse station as to the history of the treatment in the unit of some named patient. At that time the patient may be in a bed, whose number may not be known, or may be already transferred to the detached list. A failure to recognise the name implies that the patient has left the system or that there was an error in the name. To enable such enquiries to be handled, a name directory is required, giving the present status of all patients currently known to the system. This is supplied in the form of a package **package** PATIENT_DIRECTORY. This contains all the non critical patient data, dicussed above, together with the operations for manipulating it.

15.4 The Overall Program Structure

Figure 15.1 shows the structure of the overall program design, in its relation to the CORE diagrams. The main action boxes in 4.1 are related directly to Ada packages. At the lowest level in this outline are shown some of the units which implement the data flows, but which are primitives for the specification. In this diagram, and in figures 15.2 and 15.3, lines are used to indicate the interactions between the system components; solid lines represent subprogram calls and broken lines entry calls on tasks. In some cases, where this seems helpful, the flow of data and control signals are shown, using the conventions of the structured design technique.

15.4.1 Top-down Design

Further design involves the decomposition of the boxes illustrated in the figure, to create the program units which control the actions of the system.

The monitors for the separate patients are logically independent and concurrently active, so it is natural to create a task associated with each bed, to model the patient care and, since all the units are alike, to derive them from a common template. It is a consequence of the design of Ada that tasks may be formed into arrays, but packages cannot. On the other hand, tasks cannot be outer units, but must be contained within a package.
The specification also calls for a set of detached patient monitors, one for each patient in the detached state. Since each is waiting for the elapse of the period to the time when his record is finally removed from the system, a task is necessary to wait on a delay statement. However, since the requirement is to retain each patient in a detached state for a fixed period, 48 hours, the next patient to leave is always the oldest in the system. It is, therefore, possible to satisfy the requirements by organizing the waiting patients in a queue, with a single task waiting on the time to remove the first in the queue.

The central control monitor at the nurse station has two requirements; it must respond to alarm signals from the patient monitors and it must allow members of the medical staff to interrogate the system. The first of these requirements is modelled by a task that accepts entry calls to set or cancel alarms. This task has to be accessible by the patient monitors. The second requirement can be met by an independent code sequence that is driven by keyboard input. The decision has been made to make this the main procedure of the program.

The considerations of the previous sections thus lead to a program structured in the following units:

Figure 15.1 - Program Structure

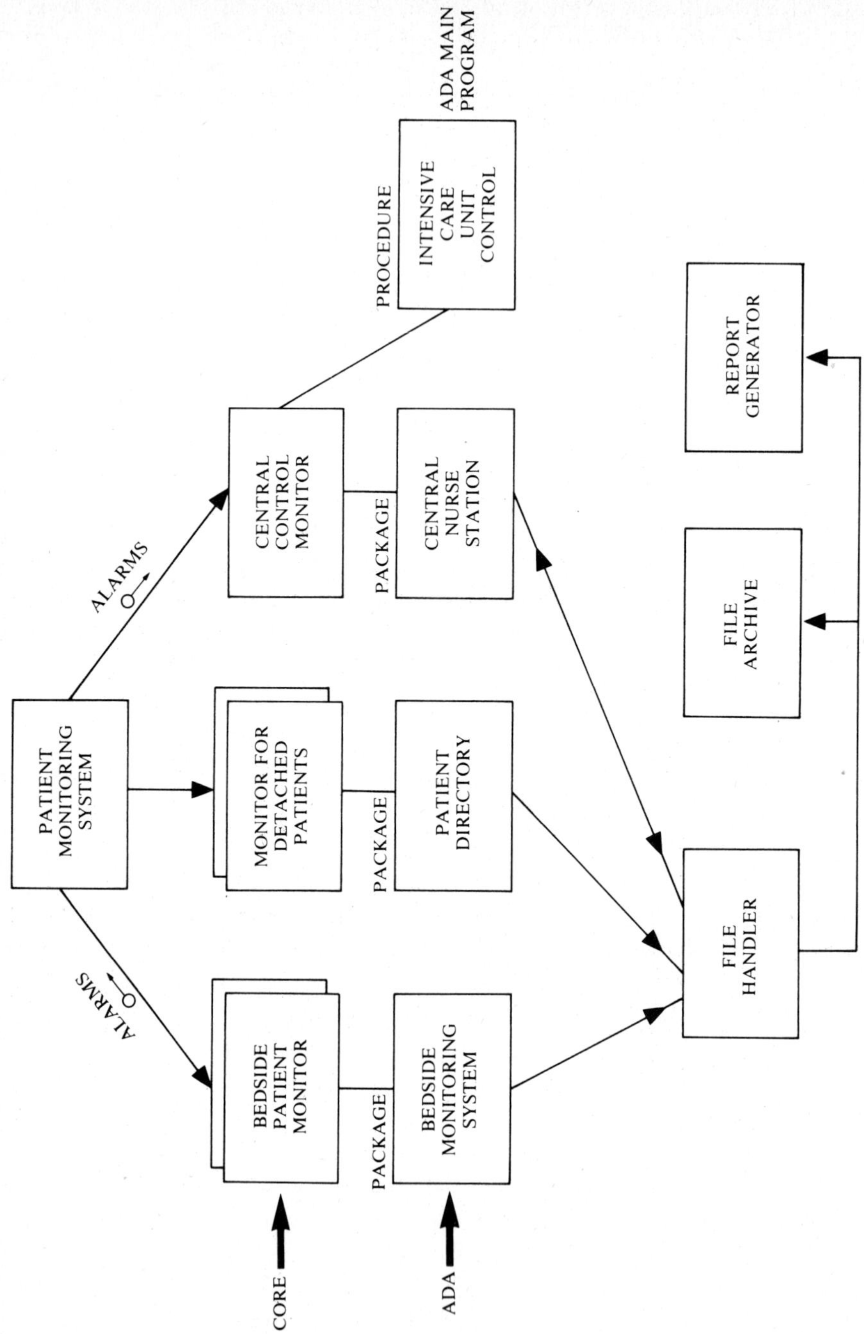

Figure 15.2 - Bedside Monitoring System

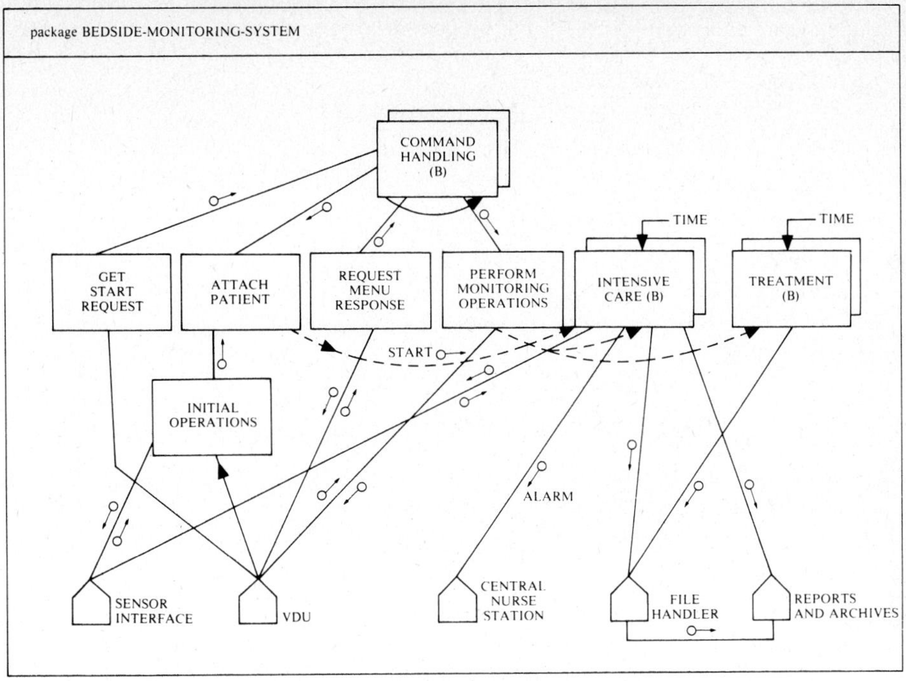

Figure 15.3 - Task Body Monitor

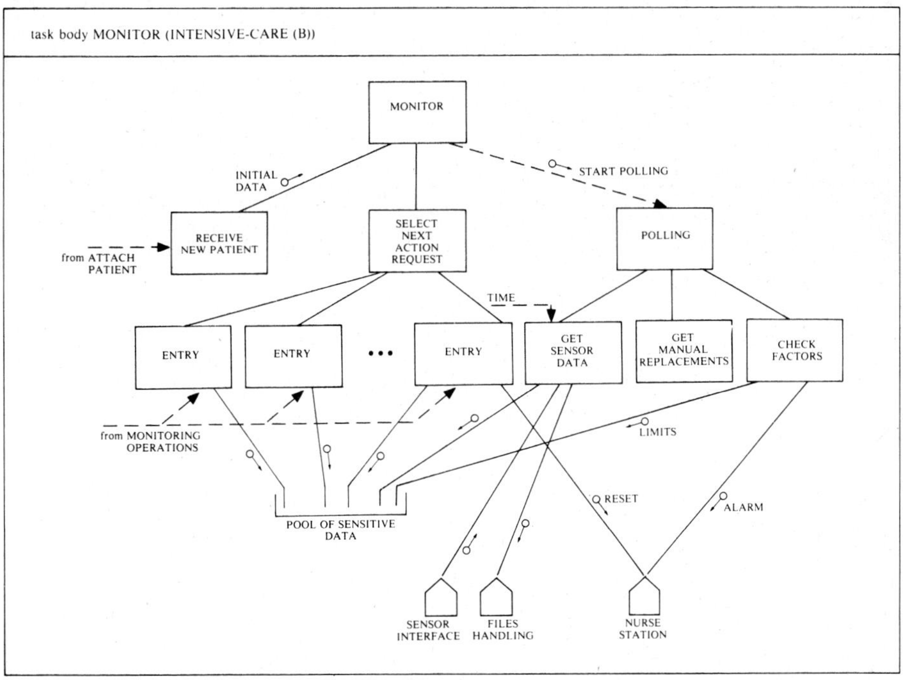

```
package SYSTEM_TYPES;
    -- defines the globally known data types for data flows;

package FILE_HANDLING;
     -- types for transaction records,
     -- procedures for file access;

package REPORT_GENERATOR;
package DISPLAY_GENERATOR;
package FILE_ARCHIVE;
     -- interfaces for output to the external world;

package TERMINAL_HANDLER;
     -- interface for input and online output

package BEDSIDE_MONITORING_SYSTEM;
     -- tasks to control bedside monitoring;
package PATIENT_DIRECTORY;
     -- contains the array of embedded patients and also
     -- encapsulates the list representing the detached
     -- patients, and the task DETACHED_PATIENT_MONITOR;

package CENTRAL_NURSE_STATION;
     -- deals with alarm signals;

procedure INTENSIVE_CARE_UNIT_CONTROL;
     -- main program which is linked with the processes
     -- in packages to form the total system, it deals with
     -- central enquiries; its initiation causes the system
     -- to start up, it explicitly controls system close down.
```

Each patient monitor must have a command interface with the bedside terminal. This will normally wait on input, so must be implemented as a separate task from the monitoring operations. As explained in the introduction, the command mechanisms are not part of the requirements, so do not appear in figure 4.1. They are implemented here as a separate set of tasks, one per bed, within the package containing the patient monitors.

Also associated with each occupied bed is a treatment schedule which may be altered and interrogated by medical staff. There is a requirement that the system prompt at the bedside terminal when treatment is due. Thus, there is a third logical process of the bedside monitor and this is also modelled by a task for each bed. These considerations led to an outline design for the patient monitoring system which is shown.

At this stage note is taken of the design requirements referred to earlier that the commands at the bedside will be implemented through a terminal located at each bed. Each terminal will have a split screen, the upper half being used to display current data, while the lower half serves to output requests and graphical information. This will be managed by a package TERMINAL_HANDLER whose specification is given below. For the same reason as with the other input and output functions, this package is regarded as primitive, and not further detailed.

```
with SYSTEM_TYPES;
package TERMINAL_HANDLER is
      package SCREEN_HANDLER is
            procedure PUT_STRING(B: BED; S: STRING):
            procedure CLEAR_SCREEN(B: BED);
      end SCREEN_HANDLER;
      package KEYBOARD_HANDLER is
            procedure GET_STRING(B: BED; N: NATURAL; S: STRING);
            procedure GET_REPLY(B: in BED; X: CHARACTER);
      end KEYBOARD_HANDLER;
end TERMINAL_HANDLER;
```

Any task calling either of the GET operations in KEYBOARD_HANDLER must wait for the reaction from the outside world. If the nurse decides to get a cup of tea, the wait might be prolonged. It is clear that such a call must be made by a separate task, so that the monitoring process is not interrupted. This is the origin of the array COMMAND_CONTROL in the design below. To ensure that data is only input when such a call is made, the first action of these procedures is to output on the screen a prompt symbol, say an asterisk.

Taking all these considerations into account, the package body of the patient monitoring system has the structure illustrated in figure 15.2, and given in outline in the package body of the BEDSIDE_PATIENT_MONITOR below:

```
package body BEDSIDE_MONITORING_SYSTEM is
     task type MONITOR is
          entry INITIALIZE (B: in BED);
          -- further entries for the commands recognized by
          -- the system affecting the patient state
     end MONITOR;


     task type COMMAND_CONTROL is
          entry INITIALIZE (B: in BED);
     end COMMAND_CONTROL;
     task type TREATMENT is
          entry INITIALIZE (B: in BED);
          -- other entries concerned with treatment of patient
     end TREATMENT;
--BEDSIDE_MONITORING_SYSTEM continued:

     INTENSIVE_CARE    : array (BED) of MONITOR;
     COMMAND_HANDLING  : array (BED) of COMMAND_CONTROL;
     TREATMENT_CONTROL: array (BED) of TREATMENT;

     -- procedures to ATTACH_PATIENT and CHECK_LIMITS;

     task body MONITOR          is separate;
     task body COMMAND_CONTROL is separate;
     task body TREATMENT        is separate;

begin
     for B in BED loop
          INTENSIVE_CARE    (B).INITIALIZE(B);
          COMMAND_HANDLER   (B).INITIALIZE(B);
          TREATMENT_CONTROL(B).INITIALIZE(B);
     end loop;
end BEDSIDE_MONITORING_SYSTEM;
```

Finally, in this section, the further design of the body of the task type MONITOR forming one member of the array INTENSIVE_CARE. This is given in outline in figure 15.3. More details of these and all the smaller units are given in connection with the actual programs in chapter 16.

15.5 Testing and Commissioning an Ada Program

This section discusses the steps that should be included in the testing procedures for such Ada control programs.

The case study in this book has been developed as far as an Ada design for the actual system. The objective of this design is to give a full definition of the data structures and control algorithms need, and so provide an understanding of the behaviour of the system. Being written in Ada, this design can be subjected to full syntactic and semantic checking by an Ada compiler. However, at this stage the program cannot be run. The compiler being used for checking will be run on a host development computer, typically a large mainframe running a full APSE. This is not the target computer for the intensive care unit, which will be a smaller machine dedicated to running the target object code that will be produced by cross compilation from the host APSE. The problems of converting the program design to a running program are not trivial.

A first consideration must be the availability and reliability of the tools that will be used in the transfer. These should include a compiler that will produce object code for the target machine, and an exporter that will load this object code into the target with a run time support system (or Kernel). An emulator of the target machine that can be run on the host, with code augmented by testing aids, will also be needed. However, such a test harness may not be a standard APSE tool and will probably have to be developed specially for each project.

Any Ada compiler in an APSE will be much more than just a simple translation system. The problems of binding together the required program components from a library file have already been described in chapter 14. The compilation system must then be capable of producing correct and efficient object code for a number of different target machines, one of which will be the host. It is intended that Ada compilers which are to be used for defence work will have to pass a rigorous validation test. Here the compiler will have to prove that it can process a number of benchmark programs correctly, the benchmarks being parameterized to avoid the danger of compiler 'tuning'. The source code of the compiler will also be subjected to a detailed analysis. A compiler that passes the validation tests can be assumed to be correct in its interpretation of Ada, and then only to the extent that is tested by the validation facility. Early validation suites are unlikely to be fully reliable. Only validated compilers should be used for all systems upon which life may depend.

Validation alone, however, is not enough. It does not guarantee the correctness of all object code that may be produced nor does it say anything about the efficiency of time critical sections of Ada code. One of the main fears voiced by those who question the wisdom of using Ada is that its complexity will necessarily lead to inefficient code, a fear that early attempts at compiling full Ada appear to endorse.

A program, such as the case study design, should first be compiled and tested in an emulator running on the host. The behaviour of the program can be monitored through test code inserts and simulated input/output channels. Some estimates can also be made about the timing of the execution, not in real time but in simulated time. At this stage in the development of the program there are bound to be some modifications which will envolve retesting. Eventually a version of the program is obtained which is considered ready for running in the target. The first tests should be made with simulated sensor input, not using real patients. When the implementors are reasonably sure that the system is correct both in function and timing, a full object code reading of the system should be undertaken. This tedious operation can be assisted by tools which can disassemble machine code and insert mnemonics alongside the original Ada text. However, even the functional behaviour of such tools may be in doubt and the only way of verifying the accuracy of code, where faults may cost lives, is by inspection of the actual code.

The system may now be considered ready for use, but testing should continue with parallel running of a manual system with the automatic monitor. This should continue for a number of weeks and a full comparison of performance evaluated before the automatic system is finally entrusted with the care of the patients.

The actual performance of Ada programs in a control environment is, as yet, a matter for speculation. It is feared that much of the error checking code inserted by the compiler, to provide the full support of strong typing and exception handling, will slow execution speeds below those acceptable in real-time interactions. Pragmas may have to be used to direct compilers to omit checking code at critical points, but this defeats most of the objectives of Ada.

15.6 Some General Comments

There follow here a few comments of a general nature concerning the use of Ada. It should first be remarked that Ada is still at an early stage of its development. It is likely that, in the course of time, methods of system design will be developed which are specific to Ada. Indeed, a great deal of work is in progress around the world on this topic. In the mean time, it has only been possible to recommend sound methods based on known techniques which can be applied with success in designing Ada systems.

An important warning concerns the fact that, like any other language, Ada can be badly used. There are among its features certain whose implications are not yet fully explored, and whose dangers may be significant in practice. Ada can be used in a simple and elegant manner, taking full advantage of its power of expression and of the protection that it offers against errors. It can also be misused, by over indulgence in its more complex features. Programs with complicated multitask structures can be difficult to comprehend, and will probably be inefficiently implemented by the early compilers. Programs which generate and destroy tasks during program execution may have behaviours which are difficult to predict. Until experience has been gained of these more difficult aspects of Ada, it will be advisable to keep things as simple as possible, using only features which are well understood and known to be secure. Similar remarks may be made about all but the simplest examples of generics and of exceptions.

The strongest features of Ada lie in its typing and data structuring and in the use of packages to provide modules with well defined interfaces. Separate compilation of library units and of separate subunits is a powerful aid to construction of large programs. Constructing a program in terms of separately compiled library units permits restriction of visibility between units which are unrelated, thus reducing risks of error.

The code of modules should not be larger than neccessary, generally not more than one or two pages of printer output. This enables each program unit to be fully understood by the programmer and by the subsequent generations of programmers who will maintain it. Larger program units should be subdivided by the use of procedures and functions, whose bodies can be declared **separate.** Of course, it would be foolish to follow such an arbitrary guideline slavishly. The logical program structure must be paramount, and larger modules may be justified in particular cases.

Tasks are needed to model the behaviour of independent, or almost independent, components of a system. Used in this way the tasks are mainly static, created during the system initialisation and lasting until system close down. Where an application involves a collection of identical subsystems, such as the patients in the hospital intensive care unit, the use of task types to create an array of identical tasks is appropriate, but these are still static tasks.

The correctness and efficiency of Ada code is a subject which must receive a great deal of study before Ada is used for real-time embedded systems. In the mean time, it seems wise to reiterate the advice given above, to utilise only the simple and elegant parts of Ada in real systems. These are based on 'state of the art' knowledge of compiling techniques, and will be reasonably secure and efficient.

References

[15.1] "Structured Design"; Yourdon and Constantine; Prentice Hall 1978.

[15.2] "A Relational Model for Data for Large Shared Data Banks"; Codd; CACM, Vol 13. 1970 pp377-387.

CHAPTER 16

CASE STUDY - ADA PROGRAM

16.1 Introduction

In this chapter program units are presented implementing the patient monitoring system, according to the designs discussed in chapters 4 and 15. Inevitably, the complete collection of program units will fall short of the needs of a realistic system in some respects. Some have been simplified to avoid unnecessarily lengthening the text without introducing new concepts, while others may have been made more complicated than absolutely necessary in order to illustrate features of the language. Where the reader feels that the proposed system is unrealistic for any reason, the authors hope that allowance will be made for these pedagogical considerations, and that the reader will, in the words of W.Shakespeare[16.1]:

"Piece out our imperfections with your thoughts.."

Well written programs in Ada are, to a large extent, self-documenting, since they use clear identifiers and well understood constructs. Nevertheless, comments should be included to increase the information available to the reader to understand the operation of the programs. However, in view of the limited page-size available in the present work, these programs have only a few comments in the text. For the purpose of the book, fuller explanation of most of the components is included as narrative text, and extensive comments would be redundant.

16.2 Implementation Considerations

It is worth re-iterating at this point the warnings of section 15.3. Before any program is put in control of a critical system, such as the hospital intensive care unit, it must be subjected to extensive checking and testing. As explained in chapter 3, programs which are to be used to control embedded systems, especially those on which life may depend, must be free of serious errors before they can be tested in their intended environment. Validation of programs for embedded systems involves careful testing of the correctness of the behaviour both in response to valid and invalid inputs, and cannot be entirely conducted in a host environment, without special features being added to simulate the real world. This topic has already been discussed in chapter 15.

As explained in the preface, these program units have been checked by the Ada/Ed compiler, and they are believed to be free from syntactic and elementary semantic errors. They have not, however, been subjected to the rigours of testing discussed earlier, and it would be totally inappropriate to attempt to use them for a real hospital without these tests.

16.3 System Types

The first unit to be presented for compilation into the project library, is a package called SYSTEM_TYPES containing a set of definitions of data types for objects which form the 'universe of discourse' of the complete program system. The type definitions capture concepts which are known to almost all parts of the program, and which, in the main, are the types for the data flows between the system components. Such type declarations provide a formal definition of the vocabulary used in the application domain.

It should be observed that no variables are declared at this level, only data types, defining value-sets and structures modelling the hospital environment and a few related constants.

The patient is modelled by the type PERSONAL_INFO, defining a structure to contain all information about the patient which is of 'social' concern, such as would be gained at the admissions interview, or from the doctor who referred the patient for treatment. The data derived from the automatic measurements are defined in the structure FACTORS, while the structures LIMITS and FLUID_LIMITS are used to contain the acceptable ranges of the FACTORS, within which it is considered that the health of the patient is satisfactory. Finally, there is a small collection of types for items of global concern, but not falling into the above two classes.

```
package SYSTEM_TYPES is

    --types for personal details of patients
    subtype NAME_TYPE       is STRING (1 .. 20);
    subtype ADDRESS_TYPE    is STRING (1 .. 50);
    subtype PHONE_NO        is STRING (1 .. 15);
    subtype RELIGION        is STRING (1 .. 20);
    subtype RELATIONSHIP    is STRING (1 .. 20);
    type DAY   is range 1 .. 31;
    type MONTH is range 1 .. 12;
    type YEAR  is range 1890 .. 1999;
    type DATE  is
        record
            D: DAY;
            M: MONTH;
            Y: YEAR;
        end record;
    type SEX is (MALE, FEMALE);
    type KIN is
        record
            NAME            : NAME_TYPE;
            ADDRESS         : ADDRESS_TYPE;
            TELEPHONE_NUMBER: PHONE_NO;
            KINSHIP         : RELATIONSHIP;
        end record;

    type PERSONAL_INFO is
        record
            NAME            : NAME_TYPE;
            DATE_OF_BIRTH   : DATE;
            ADDRESS         : ADDRESS_TYPE;
            GENDER          : SEX;
            TELEPHONE_NUMBER: PHONE_NO;
            NEXT_OF_KIN     : KIN;
            BELIEF          : RELIGION;
        end record;
```

```
--types for patient factors
type CENTIGRADE      is digits 3 range 20.0 .. 50.0;
type MILLIMETRES     is range  0 .. 500;
type PER_MINUTE      is range  0 .. 300;
type LITRES          is digits 3 range -5.0 .. 5.0;
type FACTOR is (TEMPERATURE, BLOOD_PRESSURE, HEART_RATE, FLUIDS);
type FACTORS is
     record
          BODY_TEMP        : CENTIGRADE;
          RIGHT_ATRIAL,
          LEFT_ATRIAL,
          DIASTOLIC,
          SYSTOLIC         : MILLIMETRES;
          PULSE_RATE       : PER_MINUTE;
     end record;

type LIMITS is
     record
          LOWER,UPPER: FACTORS;
     end record;

 type FLUID_LIMITS is
     record
          LOWER,UPPER: LITRES;
     end record;

  --types for hospital organization
MAXBEDS: constant := 16;
type TERMINAL_INDEX is range 0 ..  MAXBEDS;
subtype BED is TERMINAL_INDEX range 1 ..  MAXBEDS;
subtype HOSPITAL_PATIENT_NUMBER is STRING(1 ..  9);
type FLUID is (DRINK, DRIP, TRANSFUSION, INJECTION,
                                        URINE, BLEEDING, VOMIT);
subtype FLUID_GAIN is FLUID range DRINK ..  INJECTION;
subtype FLUID_LOSS is FLUID range URINE ..  VOMIT;
type WARNING is (BLOOD_PRESSURE, TEMPERATURE, PULSE,
                          FLUIDS, INTERFACE_TIME_OUT, SENSOR_ERROR);
subtype LINE is STRING(1 ..  64);
end SYSTEM_TYPES;
```

16.4 Input and Output to Terminals and Files

Next in the sequence of compilation units come packages providing commands for input and output on the VDU terminals, and for the handling of files.

Terminal handling is considered 'primitive'. It is provided by a package whose specification is given below. Since the body would contain details of interface features of a particular computer, it has not been developed. This does not prevent the rest of the program from being checked by compilation, but the complete program could not be run without bodies being supplied. A system test could, of course, be conducted with dummy bodies, in which the I/O is diverted to a printer, or to the system control console of the host computer.

16.4.1 Terminal Handling

The facilities for communication with the system via VDU terminals are defined in package TERMINAL_HANDLER; this provides two separate internal packages managing, respectively, the screens and the keyboards of the bedside terminals. Each screen is split into an upper and lower part, so functions are provided to output information to these two screen areas. Successive lines of output are automatically 'scrolled' when the relevant screen area is full. Each function receives a parameter of type TERMINAL_INDEX, covering the range 0 .. MAXBEDS. The value 0 refers to the console at the nurse station. The other values are bed-numbers, so can be accessed using a value of subtype BED.

Characters received from the key-board are first stored in a line buffer. Normal editing functions, delete, backspace, etc., are available to the user to modify the contents of the buffer before it has been transmitted to the program by typing 'carriage return'. Errors recognized by the user at a later stage are corrected by typing 'escape' to abort the input for the current command. It may be noted, that such abortion is exactly what the Ada exception mechanism provides, so the package provides the exception ESCAPE which is raised, by the software implementing the package body, on receiving the 'escape' character from the keyboard.

'Get' operations are provided for strings whose length is implicit as an attribute of the corresponding parameter type. If the 'return' key is pressed before the string is full, it is filled out with blanks. Typing a longer string than can be handled by the type does not produce an error; the string is simply truncated to the size acceptable, extra characters being ignored. A second procedure, GET_REPLY, to return a single character, is included to allow for responses to menu enquiries. A call on either 'get' involves placing a prompt on the lower part of the screen, and then entering a wait on input.

```
with SYSTEM_TYPES;
use  SYSTEM_TYPES;
package TERMINAL_HANDLER is

    -- this package provides the interface to the collection
    -- of  bedside terminals (1 .. MAXBEDS) and the single terminal at the
    -- nurse station.  It is not detailed further here.

    package SCREEN_HANDLER is
        procedure PUT_STRING_UPPER(B: in TERMINAL_INDEX; S: in STRING);
        procedure PUT_STRING_LOWER(B: in TERMINAL_INDEX; S: in STRING);
        procedure CLEAR_SCREEN_UPPER(B: in TERMINAL_INDEX);
        procedure CLEAR_SCREEN_LOWER(B: in TERMINAL_INDEX);
    end SCREEN_HANDLER;

    package KEYBOARD_HANDLER is
        procedure GET_STRING (B: in TERMINAL_INDEX;  S:  out STRING);
        procedure GET_REPLY  (B: in TERMINAL_INDEX; CH: out CHARACTER);
        ESCAPE: exception;
    end KEYBOARD_HANDLER;

end TERMINAL_HANDLER;
```

16.4.2 File Handling

File storage is provided by the package FILE_HANDLING. A requirement of the patient monitor is to provide on-line file stores for all patients in the system. During the period when the patient is in bed, all transactions involving his treatment are recorded in his file. Thus, the system records, for example, the receipt of data from the sensors, the provision of treatment, or changes in the medically acceptable limits for the patient factors. These files are used for the generation of reports, and for the creation of graphical displays of the patient histories, as required. They are transferred to the hospital archives when the patient leaves the ward.

The file type, defined in package FILE_HANDLING, is derived from the generic input-output package defined in the standard environment, as explained in chapter 11. The generic package INPUT_OUTPUT is instantiated for elements whose type is that of a patient transaction. This provides a package containing definitions of types for files of patient transactions. Since transactions involve different information on different occasions, the elementary transaction unit is a variant record, defining, for each transaction, its class, its time, and additional information according to the class of transaction. The generic instantiation provides the definition of a file type for the transaction file named PATIENT_IO.INOUT_FILE, a rather clumsy name. As a cosmetic refinement, the type is immediately re-named as a sub-type TRANSACTION_FILE.

Facilities to read from, or write to, a transaction file are similarly provided by the package, in the form of procedures PATIENT_IO.READ and PATIENT_IO.WRITE. There is a possible difficulty, however, concerning the use of the disc filing system by the various patients, and the central nurse station. It is probable that the read and write operations will utilise facilities for disc handling which will ensure that no errors arise if a disc access is currently in progress when a new call occurs. The new action will simply be delayed. However, such unpredictable delays would not be acceptable in the monitoring system. To avoid such delays reacting in the calling program, it is essential to provide a buffer, so that the calls on WRITE are queued, but the calling tasks are not held up. This is a classical problem of buffering, discussed in chapter 9. To provide buffered writing, the package FILE_HANDLING provides also a procedure WRITE, to handle the writing of unit records to transaction files. The body of the package uses a bounded buffer, and calls on the procedure PATIENT_IO.WRITE.

```
with      SYSTEM_TYPES, INPUT_OUTPUT, CALENDAR;
use       SYSTEM_TYPES, INPUT_OUTPUT;

package FILE_HANDLING is

    type  TRANSACTION_CLASS is (START_UP, VITAL_SIGNS, TREATMENT_SCHEDULE,
              TREATMENT_GIVEN, FLUID_TRANSACTION, NEW_LIMITS, NEW_TIMINGS,
              DETACHED_NOTICE);
    type UNIT_RECORD (CLASS: TRANSACTION_CLASS:=VITAL_SIGNS) is
          record
               T: CALENDAR.TIME;
               case CLASS is
                    when START_UP    =>
                                   null;
                    when VITAL_SIGNS   =>
                                   DATA    : FACTORS;
                    when NEW_LIMITS   =>
                                   RANGES  : LIMITS;
                                   FLUID_RANGES: FLUID_LIMITS;
                    when NEW_TIMINGS   =>
                                   INTERVAL: DURATION;
                    when FLUID_TRANSACTION   =>
                                   WHICH_FLUID  : FLUID;
                                   VOLUME:   LITRES;
                    when others  =>
                                   TEXT: LINE;
               end case;
          end record;

     package PATIENT_IO is new INPUT_OUTPUT(ELEMENT => UNIT_RECORD);
     subtype TRANSACTION_FILE is PATIENT_IO.INOUT_FILE;
          -- a naming convenience

     procedure WRITE ( T : in TRANSACTION_FILE;
                       U : in UNIT_RECORD);
end FILE_HANDLING;
```

The body of this package contains the tasks that implement the bounded buffer, along the lines explained in chapter 9.

```
package body FILE_HANDLING is
    -- global declaration of type for buffered items
    type TRANSACTION_ITEM is
       record
        T : TRANSACTION_FILE;
        U : UNIT_RECORD;
     end record;

    -- task specifications
    task BUFFERING is
       entry READ_TRANSACTION_ITEM  (X : out TRANSACTION_ITEM);
       entry WRITE_TRANSACTION_ITEM (X : in TRANSACTION_ITEM);
    end BUFFERING;
    task DISC_WRITER;

     -- task bodies
    task body BUFFERING    is separate;
    task body DISC_WRITER  is separate;

    -- WRITE is visible to all tasks which record transactions
    procedure WRITE ( T : in TRANSACTION_FILE;
                      U : in UNIT_RECORD) is
       I : TRANSACTION_ITEM := (T,U);
    begin
       BUFFERING.WRITE_TRANSACTION_ITEM(I);
    end WRITE;

end FILE_HANDLING;
```

BUFFERING provides a circular buffer for 100 transaction items. This size can be easily increased, if test runs show that it is insufficient, since the task is written in terms of MAXBUF.

```
separate(FILE_HANDLING)
task body BUFFERING is

    -- maximum buffer size
    MAXBUF : constant INTEGER:= 100;
    -- buffer space to hold items
    BUFFER : array(1..MAXBUF) of TRANSACTION_ITEM;
    -- BUFFER is used as a circular buffer, INPOINT and OUTPOINT are used
    -- respectively to index the next free slot and the next slot to be read,
    subtype BUFFER_POINTER is INTEGER range 1..MAXBUF;
    INPOINT, OUTPOINT : BUFFER_POINTER := 1;
    subtype FREE_SLOTS is INTEGER range 0..MAXBUF;
    COUNT : FREE_SLOTS := MAXBUF; -- a count of empty buffer slots

begin
    loop
      select
          when COUNT > 0 => -- stop when buffer is full
                accept WRITE_TRANSACTION_ITEM (X : in TRANSACTION_ITEM) do
                   -- insert an item in the circular buffer
                   BUFFER(INPOINT) := X;
                end WRITE_TRANSACTION_ITEM;
                -- update pointer and count
                INPOINT := INPOINT mod MAXBUF + 1;
                COUNT := COUNT - 1;
                end if;
       or
         when COUNT < MAXBUF => -- stop when buffer is empty
                accept READ_TRANSACTION_ITEM (X : out TRANSACTION_ITEM) do
                   -- remove an item from the buffer
                   X := BUFFER(OUTPOINT);
                end READ_TRANSACTION_ITEM;
                -- update pointer and count
                OUTPOINT := OUTPOINT mod MAXBUF + 1;
                COUNT := COUNT + 1;
       end select;
    end loop;
end BUFFERING;
```

The task DISC_WRITER spends most of its time waiting for a disc transfer or waiting to receive transaction records from the buffer for recording in a patient's file.

```
separate (FILE_HANDLING)
task body DISC_WRITER is
   T : TRANSACTION_FILE;
   U : UNIT_RECORD;
begin
   loop
      -- reads next item from the buffer
      BUFFERING.READ_TRANSACTION_ITEM((T,U));
      -- writes unit record to patient's transaction file
      PATIENT_IO.WRITE(T,U);
   end loop;
end DISC_WRITER;
```

16.5 Alarm Handling by the Central Nurse Station

When an alarm condition occurs at any bed the central console is informed so that a warning display can be generated. This display continues until the alarm is cancelled. The control of these alarm displays is effected by a task NURSE_STATION_MONITOR within a package CENTRAL_NURSE_STATION. The specification of this package makes visible the entries to the task; monitors calling these entries will identify the bed for which the critical situation exists and the nature of the warning.

```
with SYSTEM_TYPES;
use  SYSTEM_TYPES;
package CENTRAL_NURSE_STATION is
     task NURSE_STATION_MONITOR is
          entry  ALARM        (B : in BED; W : in WARNING);
          entry  CANCEL_ALARM (B : in BED; W : in WARNING);
     end NURSE_STATION_MONITOR;
end CENTRAL_NURSE_STATION;
```

16.6 The Interface with the Sensors

Input to the system from the sensors is provided by a package INTERFACE_DETAILS. This provides a function INTERFACE which, when called with a bed-number as parameter, reads the instruments of the corresponding patient. To provide for possible malfunction of the interface, an array is included, for each bed, of flags, giving a signal for each of four possible error conditions.

Consideration was given to the possibility of defining a general exception raised in the package to signal to the calling program that errors had occurred. This was not found to be helpful in coding the POLLER which takes defensive action against such errors. Exceptions are, of course, the mechanism by which the interface errors are recognized in the package body, and the appropriate error flags set. This will be seen in the implementation of the body of INTERFACE_DETAILS, below.

```
with SYSTEM_TYPES;
use  SYSTEM_TYPES;

package INTERFACE_DETAILS is

     -- this package provides a function hiding the machine-dependent
     -- details of the instrument interfaces.
     -- interface errors for each bed are transmitted as boolean
     -- values stored in an  array. This may be interrogated after
     -- any call on the INTERFACE function.
     -- the interface is shared, but the array of flags must be
     -- replicated for each bed, or intolerable waiting may occur.
     -- the flags are reset to false on entry to the interface program

     type ERROR is (BODY_TEMP, BLOOD_PRESSURE, PULSE, TIME_OUT);
     type INTERFACE_ERRORS  is array (ERROR) of BOOLEAN;
     MALFUNCTION : array (BED) of  INTERFACE_ERRORS;
     function INTERFACE(B : BED) return FACTORS;

end INTERFACE_DETAILS;
```

To illustrate the use of low-level features, an account will be given in a later section (16.11) of the way in which the interface is handled by the package body.

16.7 The Patient Database

All patient data, other than the medically sensitive data whose values are of transient importance, and are protected by the appropriate monitor, is defined in the package PATIENT_DIRECTORY. This contains the array to represent the patients in bed, and an open-ended list of detached patients. The latter are stored in a conventional queue, whose details are hidden from the external program parts by enclosing it in the package body. Data for each patient is stored as a record of type PATIENT_DATA containing the personal information, a unique hospital number, and the logical name of the transaction file.

Since the total number of these patients is indefinite and, during his life in the system, each patient passes from the bed to the detached state, it seems best to use access variables to name them. Moving a patient into the detached state requires only the copying of the access variable. The access type is called PATIENT_DETAILS.

The visible part of the package defines the functions to detach the patient from his state in bed, and insert him in the detached list. The function to delete the patient at the head of the list has not been made visible to the rest of the program, since only the detached monitor can have the right to call it. Nevertheless, the possibility has been provided of purging the complete list. This is to allow for orderly closing of the system. If the ward is to be closed for some reason, then, after the last patient is removed from bed, it will be necessary to archive all files, without waiting 48 hours. PURGE might also be called if length specifications are given to control the storage allocated to objects of type PATIENT_DETAILS, (see chapter 14) and the allocated space for detached patients became full.

Functions are also provided to search in the directory, to find some named patient, or some patient known by his hospital number. This is provided by a pair of overloaded functions called FIND_PATIENT. These return values of type SEARCH_RESULT which indicates whether the patient is in the system, and, if so, which state he is in. If he is in bed, they also return his bed number.

More details of the package PATIENT_DIRECTORY will be given in connection with the implementation of its body. It will be found to be a much more complex component than may appear from the specification. It is necessary to provide mutual exclusion between many of its operations, and patients inserted in the detached list are automatically removed after the prescribed delay of 48 hours.

The specification part is the next unit to be compiled. It is needed to enable the units following to be compiled, but could not itself be compiled until after the file handling was defined. It needs access to the declarations in SYSTEM_TYPES and FILE_HANDLING.

```
with SYSTEM_TYPES, FILE_HANDLING;
use  SYSTEM_TYPES, FILE_HANDLING;

package PATIENT_DIRECTORY is

     type PATIENT_DATA is
          record
               HOSPITAL_NUMBER: HOSPITAL_PATIENT_NUMBER;
               PERSONAL_DATA  : PERSONAL_INFO;
               TRANSACTION_RECORD: TRANSACTION_FILE;
          end record;
     type PATIENT_DETAILS is access PATIENT_DATA;

     type PATIENT_STATUS is (IN_BED, DETACHED, NONE);
     type SEARCH_RESULT(STATUS: PATIENT_STATUS := NONE) is
          record
               PATIENT : PATIENT_DETAILS;
               case STATUS is
                    when   IN_BED   => BED_NO: BED;
                    when   DETACHED => null;
                    when   NONE     => null;
               end case;
          end record;
```

```
            -- reference list of attached patients
    BED_ALLOCATION: array (BED) of PATIENT_DETAILS;

    -- list  management for detached patients.  The list  follows
    -- the first in first out discipline of a queue.

            -- transfer patient currently in bed B to detached list.
            -- patients are automatically deleted after 48 hours
    procedure DETACH(B: in BED);

            -- search  both  lists to find patient
            -- by name or number
    function  FIND_PATIENT (NAME  : NAME_TYPE)  return SEARCH_RESULT;
    function  FIND_PATIENT (NUMBER: HOSPITAL_PATIENT_NUMBER)
                                                return SEARCH_RESULT;

            -- prints and archives all remaining detached patients,
            -- then deletes the list;
    procedure PURGE;

end PATIENT_DIRECTORY;
```

16.8 Further Primitive Operations

Next, package specifications are defined to handle the archiving of a patient's transaction file. This will be done following the deletion of a patient, or during a purge. Similarly, the creation of reports, and the formation of graphical displays are provided by packages whose internal operation will not be further described.

In the operations of archiving and report generation, the patient information is provided as a parameter of type PATIENT_DETAILS, which provides access to all the patient data, including the file of transactions giving the history. The display generator does not need the patient's personal details, so receives only the name of the transaction file, the factor whose values are to be displayed, and the index of the terminal which is to receive the display.

The body of SAVE_TO_ARCHIVE may use UNSAFE_DEALLOCATION to notify the freeing of space in the heap for items of type PATIENT-DETAILS.

```
with PATIENT_DIRECTORY;
use  PATIENT_DIRECTORY;
package FILE_ARCHIVE is
     procedure SAVE_TO_ARCHIVE(F: in PATIENT_DETAILS);
end FILE_ARCHIVE;


with PATIENT_DIRECTORY;
use  PATIENT_DIRECTORY;
package REPORT_GENERATOR is
     procedure PRINT_SUMMARY_REPORT   (P: in PATIENT_DETAILS);
     procedure PRINT_FINAL_REPORT     (P: in PATIENT_DETAILS);
     procedure PRINT_TREATMENT_SUMMARY(P: in PATIENT_DETAILS);
end REPORT_GENERATOR;

with FILE_HANDLING, SYSTEM_TYPES;
use  FILE_HANDLING, SYSTEM_TYPES;
package DISPLAY_GENERATOR is
     procedure DISPLAY(B: in TERMINAL_INDEX; F: in TRANSACTION_FILE;
                                         DATA: in FACTOR);
end DISPLAY_GENERATOR;
```

16.9 The Patient Monitoring Package

Central to the whole system is the package which manages the monitoring of the patients, and the command interface with the doctors and nurses at the bedsides. This is called BEDSIDE_MONITORING_SYSTEM. Since it contains no declarations visible to other program units, it has the trivial specification:

```
package BEDSIDE_MONITORING_SYSTEM is
end BEDSIDE_MONITORING_SYSTEM;
```

Its body contains the definition of the array of tasks to conduct the monitoring for each bed. The task type MONITOR has entries for each of the commands which involve access to the medically sensitive data. As explained in chapter 15, there is also an array of command handlers. Commands concerned with the treatment of patients were felt to be logically of a different nature to those interacting with the (time-critical) sensor data. It was therefore decided to provide separate tasks to manage this aspect of the patient supervision.

Each command handler calls the service of a procedure to attach the patient, as shown in figure 4.3 of the CORE analysis. This is declared in the package, in the scope of the body of the command handlers, but its body is replaced by a stub, for later compilation. The procedure used by the monitors to check that the measured factors are in range is treated similarly. Also, the bodies of each of the task types are declared **separate.** This package is the centrally important one, defining the communiations between the major parts of the system.

```
with SYSTEM_TYPES;
use  SYSTEM_TYPES;

package body BEDSIDE_MONITORING_SYSTEM is

  task type MONITOR is
       entry INITIALIZE              (B: in BED);
       entry MONITOR_NEW_PATIENT     (L: in LIMITS; FL: in FLUID_LIMITS;
                                                    T: in DURATION);
       entry SET_LIMITS              (L: in LIMITS);
       entry SET_TIMING              (T: in DURATION);
       entry SET_FLUID_LIMITS        (UPPER, LOWER: in LITRES);
       entry ENTER_FLUID_TRANSACTION (F: in FLUID; V: in LITRES);
       entry MANUAL_INPUT            (F: in FACTORS);
       entry DISCHARGE_PATIENT;
  end MONITOR;

  task type COMMAND_CONTROL is
       entry INITIALIZE (B: in BED);
  end COMMAND_CONTROL;
```

```
  task type TREATMENT is
       entry INITIALIZE             (B: in BED);
       entry DEFINE_TREATMENT       (S: in LINE; W: in DURATION);
       entry ENTER_TREATMENT_GIVEN (S: in LINE)
       entry CONSULT_TREATMENT_SCHEDULE;
  end TREATMENT;

  INTENSIVE_CARE   : array (BED) of MONITOR;
  COMMAND_HANDLING : array (BED) of COMMAND_CONTROL;
  TREATMENT_CONTROL: array (BED) of TREATMENT;
  procedure ATTACH_PATIENT(B: in BED) is separate ;
  procedure CHECK_LIMITS  (B: in BED; F: in FACTORS; L: in LIMITS)
                                                    is separate;
  task body MONITOR         is separate;
  task body COMMAND_CONTROL is separate;
  task body TREATMENT       is separate;

begin                              -- initialisation of package
  for B in BED loop
       -- explicit entry calls are used to initialize tasks
       -- in order, and to pass to each of them their bed number
       INTENSIVE_CARE   (B).INITIALIZE(B);
       TREATMENT_CONTROL(B).INITIALIZE(B);
       COMMAND_HANDLING (B).INITIALIZE(B);
  end loop;

end BEDSIDE_MONITORING_SYSTEM;
```

Attaching a new patient is performed by a procedure that may be called by the command handling task associated with any of the beds. This procedure will inherit the visibility of SYSTEM_TYPES from the **with** list of the body of BEDSIDE_MONITOR_SYSTEM. It also uses the facilities provided by the specifications of FILE_HANDLING and TERMINAL_HANDLER. Procedures used for each of the stages in connecting and logging in a new patient are contained in the internal package INITIALIZING_OPERATIONS, the body of which is compiled separately and will be shown in a later section (16.14).

After logging in the new patient, this procedure calls the entry MONITOR_NEW_PATIENT in the monitor task controlling the bed. This initiates the automatic monitoring of sensor data and makes the monitor ready to respond to terminal inputs. The detail of the monitor task is shown in section 16.13.

```
with       FILE_HANDLING, PATIENT_DIRECTORY;
use        FILE_HANDLING, PATIENT_DIRECTORY;
separate   (BEDSIDE_MONITORING_SYSTEM)

procedure ATTACH_PATIENT (B: in BED) is

  package INITIALIZING_OPERATIONS is
     procedure GET_PERSONAL_DATA    (B: in BED; DATA: out PERSONAL_INFO);
     procedure GET_HOSPITAL_NUMBER  (B: in BED;
                                NUMBER: out HOSPITAL_PATIENT_NUMBER);
     procedure GET_INITIAL_LIMITS   (B: in BED;  L: out LIMITS);
     procedure GET_POLLING_INTERVAL (B: in BED;  T: out DURATION);
     procedure GET_FLUID_LIMITS     (B: in BED; FL: out FLUID_LIMITS);
     procedure ATTACH_SENSORS       (B: in BED);
  end  INITIALIZING_OPERATIONS;
  package body INITIALIZING_OPERATIONS is separate;

  use INITIALIZING_OPERATIONS, SCREEN_HANDLER, KEYBOARD_HANDLER;

  IN_LIMITS: LIMITS;
  IN_FLUID_LIMITS : FLUID_LIMITS;
  INTERVAL : DURATION;
  LOCAL    : PATIENT_DETAILS := new PATIENT_DATA;

begin
  GET_PERSONAL_DATA(B, LOCAL.PERSONAL_DATA);
  GET_HOSPITAL_NUMBER(B, LOCAL.HOSPITAL_NUMBER);
  ATTACH_SENSORS(B);
  GET_INITIAL_LIMITS   (B, IN_LIMITS);
  GET_FLUID_LIMITS     (B, IN_FLUID_LIMITS);
  GET_POLLING_INTERVAL (B, INTERVAL);
```

```
          -- use the hospital number to name the external file
  PATIENT_IO.CREATE  (LOCAL.TRANSACTION_RECORD, LOCAL.HOSPITAL_NUMBER);
  PATIENT_IO.OPEN    (LOCAL.TRANSACTION_RECORD);
  BED_ALLOCATION(B) := LOCAL;
  INTENSIVE_CARE(B).MONITOR_NEW_PATIENT(IN_LIMITS,
                                   IN_FLUID_LIMITS, INTERVAL);

end ATTACH_PATIENT;
```

The procedure CHECK_FACTORS, which checks the limits of a patient's monitored factors, may also be called by any tasks responsible for sensor monitoring. This procedure uses the SCREEN_HANDLER package of TERMINAL_HANDLER to display warning messages on the upper section of the screen of the bedside terminal. It also may call the ALARM entry in the NURSE_STATION_MONITOR of CENTRAL_NURSE_STATION to pass on warning messages.

```
with TERMINAL_HANDLER, CENTRAL_NURSE_STATION;
use  TERMINAL_HANDLER, SCREEN_HANDLER, CENTRAL_NURSE_STATION;

separate (PATIEMT_MONITORING_SYSTEM )
procedure CHECK_FACTORS(B: in BED; F: in FACTORS; L: in LIMITS) is

    procedure ALARM_DISPLAY (T : in STRING) is
    begin
       PUT_STRING_UPPER(B, " ALARM " & T);
       -- switch on bedside warning light
    end ALARM_DISPLAY;

    HIGH: FACTORS renames L.UPPER;
    LOW : FACTORS renames L.LOWER;

begin
    if F.BODY_TEMP < LOW.BODY_TEMP or else
       F.BODY_TEMP > HIGH.BODY_TEMP then
             -- notify the central nurse station
             NURSE_STATION_MONITOR.ALARM(B, TEMPERATURE);
             -- and display a local warning
             ALARM_DISPLAY("TEMPERATURE CRITICAL");
    end if;
```

```
    -- or else used to improve efficiency of execution

    if F.SYSTOLIC  < LOW.SYSTOLIC  or else
       F.DIASTOLIC < LOW.DIASTOLIC or else
       F.SYSTOLIC  > HIGH.SYSTOLIC  or else
       F.DIASTOLIC > HIGH.DIASTOLIC then
               -- notify the central nurse station
               NURSE_STATION_MONITOR.ALARM(B, BLOOD_PRESSURE);
               -- and display a local warning
               ALARM_DISPLAY("BLOOD PRESSURE CRITICAL");
    end if;

    if F.PULSE_RATE < LOW.PULSE_RATE or else
       F.PULSE_RATE > HIGH.PULSE_RATE then
               -- notify the central nurse station
               NURSE_STATION_MONITOR.ALARM(B, PULSE);
               -- and display a local warning
               ALARM_DISPLAY("PULSE CRITICAL");
    end if;

end CHECK_FACTORS;
```

Each command handling task has a body as defined below. This task uses the terminal handling facilities to display requests for input data on the lower part of the bedside VDU, and to get replies. The command functions are encapsulated in the package MONITORING_OPERATIONS, the body of which is separately compiled.

Initally, each terminal has a display indicating that the bed is empty. Any key pressed on the bedside terminal will activate the patient log in procedure, and then a standard menu of command functions is displayed. Many of the procedures that handle the monitoring operations contain further menus, as will be seen in section 16.14.

```
with       TERMINAL_HANDLER;
use        TERMINAL_HANDLER;
separate (BEDSIDE_MONITORING_SYSTEM)

task body COMMAND_CONTROL is

   use KEYBOARD_HANDLER, SCREEN_HANDLER;

   package MONITORING_OPERATIONS is
       procedure ENTER_NEW_LIMITS        (B: in BED);
       procedure NEW_FLUID_LIMITS        (B: in BED);
       procedure ENTER_NEW_TIMING        (B: in BED);
       procedure ENTER_FLUID_DATA        (B: in BED);
       procedure ENTER_TREATMENT_INFO    (B: in BED);
       procedure GENERATE_DISPLAY        (B: in BED);
       procedure REQUEST_REPEAT          (B: in BED);
       procedure MANUAL_INPUT            (B: in BED);
       procedure LOG_OUT_PATIENT         (B: in BED);
   end MONITORING_OPERATIONS;
   package body MONITORING_OPERATIONS is separate;
   use MONITORING_OPERATIONS;

   BED_NUMBER: BED;
   CHOICE: CHARACTER;

   INITIAL_DISPLAY: constant STRING :=

   "     *** Ada EXAMPLE: PATIENT MONITORING SYSTEM ***"    & ASCII.CR &
   "                                                  "    & ASCII.CR &
   "        BED EMPTY: To start monitoring new patient "    & ASCII.CR &
   "                   press any key                  "    & ASCII.CR;
```

```
   MENU: constant STRING :=
   "               Please Choose Operation:            "& ASCII.CR &
   "                   1) Enter New Safe Ranges        "& ASCII.CR &
   "                   2) Enter New Timing             "& ASCII.CR &
   "                   3) Enter Fluid Data             "& ASCII.CR &
   "                   4) Enter Treatment Information"& ASCII.CR &
   "                   5) Generate Report              "& ASCII.CR &
   "                   6) Log Out Patient              "& ASCII.CR &
   "                   7) Reset Alarm                  "& ACSII.CR &
   "                   8) Manual Input for sensors     "& ASCII.CR;

begin

   accept INITIALIZE(B: in BED) do
      BED_NUMBER := B;
   end INITIALIZE;

   loop
      CLEAR_SCREEN_UPPER(BED_NUMBER);
      CLEAR_SCREEN_LOWER(BED_NUMBER);
      PUT_STRING_LOWER  (BED_NUMBER, INITIAL_DISPLAY);
      -- any character will activate log-in
      GET_REPLY          (BED_NUMBER,   CHOICE);

      PUT_STRING_LOWER  (BED_NUMBER,
         "Logging in Patient in Bed" & BED'IMAGE(BED_NUMBER));
      ATTACH_PATIENT(BED_NUMBER);

      -- block used to couple ESCAPE exception handler with dialogue
      begin
         loop
            CLEAR_SCREEN_LOWER (BED_NUMBER);
            PUT_STRING_LOWER   (BED_NUMBER, MENU);
            GET_REPLY          (BED_NUMBER, CHOICE);
            case CHOICE is
               when '1'    => ENTER_NEW_LIMITS      (BED_NUMBER);
               when '2'    => ENTER_NEW_TIMING      (BED_NUMBER);
               when '3'    => ENTER_FLUID_DATA      (BED_NUMBER);
               when '4'    => ENTER_TREATMENT_INFO (BED_NUMBER);
```

```
            when '5'     => GENERATE_DISPLAY      (BED_NUMBER);
            when '6'     => LOG_OUT_PATIENT       (BED_NUMBER);
                                exit;
            when '7'     => RESET_ALARM           (BED_NUMBER);
            when '8'     => MANUAL_INPUT          (BED_NUMBER);
            when others => REQUEST_REPEAT        (BED_NUMBER);
        end case;
      end loop;

   exception
      when ESCAPE  => REQUEST_REPEAT (BED_NUMBER);
   end;

 end loop;

end COMMAND_CONTROL;
```

The body of treatment may accept three different entries issued in response to commands processed by the command control task for the same bed. These define a treatment, both as a text of instruction and a time interval, allow treatment given to be recorded and display details of the treatment text on request. There is an internal task that acts as the time signal to prompt for each treatment.

```
with FILE_HANDLING, TERMINAL_HANDLER, CALENDAR;
use  FILE_HANDLING, TERMINAL_HANDLER, SCREEN_HANDLER, KEYBOARD_HANDLER;
separate  (BEDSIDE_MONITORING_SYSTEM)

task body TREATMENT is
    TREATMENT_PRESCRIBED, TREATMENT_RECEIVED : LINE;
    BED_NUMBER : BED;

  task TREATMENT_TIMER is
     entry NEXT_TREATMENT (WAIT : DURATION);
  end TREATMENT_TIMER;
```

```
    task body TREATMENT_TIMER is
        HOLD : DURATION;
    begin
     -- waits for initial timing schedule
       accept NEXT_TREATMENT (WAIT : DURATION) do
          HOLD := WAIT;
       end NEXT_TREATMENT;
       -- waits for a new timing instruction or
       -- signals repeat treatments;
       loop
          select
             accept NEXT_TREATMENT (WAIT : DURATION) do
                HOLD := WAIT;
             end NEXT_TREATMENT;
          or
             delay HOLD;
             PUT_SCREEN_LOWER(BED_NUMBER,
                              " Next Treatment Due Now ");
             TREATMENT_CONTROL(BED_NUMBER).CONSULT_TREATMENT_SCHEDULE;
          end select;
       end loop;

begin
     accept INITIALIZE(B : in BED) do
          BED_NUMBER := B;
     end INITIALIZE;
     loop
          select
               accept DEFINE_TREATMENT(S: in LINE
                                       W: in DURATION) do
                    TREATMENT_PRESCRIBED := S;
                    TREATMENT_TIMER.NEXT_TREATMENT(W);
               end DEFINE_TREATMENT;
               WRITE(BED_ALLOCATION(B).TRANSACTION_RECORD,
                     UNIT_RECORD' ( CLASS  => TREATMENT_SCHEDULE,
                                    T      => CALENDAR.CLOCK;
                                    TEXT   => TREATMENT_PRESCRIBED));
```

```
        or
            accept ENTER_TREATMENT_GIVEN(S: in LINE) do
                TREATMENT_RECEIVED      := S;
            end ENTER_TREATMENT_GIVEN;
            WRITE(BED_ALLOCATION(B).TRANSACTION_RECORD,
                 UNIT_RECORD' ( CLASS  => TREATMENT_GIVEN;
                                T      => CALENDAR.CLOCK;
                                TEXT   => TREATMENT_RECEIVED));

        or
            accept CONSULT_TREATMENT_SCHEDULE;
             PUT_STRING_LOWER(BED_NUMBER,
                           "Treatment Prescribed is:" & ASCII.CR &
                            TREATMENT_PRESCRIBED);
            end CONSULT_TREATMENT_SCHEDULE;
        end select;

    end loop;

end TREATMENT;
```

16.10 The Central Control Module

The central control module of the CORE diagrams 4.1 and 4.8 is controlled by the body of the package specified in section 16.5 and by the main procedure INTENSIVE_CARE_UNIT_CONTROL. The first of these units responds to entry calls to set or cancel alarms signals. The alarm signals are represented by an array of warning alarms, each element of which is an array by bed of Boolean status flags. Every time an alarm status changes the upper part of the screen of the central terminal is cleared and fresh messages displayed to show the new alarm conditions.

```
with SYSTEM_TYPES, TERMINAL_HANDLER;
use  SYSTEM_TYPES, TERMINAL_HANDLER;

package body CENTRAL_NURSE_STATION is
     use SCREEN_HANDLER, KEYBOARD_HANDLER;

     --task responds to alarm signals and displays messages on upper screen
     task body NURSE_STATION_MONITOR is
     -- alarm status flags
     type BED_ALARM is array (BED) of BOOLEAN;
     ALARMS_SET  :  array  (WARNING) of BED_ALARM
                 := (WARNING'FIRST..WARNING'LAST =>
                      (BED'FIRST..BED'LAST => FALSE));

     -- a message for each alarm condition;
     ALARM_MESSAGES : constant array (WARNING) of STRING :=
     ("     BLOOD PRESSURE ALARM in bed(s): ",
      "     TEMPERATURE ALARM in bed(s):    ",
      "     PULSE ALARM in bed(s):          ",
      "     FLUID BALANCE ALARM in bed(s):  ",
      "     INTERFACE TIME OUT in bed(s)    ",
      "     SENSOR FAILURE in bed(s)        ");

    begin

     loop
      select
         accept ALARM (B : in BED; W : in WARNING) do
            ALARMS_SET(W)(B) := TRUE;
         end ALARM;

      or
         accept CANCEL_ALARM (B : in BED; W : in WARNING) do
            ALARMS_SET(W)(B) := FALSE;
         end CANCEL_ALARM;

      end select;
```

```
      CLEAR_SCREEN_UPPER (0);
       for W in WARNING  loop
            if ALARMS_SET (W) /= (WARNING'FIRST..WARNING'LAST => FALSE)
              then
             PUT_STRING_UPPER (0,ALARM_MESSAGE(W));
             -- list bed(s)
             for B in BED loop
                if ALARMS_SET(W)(B) then
                    PUT_STRING_UPPER(0,BED'IMAGE(B));
                end if;
             end loop;
            end if;
       end loop;
     end loop;

   end NURSE_STATION_MONITOR;

end CENTRAL_NURSE_STATION;
```

The second unit is responsible for initializing the complete system, for responding to enquiries at the central console for reports and graphs, and for closing down the program controlling the unit. Close down can only be done when all the beds are empty, and there is also a check that the close down instruction was intentional.

To start up the unit this procedure contains in its **with** list all the packages that enclose the main system components. The Ada language system will then incorporate all these units in the load module for the target hardware, and the tasks contained in the library packages will be initiated concurrently with the main procedure.

```
with SYSTEM_TYPES, PATIENT_DIRECTORY, REPORT_GENERATOR, TERMINAL_HANDLER,
        BEDSIDE_MONITOR_SYSTEM, CENTRAL_NURSE_STATION, DISPLAY_GENERATOR;

use  SYSTEM_TYPES, PATIENT_DIRECTORY, REPORT_GENERATOR, TERMINAL_HANDLER,
        DISPLAY_GENERATOR;
```

```
procedure INTENSIVE_CARE_UNIT_CONTROL is
   use SCREEN_HANDLER, KEYBOARD_HANDLER;

   -- Deals with input requests at the central console
   NAME : NAME_TYPE;
   NUMBER: HOSPITAL_PATIENT_NUMBER;
   FINDINGS: SEARCH_RESULT;
   C : CHARACTER;
   TRIES : INTEGER;
   VALIDATION_ERROR: exception; -- raised on invalid input data,
   MENU : constant STRING :=
   "         PATIENT MONITORING SYSTEM          "& ASCII.CR & ASCII.CR &
   "          Please Choose Operation:          " & ASCII.CR &
   "           1    Print Patient Report        " & ASCII.CR &
   "           2    Display Graph of Factors    " & ASCII.CR &
   "           3    Close Down System           " & ASCII.CR;

   procedure VALIDATE_PATIENT is separate;
    -- checks to see if patient on whom information is requested exists,
    -- and if so, whether in bed or detached

   procedure PRODUCE_REPORT is
   begin
      VALIDATE_PATIENT;
      -- if OK then print report
      PUT_SCREEN_LOWER (0," Report is being printed for patient number " &
                        FINDINGS.PATIENT.HOSPITAL_NUMBER);
      PRINT_SUMMARY_REPORT(FINDINGS.PATIENT);
   end PRODUCE_REPORT;

   procedure PRODUCE_GRAPH is
      F : FACTOR;
   begin
      VALIDATE_PATIENT;
      CLEAR_SCREEN_LOWER(0);
      PUT_SCREEN_LOWER (0," Graph will be displayed for patient number " &
                        FINDINGS.PATIENT.HOSPITAL_NUMBER);
```

```
   PUT_SCREEN_LOWER(0,
   " Please Indicate Which Factor is to be displayed" & ASCII.CR &
   "       1         for  Temperature                   " & ASCII.CR &
   "       2         for  Blood Pressure                " & ASCII.CR &
   "       3         for  Heart Rate                    " & ASCII.CR &
   "       4         for  Fluid Gain                    " & ASCII.CR &
   "       any other character to cancel graph display" & ASCII.CR);

   GET_REPLY(0,C);

   case C is
      when  CHARACTER range '1'..'4'  =>
                  F := FACTOR'VAL(CHARACTER'POS(C)-CHARACTER'POS('1'));
                  DISPLAY(0,FINDINGS.PATIENT.TRANSACTION_RECORD,F);
      when others  =>
                     PUT_STRING_LOWER(0,
                     "  Error in choice - Display abandoned ");
   end case;

end PRODUCE_GRAPH;

procedure CLOSE_DOWN is
-- checks that all beds are empty, then clears out the detached
-- patient list and aborts all system tasks before terminating
-- the main program:
begin

   PUT_SCREEN_LOWER(0," Confirm Close Down request by pressing 'Y' ");
   GET_REPLY (0,C);
   if C = 'Y' then
      if BED_ALLOCATION = (BED'FIRST..BED'LAST => null) then
         for B in BED loop
            abort INTENSIVE_CARE(BED);
            abort COMMAND_HANDLING(BED);
            abort TREATMENT_CONTROL(BED);
         end loop;
         PURGE;
         PUT_SCREEN_LOWER(0,"System Being Shut Down");
```

```
         else -- reject close down;
            PUT_SCREEN_LOWER(0,
            "  Close Down rejected because beds are still in use ");
         end if;

      else PUT_SCREEN_LOWER(0," Close Down Cancelled");
      end if;

   end CLOSE_DOWN;

begin
MAINLOOP:
   loop
   begin
      delay 5.0;
      CLEAR_SCREEN_LOWER(0);
      -- put out standard message
      PUT_STRING_LOWER(0, MENU);
      TRIES := 0;
      while TRIES < 5 loop
         GET_REPLY(0, C);
         case C is
            when '1'        =>  PRODUCE_REPORT; exit;
            when '2'        =>  PRODUCE_GRAPH; exit;
            when '3'        =>  CLOSE_DOWN; exit MAINLOOP;
            when others     =>  PUT_SCREEN_LOWER(0,
                                       " Illegal Choice - Try again ");
         end case;
         TRIES := TRIES + 1;
      end loop;
     exception
         when ESCAPE =>
              PUT_STRING_LOWER(0," Input Aborted ");
   end;
   end loop MAINLOOP;

end INTENSIVE_CARE_UNIT_CONTROL;
```

```
separate (INTENSIVE_CARE_UNIT_CONTROL)
procedure VALIDATE_PATIENT is

begin
   CLEAR_SCREEN_LOWER(0);
   PUT_SCREEN_LOWER(0,
   " Please Indicate How Patient Will Be Identified" & ASCII.CR &
   "       1    if by name                         " & ASCII.CR &
   "       2    if by hospital number              " & ASCII.CR &
   "       Any other character to cancel  request  " & ASCII.CR );

   GET_REPLY(0,C);
   case C is
      when '1'    =>   PUT_SCREEN_LOWER(0," Input patient's name");
                       GET_STRING(0,NAME);
                       FINDINGS := FIND_PATIENT(NAME);
      when '2'    =>   PUT_SCREEN_LOWER(0, " Input patient's number");
                       GET_STRING(0,NUMBER);
                       FINDINGS := FIND_PATIENT(NUMBER);
      when others =>   raise VALIDATION_ERROR;
   end case;
   CLEAR_SCREEN_LOWER(0);
   case FINDINGS.STATUS is
        when IN_BED   =>  PUT_SCREEN_LOWER (0, " Patient Found in Bed "&
                          BED'IMAGE(FINDINGS.BED_NO));
        when DETACHED =>  PUT_SCREEN_LOWER(0,
                          " Patient Found in detached list");
        when NONE     =>  PUT_SCREEN_LOWER(0," Patient Not Found ");
                          raise VALIDATION_ERROR;
    end case;
```

16.11 Interface To the Sensors

This section presents the program implementing the body of the package INTERFACE_DETAILS, serving to hide the machine-oriented aspects of the interface from the user.

The details will differ radically in different machines, and will depend on how the system designer has chosen to implement the interface. In the present system, the arrangement assumed is the following.

All interfaces are 'store mapped'. That means that states of registers connected to external signals are read from store addresses dedicated for the purpose. This is typical of the PDP 11 and of many micros, which use peripheral interface adapters (PIA's) accessed in that way.

There are six values to be read from each of 16 beds. It has been decided to multiplex the 16 beds on a single interface, but to provide six registers for the factors, so that they can be read simultaneously. The interface responds to a signal transmitted by a write command, ie. an assignment statement, to the (arbitrarily chosen) address Hex 8000, where, it is assumed, is located an ouput PIA eight bits wide. The value transmitted selects a bed, switching the interface multiplexor to connect the appropriate collection of sensors to the shared interface. The interface then waits on an interrupt at the address 0000. When the interrupt occurs, it reads the values transmitted by the interface. If the interrupt is delayed more than one second, a time-out error is recorded.

The instruments are connected to sixteen bit interface registers mapped to the sequence of store addresses starting at 8002. They each transmit a bit pattern of sixteen bits, corresponding to an integer value, which is initially interpreted as a value of type INTERFACE_VALUE.

The package INTERFACE_DATA defines the representation specifications for this purpose. The variable CHANNEL is mapped to the output address, and constrained to an 8 bit representation. The record X of type SENSOR_VALUES provides a structure of six fields each of type INTERFACE_VALUE mapped to the interface area. The values there detected are converted to types specified for factors in the function CONVERT. If any sensor delivers a value which is outside the safe region for the instrument, an interface error is created. The values are converted in procedure CONVERT, which produces a constraint error exception if it computes a value outside the range for the type corresponding to the internal representation. Such an error is assumed to arise from an error in the instruments or in the interface. Rather than permit this to propagate outside the interface handler, it was decided to introduce a set of boolean flags for each bed, and set a flag for each of the possible error conditions. For this purpose the four instruments measuring blood pressure are 'orred' to a common flag.

Each error is trapped by a local exception handler, so that the source of the error can be identified.

```
with      SYSTEM_TYPES;
use       SYSTEM_TYPES;
package INTERFACE_DATA is

     WORD : constant := 16;
     type SELECTOR is new BED;
     type INTERFACE_VALUE is range 0 ..  65535;
     type SENSOR_VALUES is
          record
               BODY_TEMP,
               RIGHT_ATRIAL,
               LEFT_ATRIAL,
               DIASTOLIC,
               SYSTOLIC,
               PULSE_RATE: INTERFACE_VALUE;
          end record;
     CHANNEL: SELECTOR;
     X: SENSOR_VALUES;
          -- and now the representation specs
     for INTERFACE_VALUE'SIZE use WORD;
     for SENSOR_VALUES use
          record
               BODY_TEMP        at 0*WORD range  0 ..  15;
               RIGHT_ATRIAL     at 1*WORD range  0 ..  15;
               LEFT_ATRIAL      at 2*WORD range  0 ..  15;
               DIASTOLIC        at 3*WORD range  0 ..  15;
               SYSTOLIC         at 4*WORD range  0 ..  15;
               PULSE_RATE       at 5*WORD range  0 ..  15;
           end record;
     for SELECTOR'SIZE use 8;
     for CHANNEL use at 16 #8000# ;-- an 8 bit output PIA
     for X use at 16 #8002# ;

end INTERFACE_DATA;
```

```
with SYSTEM_TYPES, INTERFACE_DATA;
use  SYSTEM_TYPES, INTERFACE_DATA;
package body INTERFACE_DETAILS is

     function CONVERT(B : BED; X : in SENSOR_VALUES)
                         return FACTORS is separate;

     task INTERRUPT_HANDLER is
          entry CALL(B: in BED);
          entry FINISH(DATA: out FACTORS);
          entry DATA_READY;
          for DATA_READY use at 16 #0000# ;
     end  INTERRUPT_HANDLER;

     task body INTERRUPT_HANDLER is separate;

     function INTERFACE(B: BED) return FACTORS is
          BUFFER: FACTORS;
     begin
          MALFUNCTION(B) := (ERROR'FIRST ..  ERROR'LAST => FALSE);
          INTERRUPT_HANDLER.CALL(B);
          INTERRUPT_HANDLER.FINISH(BUFFER);
          return BUFFER;
     end INTERFACE;

end INTERFACE_DETAILS;


separate (INTERFACE_DETAILS)
function CONVERT(B : BED; X : in SENSOR_VALUES)
                    return FACTORS is
     BUFFER: FACTORS;
begin
     begin
          BUFFER.BODY_TEMP := CENTIGRADE (FLOAT(X.BODY_TEMP)/1000.0);
     exception
          when others =>  MALFUNCTION(B)(TEMPERATURE) := TRUE;
     end;
```

```
     begin
          BUFFER.RIGHT_ATRIAL := MILLIMETRES  (X.RIGHT_ATRIAL);
          BUFFER.LEFT_ATRIAL  := MILLIMETRES  (X.LEFT_ATRIAL);
          BUFFER.DIASTOLIC    := MILLIMETRES  (X.DIASTOLIC);
          BUFFER.SYSTOLIC     := MILLIMETRES  (X.SYSTOLIC);
     exception
          when others => MALFUNCTION(B)(BLOOD_PRESSURE) := TRUE;
     end;

     begin
          BUFFER.PULSE_RATE := PER_MINUTE (X.PULSE_RATE);
     exception
          when others => MALFUNCTION(B)(PULSE) := TRUE;
     end;

end CONVERT;


separate (INTERFACE_DETAILS)
task body INTERRUPT_HANDLER is
     CURRENT_BED : BED;
begin
     loop
          accept CALL(B: in BED) do
               CHANNEL := SELECTOR(B);
               CURRENT_BED := B;
          end;
          select
               accept DATA_READY;
          or
               delay 1.0;
               MALFUNCTION(CURRENT_BED)(TIME_OUT) := TRUE;
          end select;
          accept FINISH(DATA: out FACTORS) do
               DATA := CONVERT(CURRENT_BED,X);
          end;
     end loop;

end INTERRUPT_HANDLER;
```

16.12 Body of the Patient Database

Section 16.7 contained the specification of the package PATIENT_DIRECTORY which provides the database for all patients in the intensive care system and those detached within the last 48 hours. The body of this package is now included. It contains two tasks, one to provide the detached patient monitor which archives a patient's records after 48 hours in a detached state, the other to ensure that access to the database is an indivisible action, thus avoiding any contention between tasks which use the database.

```
with SYSTEM_TYPES, CALENDAR;
use SYSTEM_TYPES;
package body PATIENT_DIRECTORY is

      task DETACHED_PATIENT_MONITOR;

      task DATA_PROTECTION is
            -- entries to implement list handling and searches
            entry DETACH_PATIENT            ( B: in BED);
            entry DELETE;
            entry GET_NEXT_TIME             ( T: out CALENDAR.TIME);
            entry FIND_PATIENT_BY_NAME      ( N: in NAME_TYPE;
                                              X: out SEARCH_RESULT);
            entry FIND_PATIENT_BY_NUMBER    (NO: in HOSPITAL_PATIENT_NUMBER;
                                              X: out SEARCH_RESULT);
            entry PURGE_LIST;
      end DATA_PROTECTION;

      task body DETACHED_PATIENT_MONITOR is separate;
      task body DATA_PROTECTION is separate;
      function  FIND_PATIENT(N: NAME_TYPE)
                        return  SEARCH_RESULT  is separate;
      function  FIND_PATIENT(NO: HOSPITAL_PATIENT_NUMBER)
                        return  SEARCH_RESULT  is separate;
      procedure DETACH_PATIENT(B: in BED)  renames
                         DATA_PROTECTION.DETACH_PATIENT(B: in BED);
      procedure PURGE is separate;
end PATIENT_DIRECTORY;
```

The procedure PURGE causes immediate archiving of all the detached patients' records and then aborts the tasks DETACHED_PATIENT_MONITOR and DATA_PROTECTION. This is only called on system shut-down.

```
separate (PATIENT_DIRECTORY)
procedure PURGE is
begin
   DATA_PROTECTION.PURGE_LIST;
   abort DETACHED_PATIENT_MONITOR;
   abort DATA_PROTECTION;
end PURGE;
```

Overloaded procedures to find a patient call the appropriate entry in DATA_PROTECTION:

```
separate (PATIENT_DIRECTORY)
function FIND_PATIENT(N: NAME_TYPE) return SEARCH_RESULT is
     X: SEARCH_RESULT;
begin
     DATA_PROTECTION.FIND_PATIENT_BY_NAME(N, X);
     return X;
end FIND_PATIENT;

separate (PATIENT_DIRECTORY)
function FIND_PATIENT(NO : HOSPITAL_PATIENT_NUMBER)
                                    return SEARCH_RESULT is
     X: SEARCH_RESULT;
begin
     DATA_PROTECTION.FIND_PATIENT_BY_NUMBER(NO, X);
     return X;
end FIND_PATIENT;
```

The body of DATA_PROTECTION implements the list handling:

```
with      REPORT_GENERATOR, FILE_ARCHIVE, FILE_HANDLING, CALENDAR;
use       REPORT_GENERATOR, FILE_ARCHIVE, FILE_HANDLING;
separate (PATIENT_DIRECTORY)
```

```
task body DATA_PROTECTION is
     type LINK;
     type NODE is
          record
               PATIENT: PATIENT_DETAILS;
               T      : CALENDAR.TIME;
               NEXT   : LINK;
          end record;
     type LINK is access NODE;

     HEAD, TAIL, TEMP: LINK;

begin

     loop

          select
               accept DETACH_PATIENT (B: in BED) do
                    TEMP := new NODE(BED_ALLOCATION(B),
                                              CALENDAR.CLOCK, null);
                    if HEAD = null then
                         HEAD := TEMP;
                         TAIL := TEMP;
                    else
                         TAIL.NEXT := TEMP;
                         TAIL := TAIL.NEXT;
                    end if;
                    BED_ALLOCATION(B) := null;
               end DETACH_PATIENT;

          or
               when HEAD /= null =>
                    accept DELETE do
                         PATIENT_IO.CLOSE(HEAD.PATIENT.TRANSACTION_RECORD);
                         PRINT_FINAL_REPORT(HEAD.PATIENT);
                         SAVE_TO_ARCHIVE   (HEAD.PATIENT);
                         if HEAD = TAIL then
                              HEAD := null;
                              TAIL := null;
```

```
                    else
                         HEAD := HEAD.NEXT;
                    end if;
               end DELETE;

     or
          when HEAD /= null =>
               accept GET_NEXT_TIME ( T: out CALENDAR.TIME) do
                         T:= HEAD.T;
               end GET_NEXT_TIME;
     or

          accept  FIND_PATIENT_BY_NAME (N: in NAME_TYPE;
               X: out SEARCH_RESULT) do
               declare
                    FOUND: BOOLEAN := FALSE;
               begin
                    for B in BED loop
                         if N = BED_ALLOCATION(B).PATIENT.NAME then
                              X := (IN_BED, B, BED_ALLOCATION(B));
                              FOUND := TRUE;
                              exit;
                         end if;
                    end loop;

                    if not FOUND then
                         TEMP := HEAD;
                         while  TEMP /= null and not FOUND loop
                              if N = TEMP.PATIENT.NAME then
                                   X := (DETACHED, TEMP.PATIENT);
                                   FOUND := TRUE;
                              else
                                   TEMP := TEMP.NEXT;
                              end if;
                         end loop;
                    end if;
```

```
            if not FOUND then
                  X := (NONE);
            end if;
      end;
end FIND_PATIENT_BY_NAME;

or
      accept FIND_PATIENT_BY_NUMBER (NO: in  PATIENT_NO;
                                  X: out SEARCH_RESULT) do
            declare
                  FOUND: BOOLEAN := FALSE;
            begin
                  for B in BED loop
                        if  NO  = BED_ALLOCATION(B).HOSPITAL_NUMBER
                             then
                               X := (IN_BED, B, BED_ALLOCATION(B));
                               FOUND := TRUE;
                               exit;
                        end if;
                  end loop;

                  if not FOUND then
                        TEMP := HEAD;
                        while  TEMP /= null and not FOUND loop
                              if NO = TEMP.HOSPITAL_NUMBER then
                                    X := (DETACHED, TEMP.PATIENT);
                                    FOUND := TRUE;
                              else
                                    TEMP := TEMP.NEXT;
                              end if;
                        end loop;
                  end if;

                  if not FOUND then
                        X := (NONE);
                  end if;
            end;
      end FIND_PATIENT_BY_NUMBER;
```

```
        or
                accept PURGE_LIST do
                   while HEAD /= null loop
                       PATIENT.IO.CLOSE  (HEAD.PATIENT.TRANSACTION_RECORD);
                       PRINT_FINAL_REPORT(HEAD.PATIENT);
                       SAVE_TO_ARCHIVE   (HEAD.PATIENT);
                       HEAD := HEAD.NEXT;
                   end loop;
                end PURGE_LIST;

        end select;
    end loop;

end DATA_PROTECTION;
```

The body of DETACHED_PATIENT_MONITOR repeatedly finds the time for deletion of the first data record in the detached list, waits until the time specified, and then calls DELETE.

```
with CALENDAR;
separate (PATIENT_DIRECTORY)

task body DETACHED_PATIENT_MONITOR is
    T: CALENDAR.TIME;
begin
    HOURS: constant DURATION := 3600.0;
    loop
        DATA_PROTECTION.GET_NEXT_TIME(T);
        delay T + 48.0*HOURS - CALENDAR.CLOCK();
        DATA_PROTECTION.DELETE;
    end loop;
end DETACHED_PATIENT_MONITOR;
```

16.13 Monitoring of Sensor Data

The task body for MONITOR comes next. It defines the control operations for monitoring a patient's vital signs at each bedside. After accepting an initializing entry call, which gives the bed number, the task waits for a signal to monitor a new patient. Entries which change the local values are then accepted repeatedly until the patient is discharged. When this happens, the poller is stopped and the monitor waits for another patient.

These tasks will continue to be active until aborted on system shut down.

```
with TERMINAL_HANDLER, FILE_HANDLING, CENTRAL_NURSE_STATION, CALENDAR;
use  TERMINAL_HANDLER, FILE_HANDLING, CENTRAL_NURSE_STATION,
     SCREEN_HANDLER;
separate (BEDSIDE_MONITORING_SYSTEM)

task body MONITOR is

     BED_NO      : BED;
     SENSOR_DATA, MANUAL_DATA : FACTORS;
     INTERVAL    : DURATION;
     SAFE_RANGES: LIMITS;
     TOTAL_FLUID_GAIN : LITRES;
     SAFE_FLUID_GAIN  : FLUID_LIMITS;

     -- CONTROL acts as a semphore to provide mutual exclusion
     -- on access to the data values held in monitor by POLLING
     -- and MONITOR,
     task CONTROL is;
          entry CLAIM;
          entry RELEASE;
     end CONTROL;

     -- polling task causes timed access to the sensors,
     -- it uses globally visible INTERVAL for timing
     -- and puts values in SENSOR_DATA,
     -- the entries are used to START polling when a patient
     -- is put into a bed and STOP polling when he leaves
     task POLLING is
          entry START;
          entry STOP;
     end  POLLING;
```

```
     task body CONTROL is
     begin
          loop
               accept CLAIM;
               accept RELEASE;
          end loop;
     end CONTROL;

     task body POLLING is separate;

     DISCHARGE_REASON : LINE;

begin --body of MONITOR

     accept INITIALIZE(B: in BED) do
          BED_NO := B;
     end;

     loop
         accept MONITOR_NEW_PATIENT
               (L: in LIMITS; FL: FLUID_LIMITS; T: in DURATION) do
                 --note: POLLING is inactive so no protection is needed
                 SAFE_RANGES := L;
                 INTERVAL := T;
                 SAFE_FLUID_GAIN := FL;
         end MONITOR_NEW_PATIENT;

         WRITE (BED_ALLOCATION(BED_NO).TRANSACTION_FILE,
                 UNIT_RECORD'(CLASS => START_UP,
                 T     => CALENDAR.CLOCK);

         POLLING.START;
        loop
               select

                    accept SET_LIMITS (L: LIMITS) do
                         --protect from concurrent access by POLLING
                         CONTROL.CLAIM;
                         SAFE_RANGES:= L;
```

```
            CONTROL.RELEASE;
            WRITE(BED_ALLOCATION(BED_NO).TRANSACTION_RECORD,
                  UNIT_RECORD'(CLASS        => NEW_LIMITS,
                               T            => CALENDAR.CLOCK,
                               SAFE_RANGES  => L));
        end SET_LIMITS ;

or
        accept SET_TIMING (D: in DURATION) do
            --protect from concurrent access by POLLING
            CONTROL.CLAIM;
            INTERVAL := T;
            CONTROL.RELEASE;
            WRITE(BED_ALLOCATION(BED_NO).TRANSACTION_RECORD,
                  UNIT_RECORD'(CLASS     => NEW_TIMINGS,
                               T         => CALENDAR.CLOCK,
                               INTERVAL  => D));
        end SET_TIMING ;

or
        accept SET_FLUID_LIMITS (FL: FLUID_LIMITS) do
            SAFE_FLUID_GAIN := FL;
            WRITE(BED_ALLOCATION(BED_NO).TRANSACTION_RECORD,
                  UNIT_RECORD'(CLASS     => NEW_FLUID_LIMITS,
                               T         => CALENDAR.CLOCK,
                               SAFE_FLUID_GAIN => FL));
        end SET_FLUID_LIMITS ;

or
        accept ENTER_FLUID_TRANSACTION(F:in FLUID;
                                       V:in LITRES) do
            TOTAL_FLUID_GAIN := TOTAL_FLUID_GAIN + V;
            WRITE(BED_ALLOCATION(BED_NO).TRANSACTION_RECORD,
                  UNIT_RECORD'(CLASS=> FLUID_TRANSACTION,
                               T     => CALENDAR.CLOCK,
                               WHICH_FLUID => F
                               VOLUME      => V));
            if TOTAL_FLUID_GAIN > SAFE_FLUID_GAIN.UPPER or
               TOTAL_FLUID_GAIN<SAFE_FLUID_GAIN.LOWER then
```

```
                        NURSE_STATION_MONITOR.ALARM(BED_NO, FLUIDS);
                        PUT_SCREEN_UPPER(BED_NO,
                            "ALARM - FLUID LEVEL CRITICAL");
                    end if;
                end ENTER_FLUID_TRANSACTION;
            or

                accept MANUAL_INPUT(F: in FACTORS) do
                    MANUAL_DATA := F;
                end MANUAL_INPUT;
            or

                accept DISCHARGE_PATIENT do
                    PUT_SCREEN_LOWER(BED_NO,
            " Patient being detached - Please give reason for records");
                    GET_STRING(BED_NO,DISCHARGE_REASON);
                    WRITE(BED_ALLOCATION(BED_NO).TRANSACTION_RECORD,
                        UNIT_RECORD'(CLASS=>DETACHED_NOTICE,
                                     T => CALENDAR.CLOCK;
                                     TEXT => DISCHARGE_REASON);
                    DETACH(BED_NO);
                end DISCHARGE_PATIENT ;
                exit;

            end select;
        end loop;

        POLLING.STOP;
    end loop;

end MONITOR;
```

The body of POLLING requires access to the interface package which provides the facilities for interrogating the sensors.

```
with INTERFACE_DETAILS, CALENDAR;
use  INTERFACE_DETAILS;
separate (BEDSIDE_MONITORING_SYSTEM.MONITOR)
```

```
task body POLLING is
    NEXT:CALENDAR.TIME;
begin
   loop
      accept START;
      NEXT := CALENDAR.CLOCK;
      loop
         NEXT := NEXT + INTERVAL;
         select
            accept STOP;
            exit;
         or
            delay NEXT - CALENDAR.CLOCK;
         end select;
         SENSOR_DATA := INTERFACE(BED_NO);

      -- check for error conditions and replace with manual readings
         if MALFUNCTION(B) /= (ERROR'RANGE => FALSE) then
            PUT_STRING_UPPER(B,
                  " Sensor Malfunction - Manual Input Required ");
         end if                                                    ;

         for E in ERROR loop
            if MALFUNCTION(B)(E) = TRUE then
               case E is
                  when BODY_TEMP =>
                    SENSOR_DATA.BODY_TEMP := MANUAL_DATA.BODY_TEMP;
                  when BLOOD_PRESSURE =>
                    SENSOR_DATA.RIGHT_ATRIAL:= MANUAL_DATA.RIGHT_ATRIAL;
                    SENSOR_DATA.LEFT_ATRIAL:= MANUAL_DATA.LEFT_ATRIAL;
                    SENSOR_DATA.DIASTOLIC := MANUAL_DATA.DIASTOLIC;
                    SENSOR_DATA.SYSTOLIC := SENSOR_DATA.SYSTOLIC;
                  when PULSE =>
                    SENSOR_DATA.PULSE_RATE := SENSOR_DATA.PULSE_RATE;
                  when TIME_OUT =>
                    SENSOR_DATA := MANUAL_DATA;
               end case;
            end if;
         end loop;
```

```
            WRITE(BED_ALLOCATION(BED_NO).TRANSACTION_RECORD,
                 UNIT_RECORD'(CLASS=> VITAL_SIGNS,
                              T =>  CALENDAR.CLOCK,
                              F    => SENSOR_DATA));
            CONTROL.CLAIM;
            CHECK_FACTORS(SENSOR_DATA, LIMITS);
            CONTROL.RELEASE;
        end loop;
    end loop;

end POLLING;
```

16.14 Procedures to Support Dialogues at Terminals

Within the package BEDSIDE_MONITORING_SYSTEM there are two units which control lengthy dialogues with a member of the medical staff at the bedside terminal. These are ATTACH_PATIENT, where all the initial values of the patient's data records are set up, and COMMAND_CONTROL, which responds to commands entered during the patient's stay in the intensive care unit. The bodies of these units were shown in section 16.9. They both contain packages used to encapsulate the procedures for terminal interactions. The bodies of these packages were left for separate development and compilation, following the top-down style of Ada program design.

The body of the first of these packages, INITIALIZING_OPERATIONS, is compiled next. Its **separate** tag identifies its place in the program structure and it will inherit the visibility of ATTACH_PATIENT. In addition, the package INTERFACE_DETAILS is made visible because the procedure ATTACH_SENSORS uses the INTERFACE function, as described in section 16.11 above.

The procedures which convert a string input into numerical values each contain a validation check. If the conversion is successful then the procedure terminates, otherwise an exception handler is used to prompt for re-input of data. The string input of the patient's personal data is not validated. However, the input may be aborted and started again at any time by pressing the 'escape' character at the terminal. This will raise the ESCAPE exception in the package TERMINAL_HANDLER which is handled locally.

Both the following packages contain procedures that may be called simultaneously by several active tasks. This presents no problems. The language implementation will create a separate data frame for each activation, but will share the same code.

```
with INTERFACE_DETAILS, TERMINAL_HANDLER;
use  INTERFACE_DETAILS, TERMINAL_HANDLER;
separate (BEDSIDE_MONITORING_SYSTEM.ATTACH_PATIENT)

package body INITIALIZING_OPERATIONS is
   use KEYBOARD_HANDLER, SCREEN_HANDLER;

   procedure GET_TEMPERATURE(B: in BED; T: out CENTIGRADE) is
        S:STRING(1 .. 6);
   begin
      loop
          begin
              GET_STRING(B, S);
              T := CENTIGRADE'VALUE(S);
              exit;
          exception
              when CONSTRAINT_ERROR|ESCAPE =>
                   PUT_SCREEN_LOWER(B, " Invalid Entry - Try Again ");
           end;
       end loop;
   end GET_TEMPERATURE;


   procedure GET_PRESSURE(B: in BED; P: out MILLIMETRES) is
        S:STRING(1 .. 3);
   begin
      loop
          begin
              GET_STRING(B, S);
              P := MILLIMETRES'VALUE(S);
              exit;
          exception
              when CONSTRAINT_ERROR|ESCAPE =>
                   PUT_SCREEN_LOWER(B, " Invalid Entry - Try Again ");
```

```
        end;
    end loop;
end GET_PRESSURE;


procedure GET_RATE (B: in BED; R: out PER_MINUTE) is
     S:STRING(1 ..  3);
begin
   loop
        begin
            GET_STRING(B, S);
            R := PER_MINUTE'VALUE(S);
            exit;
        exception
            when CONSTRAINT_ERROR|ESCAPE =>
                 PUT_SCREEN_LOWER(B, " Invalid Entry - Try Again ");
        end;
    end loop;
end GET_RATE;


procedure GET_DATE (B: in BED; DD: out DATE) is
     S:STRING(1 ..  10);
begin
   loop
        begin
            GET_STRING(B, S);
            DD.D := DAY'VALUE(S(1 ..  2));
            DD.M := DAY'VALUE(S(4 ..  5));
            DD.Y := YEAR'VALUE(S(7 ..  10);
            exit;
        exception
            when CONSTRAINT_ERROR|ESCAPE =>
                 PUT_SCREEN_LOWER(B, " Invalid Entry - Try Again ");
        end;
    end loop;
end GET_DATE;
```

```
procedure GET_PERSONAL_DATA(B: in BED; P: out PATIENT_INFO) is
  begin     -- dialogue with staff
    loop

      begin
          PUT_STRING_LOWER (B, " Enter Patient's Name.");
          GET_STRING (B, P.NAME);
          PUT_STRING_LOWER (B,
              " Enter Date of Birth - format dd mm yyyy");
          GET_DATE(B, P.DATE_OF_BIRTH);
          PUT_STRING_LOWER (B, " Enter Patient's Address.");
          GET_STRING (B, P.ADDRESS);
              loop
                  PUT_STRING_LOWER (B, " ENTER SEX: M / F");
                  GET_REPLY   (B, CHOICE);
                  if CHOICE = 'M' then
                          P.GENDER := MALE;
                          exit;
                  elsif CHOICE = 'F' then
                          P.GENDER := FEMALE;
                          exit;
                  end if ;
               end loop;
            PUT_STRING_LOWER (B, " Enter 'phone Number.");
            GET_STRING (B, P.TELEPHONE_NUMBER);

            PUT_STRING_LOWER (B, " Enter Name of Next-of-kin.");
            GET_STRING (B, P.KIN.NAME);
            PUT_STRING_LOWER (B, " Enter Address of Next-of-kin.");
            GET_STRING (B, P.KIN.ADDRESS);
            PUT_STRING_LOWER (B, " Enter Phone Number of Next-of-kin.");
            GET_STRING (B, P.KIN.TELEPHONE_NUMBER);
            PUT_STRING_LOWER (B, " Enter Relationship of Next-of-kin.");
            GET_STRING (B, P.KIN.KINSHIP);
            PUT_STRING_LOWER (B, " Enter Patient's Religion");
            GET_STRING (B, P.BELIEF);
            exit;
```

```
    exception
          when ESCAPE =>
                PUT_STRING_LOWER(B, " Try again ?  (Y/N)");
                GET_REPLY (B, CHOICE);
                if CHOICE /= 'Y' then
                      exit;
                end if;
    end;
  end loop;

end GET_PERSONAL_DATA;


procedure GET_HOSPITAL_NUMBER(B: in BED) is separate;
     -- this follows closely the style of GET_PERSONAL_DATE


procedure GET_INITIAL_LIMITS (B: in  BED; L: out LIMITS) is
begin
                -- deal with temperature
   PUT_STRING_LOWER (B, " Enter Acceptable Limits of Body Temperature");
   PUT_STRING_LOWER (B, " DEGREES CENTIGRADE format XX.XXX");

   PUT_STRING_LOWER (B, " LOWER LIMIT:");
   GET_TEMPERATURE  (B, L.LOWER.BODY_TEMP);
   PUT_STRING_LOWER (B, " UPPER_LIMIT:");
   GET_TEMPERATURE  (B, L.UPPER.BODY_TEMP);

                -- now deal with blood pressures
   PUT_STRING_LOWER (B, " Enter acceptable limits of Blood-pressure" );
   PUT_STRING_LOWER (B, " MILLIMETRES of MERCURY format XXX");

   PUT_STRING_LOWER (B, " RIGHT_ATRIAL: LOWER LIMIT");
   GET_PRESSURE (B, L.LOWER.RIGHT_ATRIAL);
   PUT_STRING_LOWER (B, " RIGHT_ATRIAL: UPPER LIMIT");
   GET_PRESSURE (B, L.UPPER.RIGHT_ATRIAL);
   PUT_STRING_LOWER (B, " LEFT_ATRIAL: LOWER LIMIT");
   GET_PRESSURE (B, L.LOWER.LEFT_ATRIAL);
   PUT_STRING_LOWER (B, " LEFT_ATRIAL: UPPER LIMIT");
```

```
   GET_PRESSURE (B, L.UPPER.LEFT_ATRIAL);
   PUT_STRING_LOWER (B, " DIASTOLIC: LOWER LIMIT");
   GET_PRESSURE (B, L.LOWER.DIASTOLIC);
   PUT_STRING_LOWER (B, " DIASTOLIC: UPPER LIMIT");
   GET_PRESSURE (B, L.UPPER.DIASTOLIC);
   PUT_STRING_LOWER (B, " SYSTOLIC: LOWER LIMIT");
   GET_PRESSURE (B, L.LOWER.SYSTOLIC);
   PUT_STRING_LOWER (B, " SYSTOLIC: UPPER LIMIT");
   GET_PRESSURE (B, L.UPPER.SYSTOLIC);

                -- now deal with pulse rate
   PUT_STRING_LOWER (B, " ENTER LIMITS OF PULSE RATE");
   PUT_STRING_LOWER (B, " COUNT per MINUTE format XXX");

   PUT_STRING_LOWER (B, " LOWER LIMIT");
   GET_RATE(B, L.LOWER.PULSE_RATE);
   PUT_STRING_LOWER (B, " UPPER LIMIT");
   GET_RATE(B, L.UPPER.PULSE_RATE);
end GET_INITIAL_LIMITS;


procedure GET_POLLING_INTERVAL (in BED; T out DURATION)
                                                        is separate;
procedure GET_FLUID_LIMITS(B: in BED; FL: out FLUID_LIMITS)
                                                        is separate;
-- these follow closely the style of get limits,and are not given here


procedure ATTACH_SENSORS(B: in BED) is
     MESSAGE: constant STRING :=
          " Please Attach Sensors:  Press any Key when Done."
     COUNT_TRIES: INTEGER:= 0;
     BUFFER: FACTORS;

begin
     CLEAR_SCREEN_LOWER(B);
     PUT_STRING_LOWER(B, MESSAGE);
     GET_REPLY(B);  -- ignore arbitrary reply
```

```
        while COUNT_TRIES < 4 loop
            BUFFER := INTERFACE(B);
            if MALFUNCTION(B) = (FALSE, FALSE, FALSE, FALSE) then
                PUT_STRING_LOWER(B,"Successfulattachment: automatic" &
                                                 " monitoring.");
                exit;
            end if;
            COUNT_TRIES := COUNT_TRIES + 1;
            for E in ERROR loop
                if MALFUNCTION(B)(E) then
                    PUT_STRING_LOWER(B, " ERROR - "& ERROR'IMAGE(E));
                end if;
            end loop;
            if COUNT_TRIES < 4 then
                PUT_STRING_LOWER(B, " Try again to fix faulty sensors");
            else
                PUT_STRING_LOWER(B, " Unsuccessful: use manual input"&
                                                 " for faulty sensors");
            end if;
        end loop;
    end ATTACH_SENSORS;

end INITIALIZING_OPERATIONS;
```

The next package provides the procedures for use in the COMMAND_CONTROL task. Not all the procedures are given in detail since they would follow the same pattern as those of the previous package. In several cases, data is transferred to the appropriate TREATMENT or MONITOR task by calling an entry.

```
with CENTRAL_NURSE_MONITOR;
use  CENTRAL_NURSE_MONITOR;
use  SCREEN_HANDLER, KEYBOARD_HANDLER;
separate (BEDSIDE_MONITORING_SYSTEM.COMMAND_CONTROL)

package body MONITORING_OPERATIONS is
```

```
procedure GET_FLUID_VOLUME (B: in BED; L: out LITRES) is
     S: STRING(1 ..  4);
begin
   loop
       begin
           GET_STRING(B, S);
           L := LITRES(FLOAT(INTEGER'VALUE(S))/1000.0);
           exit;
       exception
           when CONSTRAINT_ERROR|ESCAPE =>
                PUT_SCREEN_LOWER(B, " Invalid Entry - Try Again ");
       end;
    end loop;
end GET_FLUID_VOLUME;


procedure TRY_AGAIN (B: in BED) is
begin
     PUT_STRING_LOWER (B, "Illegal Response: please try again");
end TRY_AGAIN;


procedure ENTER_TREATMENT_SCHEDULE(B: in BED) is
     TEXT: LINE;  W: DURATION; S: STRING(1 .. 5);
begin
     -- gets treatment schedule as text
     PUT_STRING_LOWER( B, "Please enter treatment schedule ");
     GET_STRING(B, TEXT);
     -- gets elapse time to next treatment
     PUT_STRING_LOWER(B,
       " Please enter time lapse to next treatment as hh:mm ");
     GET_STRING(B, S);
     W := DURATION(60*INTEGER'VALUE(S(1..2)) + INTEGER'VALUE(S(4..5)));
     -- passes treatment information to TREATMENT_CONTROL task
     TREATMENT_CONTROL(B).DEFINE_TREATMENT(TEXT, W);
end ENTER_TREATMENT_SCHEDULE;
```

```
procedure ENTER_TREATMENT_GIVEN(B: in BED) is
     TEXT: LINE;
begin
     PUT_STRING_LOWER( B, "PLEASE ENTER TREATMENT GIVEN:");
     GET_STRING(B, TEXT);
     TREATMENT_CONTROL(B).ENTER_TREATMENT_GIVEN(TEXT);
end ENTER_TREATMENT_GIVEN;


procedure ENTER_TREATMENT_INFO(B : in BED) is
     C : CHOICE;
begin
     PUT_STRING_LOWER(B,
 " Please indicate which treatment transaction is required "& ASCII.CR &
 "             1      Consult schedule                  "& ASCII.CR &
 "             2      Input new schedule                "& ASCII.CR &
 "             3      Record treatment given            "& ASCII.CR &
 "   any other character will cancel input              "& ASCII.CR);
     GET_REPLY(B,C);
     case C is
         when '1'  => TREATMENT_CONTROL(B).CONSULT_TREATMENT_SCHEDULE;
         when '2'  => ENTER_TREATMENT_SCHEDULE(B);
         when '3'  => ENTER_TREATMENT_GIVEN(B);
         when '4'  => null;
end ENTER_TREATMENT_INFO;


procedure ENTER_FLUID_DATA (B: in BED) is
     MENU: constant STRING :=
     "         Please Select Fluid Transaction"& ASCII.CR &
     "             1) Intake                  "& ASCII.CR &
     "             2) Loss                    "& ASCII.CR;

     INTAKE_MENU: constant STRING :=
     "         Which Fluid?       "& ASCII.CR &
     "             1) Drink       "& ASCII.CR &
     "             2) Drip        "& ASCII.CR &
     "             3) Transfusion "& ASCII.CR &
     "             4) Injection   "& ASCII.CR;
```

```
    LOSS_MENU: constant STRING :=
    "          Which Fluid?          "& ASCII.CR &
    "              1) Urine          "& ASCII.CR &
    "              2) Bleeding       "& ASCII.CR &
    "              3) Vomit          "& ASCII.CR;

    IN_FLUIDS: constant array (CHARACTER range '1' ..  '4')
                         of STRING(1.. 11)
              := ( "Drink      ",
                   "Drip_feed  ",
                   "Transfusion",
                   "Injection  " );

    OUT_FLUIDS:constant array (CHARACTER range '1' ..  '3')
                         of STRING(1 .. 8)
              := ( "Urine   ",
                   "Bleeding",
                   "Vomit   ");
    CHOICE: CHARACTER;
    F     : FLUID;
    V     : LITRES;

begin
    CLEAR_SCREEN(B);
    PUT_STRING (B, MENU);
    loop
        GET_REPLY(B, CHOICE);
        exit when CHOICE in CHARACTER range '1' ..'2';
        TRY_AGAIN (B);
    end loop;
    case CHOICE is
       when '1'    => -- intake of fluids
          PUT_STRING (INTAKE_MENU, B);
          loop
             GET_REPLY(B, CHOICE);
             exit when CHOICE in CHARACTER range '1' ..'4';
             TRY_AGAIN (B);
          end loop;
```

```
        PUT_STRING(B, " Please Enter Fluid Intake by " &
                      IN_FLUIDS(CHOICE) & " in Millilitres ");
        GET_FLUID_VOLUME (B, V);
        F:=FLUID'VAL(CHARACTER'POS(CHOICE) - CHARACTER'POS(0) - 1);
                --depends on matching order of type and menu
    when '2'    => -- loss of fluids
        PUT_STRING (LOSS_MENU, B);
        loop
            GET_REPLY(B, CHOICE);
            exit when CHOICE in CHARACTER range '1'..'2';
            TRY_AGAIN (B);
        end loop;
        PUT_STRING(B, " Please Enter Fluid Loss by " &
                      OUT_FLUIDS(CHOICE) & " in Millilitres ");
        GET_FLUID_VOLUME (B,V);
        V := -V;
        F := FLUID'VAL(CHARACTER'POS(CHOICE) - CHARACTER'POS(0) + 3);
                --comment as above
        TRY_AGAIN(B);
    end case;
    -- fluid transaction passed to MONITOR task by entry call
    INTENSIVE_CARE(B).ENTER_FLUID_TRANSACTION(F, V);

exception
    when ESCAPE => null;

end ENTER_FLUID_DATA;


procedure REQUEST_REPEAT(B: in BED) is
    ERROR_MESSAGE: constant STRING := "Illegal Choice - Start Again";
begin
    PUT_STRING(B,ERROR_MESSAGE);
    delay 2.0;      -- returns after 2 seconds delay
                    -- to display the message
end REQUEST_REPEAT;
```

```
procedure RESET_ALARM (B: in BED) is
    C : CHARACTER;
    W : WARNING;
    MENU : constant STRING :=
"  Please indicate which alarm warning is to be cancelled "& ASCII.CR &
"       1          for   Blood Pressure                   "& ASCII.CR &
"       2          for   Temperature                      "& ASCII.CR &
"       3          for   Pulse                            "& ASCII.CR &
"       4          for   Fluid Level                      "& ASCII.CR &
"       5          for   Interface Time-out               "& ASCII.CR &
"       6          for   Sensor Failure                   "& ASCII.CR &
"       any other character to cancel input               "& ASCII.CR ;

begin
    CLEAR_SCREEN_LOWER(B);
    PUT_STRING_LOWER(B, MENU);
    GET_REPLY(B,C);
    if C in CHARACTER range 1..6 then
       W := WARNING'VAL(CHARACTER'POS(C) - CHARACTER'POS(0));
       NURSE_STATION_MONITOR.CANCEL_ALARM(B,W);
    else PUT_STRING_LOWER(B, " Input Abandoned ");
    end if;
end RESET_ALARM;


-- the following procedures are not given since they follow
-- the pattern of those given above and in INITIALIZING_OPERATIONS

procedure NEW_FLUID_LIMITS (B: in BED) is separate;
procedure ENTER_NEW_LIMITS (B: in BED) is separate;
procedure ENTER_NEW_TIMING (B: in BED) is separate;
procedure GENERATE_DISPLAY (B: in BED) is separate;
procedure MANUAL_INPUT     (B: in BED) is separate;
procedure LOG_OUT_PATIENT  (B: in BED) is separate;

end MONITORING_OPERATIONS;
```

16.15 Conclusion

The aim of this book has been to give the reader an understanding of the principal features of the Ada language. This it has done by a tutorial approach, rather than a systematic and rigorous treatise based on the reference manual. It is hoped that this will prove helpful to programmers experienced in programming in less powerful languages. The development of a fairly large program as a case study was thought to be helpful in illustrating the use of Ada for significant problems.

Ada has been found to be an excellent language for the design of a moderately large embedded system. Outline code modules can be designed and then gradually 'fleshed-out' into full program units. Carefully used, the program texts can be clear and attractive to read. Strong typing proved its worth in discovering errors at compilation. The programs presented are known to be substantially error free, though a few modules have been added since the last compilation, so it is not possible to make a guarantee of their correctness.

In developing this program the authors have become very much aware of the need for software support tools for the Ada programming process. A good data dictionary with cross reference facilities is essential to eliminate naming errors and name clashes. As stated in chapter 6, the existence of names for the variables, types and access types can make it very difficult to remember which is which. The use of systematised formal names might help to keep account of all the identifiers used, but this would certainly spoil the readability of the programs. Software to help access a dictionary of readable names would be a preferable solution.

Careful attention to layout helps readability, and reduces errors. Formatters and pretty printers are important tools, and some of the programmer can be helped in coping with the verbosity of Ada by language specific editors. A program development methodology using stages of outline Ada code supported by database auditing would also be a great aid. These tools, and many more, are to be expected as part of an APSE.

In spite of the words of caution included in chapter 15, drawing attention to the possible overheads of compilation and run time efficiency which Ada programs may incur, the authors are confident that the language will make a great contribution to the discipline of software engineering, improving the quality of software throughout the world, especially software for embedded systems.

History has shown that certain languages set the style for future developments. Ada itself has a genealogy which includes important influences from many earlier languages. Algol and Pascal deserve special mention. Whatever the outcome of present endeavours to standardize methods of software production around Ada for embedded systems, there is no doubt that the interest which it has aroused will influence developments of future languages in this and other fields.

Reference

[16.1] Henry V, Prologue to Act I, William Shakespeare.

Exercise 16

16.1 Write the bodies for the missing procedures of MONITORING-OPERATIONS package.

16.2 A shortcoming of the requirements specification for the patient monitoring system has been recognized. In the present design there is no provision for patients to be re-admitted to the intensive care unit. If a patient should suffer a relapse and return to the unit before 48 hours have elapsed then he will be treated as a new patient. His previous records, although still in the detached patient list, cannot be accessed since any search on name or number will first find the patient in his new bed. The earlier data will be inaccessible. In fact the data base is inconsistent.

Consider the program modifications required to allow for the re-admission of patients so that any transaction file still in the system is recovered from the detached list and reopened. A returning patient may occupy a different bed to that occupied on his previous stay.

16.3 An increasingly important part of computing involves the use of distributed microcomputer systems, involving cooperation between a collection of machines connected in a network. A hospital system might be developed where each patient was monitored by a separate computer.

The design given in BEDSIDE_MONITORING_SYSTEM is highly central, with all the tasks enclosed in a common package. Consider how the programs could be adapted to the needs of a distributed implementation.

APPENDIX

SOLUTIONS TO SAMPLE EXERCISES

Exercise 3

3.1 This should just be a table of items such as:

- concurrency,
- access to a real-time clock,
- high maintainability,
- interfacing to hardware external to the computer,
- handling of exceptions.

3.2 They are more often concerned with handling simultaneous needs of many co-existing external activities.

3.3 Deadlock occurs when concurrent actions share resources in a way which can lead to each waiting for the other to respond.

Traffic can deadlock at an intersection if cars arrive at each entrance simultaneously, and drivers follow rigidly a protocol such as priority on the right.

Humans 'dither' trying to pass in a narrow confine.

etc.

Exercise 5

5.1 Legal identifiers are X DAYS_IN_THE_YEAR and X3H1,
4_SIGHT does not start with a letter,
LENGTH-OF-RUN contains hyphens not underscores.

5.2 The program units of Ada are packages, tasks, functions and procedures.

5.3 Tasks are the only program units which cannot be compiled as stand alone components.

5.4 Stubs are essential for top-down construction of a program following the decomposition of a problem as explained in chapter 2.

Exercise 6

6.1
```
type STATE is (ALABAMA, ALASKA, ARIZONA, ... etc.);
type STATE_POPULATION is range 0 .. 30_000_000;
type POPULATION_TABLE is array (STATE) of STATE_POPULATION;
type BATH_TEMPERATURE is delta 0.1 range 0.0 .. 100.0;
type VEHICLE_SPEED    is digits  3 range 0.0 .. 100.0;
type LONGITUDE        is delta 0.01 range 0.0 .. 360.0;
type LATITUDE         is delta 0.01 range -90.0 .. 90.0;
type POSITION         is
     record
          THETA: LATITUDE;
          PHI  : LONGITUDE;
     end record;
```

6.2 The following definitions give an indication of the kind of solution expected. There is room for the application of much imagination in selecting items for inclusion in the model.

```
subtype NAME_TYPE is STRING(1 .. 40);
subtype ADDRESS_TYPE is STRING(1 .. 200);
type DOLLARS   is range 0 .. 100_000_000;
subtype PAY is DOLLARS range 0 .. 40_000;
```

```
type DEPARTMENT is (SALES, ACCOUNTS, MANUFACTURING ..etc);
type BUDGET is array (DEPARTMENT) of DOLLARS;
type EMPLOYEE is
     record
          NAME: NAME_TYPE;
          SECTION: DEPARTMENT;
          SALARY :PAY;
          .. etc;
     end record;
type PAYROLL is array (1 .. NUMBER_OF_EMPLOYEES) of EMPLOYEE;
type COMPANY is
     record
          CORPORATE_NAME: NAME_TYPE;
          CORPORATE_ADDRESS: ADDRESS_TYPE;
          STAFF_LIST: PAYROLL;
          FINANCIAL_PLAN: BUDGET;
     end record;
```

6.3
```
type VOLTS is digits 3 range 0.0 .. 10.0;
type BUS   is array (1 .. 12) of VOLTS;
```

6.4 There is an array of lifts, and an array of button-pairs to model the calls from the floors of the building. In the following solution, the two arrays are grouped together into a single conceptual unit, as a record, parameterized by with a discriminant to control the number of lifts and the number of floors.

Since each lift contains a panel of buttons whose size depends on the number of floors, the lift type also has a parameter determining this value. This illustrates the way in which a discriminant can be used to provide a value of a discriminant of an inner structure.

```
MAX_FLOOR: constant := 10;
MAX_LIFT: constant := 4;
type DOOR_STATE is (OPEN, CLOSED);
type BRAKE_STATE is (OFF, ON);
type MOTION is (UP, DOWN, NONE);
type FLOOR_NUMBER is range 1 .. MAX_FLOOR;
```

```
type LIFT_NUMBER is range 1 .. MAX_LIFT;
type BUTTON is (PRESSED, FREE);
type PANEL_TYPE  is array (FLOOR_NUMBER) of BUTTON;
type FLOOR is
     record
          UP, DOWN: BUTTON;
     end record;
type FLOOR_ARRAY is array (FLOOR_NUMBER) of FLOOR;
type LIFT is
     record
          DOOR: DOOR_STATE;
          MOVEMENT: MOTION;
          BRAKES: BRAKE_STATE;
          LEVEL: FLOOR_NUMBER;
          PANEL: PANEL_TYPE;
     end record;

type LIFT_ARRAY is array (LIFT_NUMBER) of LIFT;
type SYSTEM is
      record
          LIFTS:  LIFT_ARRAY;
          FLOORS: FLOOR_ARRAY;
     end record;

LIFT_SYSTEM: SYSTEM;          --generates a system of four lifts
                              --in a building of ten floors
```

Access to, say, the fourth button of the panel contained in the third lift of the system would be obtained by a series of record accesses using a mixture of the dot notation and the indexing of arrays as follows:

```
LIFT_SYSTEM.LIFTS(3).PANEL(4)
```

names an object of type BUTTON, with possible values PRESSED or FREE.

Renaming could be used to simplify such access.

Exercise 7

7.1
```
F3 := F1 xor F2;
```

7.2
```
if X > Y then Z := X rem Y;
else Z := Y rem X;
end if;
```

7.3
```
I := 0;
for C in 1..N loop
     if STUDENT = CLASS_ROLL(N) then
          I := N; exit;
     end if;
end loop;
```

7.4
```
for R in ROOM loop
     if HOUSE_LIGHT(R) = ON then
          -- low level interaction with control of light R
          HOUSE_LIGHT(R) := OFF;
     end if;
end loop;
```

7.5
```
case THIS_MONTH is
     when JANUARY..APRIL         => SAFE_TO_EAT := TRUE;
     when MAY..AUGUST            => SAFE_TO_EAT := FALSE;
     when SEPTEMBER..DECEMBER    => SAFE_TO_EAT := TRUE;
end case;
```

Exercise 8

8.1
```
type MONTH is (JANUARY, FEBRUARY, MARCH, APRIL, MAY, JUNE, JULY,
               AUGUST, SEPTEMBER, OCTOBER, NOVEMBER, DECEMBER);
type YEAR is INTEGER range 1900..1999;
type DATE is record
     DAY : INTEGER range 1..31;
     M   : MONTH;
     Y   : YEAR;
end record;
```

```
function VALID_DATE (D : DATE) return BOOLEAN is
   function IS_LEAP(Y : YEAR) return BOOLEAN is
     return (Y mod 4 = 0) and not
           ((Y mod 100 = 0) and not (Y mod 400 = 0));
   end IS_LEAP;
   OK : BOOLEAN;
begin
   case D.M is
     when FEBRUARY => if IS_LEAP(D.Y) then OK := D.DAY < 30;
                      else OK := D.DAY < 29 end if;
     when APRIL|JUNE|SEPTEMBER|NOVEMBER => OK := D.DAY < 31;
     when others => OK := TRUE; -- enforced by range constraint
   end case;
   return OK;
end VALID_DATE;
```

8.2

```
function HCF(M,N : INTEGER) return INTEGER is
   T : INTEGER;
begin
   if M>N then return HCF(M,N);
   elsif M = 0 then return N;
   else T := N rem M;
        return HCF (M,T);
   end if;
end HCF;
```

8.3

```
procedure CDF(OBSERVATIONS : in INT_VECTOR;
              DISTRIBUTION : out REAL_VECTOR) is
   SUM : FLOAT := 0.0;
begin
   -- accumulate observations
   for I in INDEX_RANGE loop
     SUM := SUM + FLOAT(OBSERVATIONS(I));
     DISTRIBUTION(I) := SUM;
   end loop;
```

```
  -- then normalize
  for I in INDEX_RANGE loop
    DISTRIBUTION := DISTRIBUTION(I)/SUM;
  end loop;
end CDF;
```

8.5 A type is required that consists of three interger values, representing yards, feet and inches respectively. For each of these a subtype is used to impose an appropriate range constraint.

```
subtype YARDS is INTEGER range 0..100;
subtype FEET is INTEGER range 0..2;
subtype INCHES is INTEGER range 0..11;
type MEASURE is record
    Y : YARDS;
    F : FEET;
    I : INCHES;
end record;
```

A function to overload "+" is quite straightforward and is not given here. However, subtraction involves the possibility of a constraint error caused by a negative result:

```
function "-" (A,B : MEASURE) return MEASURE is
   X : MEASURE;  IA, IB : INTEGER;
begin
   IA := A.Y*36 + A.F*12 + A.I; -- measure A in inches
   IB := B.Y*36 + B.F*12 + B.I; -- measure B in inches
   if IB > IA then raise CONSTRAINT_ERROR;
   else IA := IA - IB;
        X.Y := IA/36;
        IA  := IA - X.Y*36;
        X.F := IA/12;
        X.I := IA - X.F*12;
        return X;
   end if;
end;
```

As a further exercise, this function could be improved by pre-defining a function to convert a MEASURE to an INTEGER value and overloading the operator ">" for MEASURE.

Exercise 9

9.1
```
task MERCURY is
     entry INPUT(M : in MESSAGE);
end MERCURY;

task type MERCURY is
     LOCAL : MESSAGE;  -- local storage for a message
begin
     loop
          accept INPUT(M : in MESSAGE) do
             LOCAL := M; -- copies message recieved
          end INPUT; -- end of rendezvous
          RECIEVER.INPUT(LOCAL);  -- call of entry in RECIEVER
     end loop;  -- infinite loop
end MERCURY;
```

9.2
```
task MAILBOX is
     -- messages can be put in the mailbox by task ID
     entry IN_MESSAGE(M : in MESSAGE; ID : in INTEGER);
     -- and read from the mailbox by tasks giving their ID
     entry READ_MESSAGE(M : out MESSAGE; ID : in INTEGER);
end MAIBOX;

task body MAILBOX is
     -- a Boolean array is used to register tasks who have
     -- read a message:
     MESSAGE_SEEN : array (1..N) of BOOLEAN;
     LOCAL : MESSAGE;
begin
     loop
          MESSAGE_SEEN := (others => FALSE);  -- not seen by any task
```

```
        accept IN_MESSAGE(M : in MESSAGE;
                          ID : in INTEGER) is
            LOCAL := M; -- copy message
            MESSAGE_SEEN(ID) := TRUE; -- seen by originator
        end IN_MESSAGE;
        while MESSAGE_SEEN /= (1..N => TRUE) loop
            accept READ_MESSAGE(M : out MESSAGE;
                                ID : in INTEGER) do
                M := LOCAL; -- give out message
                MESSAGE_SEEN(ID) := TRUE; -- record calling task
            end READ_MESSAGE;
        end loop; -- ends when all tasks have read message
    end loop; -- infinite loop
end MAILBOX;
```

9.3

```
procedure TEXT_ASSEMBLER is

    subtype LINE is STRING(1 .. 120);
    subtype WORD_TEXT is STRING(1..30);
    subtype WORD_LENGTH is INTEGER range 1..30;
    type WORD_TYPE is
        record
            TEXT: WORD_TEXT;
            LENGTH: WORD_LENGTH;
        end record;

    BLANK: constant WORD_TYPE := ((1 .. 30=> ' '), 1);
    EMPTY_LINE: constant LINE := (1 .. 120 => ' ');

    task IN_CHAR;

    task MAKE_LINE is
        entry RECEIVE_WORD(W: in WORD_TYPE);
    end;

    task OUT_LINE is
        entry RECEIVE_LINE(L: in LINE);
```

```
    end;

    task body IN_CHAR is separate;
    task body MAKE_LINE is separate;
    task body OUT_LINE is separate;

begin
     null;
end TEXT_ASSEMBLER;



separate (TEXT_ASSEMBLER) task body IN_CHAR is
     WORD: WORD_TYPE;
     CH  : CHARACTER;
begin
     loop
          WORD.LENGTH:=1;
          GET(CH);
          -- ignore leading separators
          while CH not in  CHARACTER range 'A' .. 'Z' loop
               GET(CH);
          end loop;
          loop
               WORD.TEXT(WORD.LENGTH) := CH;
               WORD.LENGTH := WORD.LENGTH + 1;
               GET(CH);
               exit when CH not in  CHARACTER range 'A' .. 'Z';
          end loop;
          WORD.TEXT(WORD.LENGTH):= ' ';
          MAKE_LINE.RECEIVE_WORD(WORD);
          exit when  CH = '!'; -- terminator
     end loop;
     MAKE_LINE.RECEIVE_WORD(BLANK); -- passes last word
end IN_CHAR;
```

```
separate (TEXT_ASSEMBLER) task body MAKE_LINE is
     WORD: WORD_TYPE;
     L: LINE;
     COUNT: INTEGER range 1 .. 120;

     procedure SEND_LINE is
     begin
          for I in COUNT .. 120 loop
               L(I) := ' ';
          end loop;
          OUT_LINE.RECEIVE_LINE(L);
          COUNT := 1;
     end SEND_LINE;
begin
MAINLOOP:
     loop     -- over lines
          COUNT := 1;
          loop     -- over words
               accept RECEIVE_WORD(W: in WORD_TYPE) do
                    WORD := W;
               end RECEIVE_WORD;
               if WORD = BLANK then
                    if COUNT /= 1 then SEND_LINE;
                    end if;
                    OUT_LINE.RECEIVE_LINE(EMPTY_LINE);
                    exit MAINLOOP;
               elsif COUNT + WORD.LENGTH - 1 < 120 then
                    L(COUNT .. COUNT + WORD.LENGTH - 1)
                         := WORD.TEXT(1 .. WORD.LENGTH);
                    COUNT := COUNT + WORD.LENGTH;
               else
                    SEND_LINE;
                    L(1..WORD.LENGTH) := WORD.TEXT(1..WORD.LENGTH);
                    COUNT := COUNT + WORD.LENGTH;
                    exit;
               end if;
          end loop;
     end loop MAINLOOP;
end MAKE_LINE;
```

```
separate (TEXT_ASSEMBLER) task_body OUT_LINE is
     LOCAL: LINE;
begin
     loop
          accept RECEIVE_LINE(L: in LINE) do
               LOCAL := L;
          end RECEIVE_LINE;
          exit when LOCAL = EMPTY_LINE;
          PUT(LOCAL) ;
     end loop;
end OUT_LINE;
```

Exercise 10

10.1 The package specifies a private type with operations. Other representations would be equally possible; for example the record could contain the modulus and argument.

```
package COMPLEX_NUMBERS is
     type COMPLEX is private;
     function "+" (X, Y: COMPLEX) return COMPLEX;
     function "-" (X, Y: COMPLEX) return COMPLEX;
     function "*" (X, Y: COMPLEX) return COMPLEX;
     function "/" (X, Y: COMPLEX) return COMPLEX;
     function "*" (X: COMPLEX, Y: INTEGER) return COMPLEX;
     function MAKE_COMPLEX (X,Y: FLOAT) return COMPLEX;
private
     type COMPLEX is
          record
               RE, IM: FLOAT:= 0.0;
          end;
end COMPLEX_NUMBERS;
```

Since the type is private, its structure is unkown to users. They must call a function MAKE_COMPLEX to compose complex numbers from the pair of reals.

The body contains the definitions of the operations on complex numbers. In the following, the functions each return a record aggregate of type COMPLEX. For clarity this is qualified by the type, but that is a cosmetic refinement. The type is known from the function signature.

The algorithms are written for simplicity and clarity, rather than efficiency.

```
package body COMPLEX_NUMBERS is

    function MAKE_COMPLEX (X,Y: FLOAT) return COMPLEX is
    begin
        return COMPLEX'(X,Y);
    end MAKE_COMPLEX;

    function "+" (X, Y: COMPLEX) return COMPLEX is
    begin
        return COMPLEX'(X.RE + Y.RE, X.IM + Y.IM);
    end "+";

    function "-" (X, Y: COMPLEX) return COMPLEX;
    begin
        return COMPLEX'(X.RE - Y.RE, X.IM - Y.IM);
    end "-";

    function "*" (X, Y: COMPLEX) return COMPLEX;
    begin
        return COMPLEX'(X.RE * Y.RE + X.IM * Y.IM,
                        X.RE * Y.RE - X.IM * Y.IM);
    end "*";

    function "/" (X, Y: COMPLEX) return COMPLEX;
        D:FLOAT := Y.RE ** 2 + Y.IM ** 2;
    begin
        return COMPLEX'((X.RE * Y.RE + X.IM * Y.IM)/D,
                        (X.RE * Y.RE - X.IM * Y.IM)/D);
    end "/";
```

```
     function "*" (X: COMPLEX, Y: INTEGER) return COMPLEX;
     begin
          return COMPLEX'(X.RE * FLOAT(Y), X.IM * FLOAT(Y));
     end "*";

end COMPLEX_NUMBERS;
```

10.2 The following is a possible representation of Rubik's cube. It makes no attempt to be clever, and the solution is simple minded. Each face is an array of eight colours corresponding to the eight small faces surrounding each centre face. The array is a convenient representation since rotation of that face gives a cyclic shift of the existing pattern. To enable the other affected sides to be discovered, each edge of each side has an array of 'adjacencies', defining the connectivity of the cube. Each adjacency defines the name of the adjacent face, by colour, and the edge of that face to which it is attached. Since the cublet number 1 on each face belongs to both the edges numbered 1 and 4 it is convenient to introduce a guard element. Whenever edge 4 is addressed, the equivalence of elements 1 and 9 must be maintained.

As well as being an example of Ada data structuring, this solution uses many features of Ada which deserve mention. Particularly, the use of slice assignments, and renaming, both of which are extensively used. The aggregate assignment to initialize the data structure deserves examination.

Abbreviations have been used for colours as a compromise, to enable the lay out of the aggregates to be neatly tabulated.

```
package RUBIK is

     type COLOUR is (R, B, G, W, O, Y);
     subtype ROTATION is INTEGER range 1 .. 3;
     procedure ROTATE (SIDE: in COLOUR; SHIFT: in ROTATION);
     procedure DISPLAY;

end RUBIK;
```

```
package body RUBIK is

    type COLOUR_SEQUENCE is array (INTEGER range <>) of COLOUR;
    subtype SURFACE is COLOUR_SEQUENCE (1 .. 9);
    subtype EDGE is INTEGER range 1 .. 4;
    type ADJACENCY is
        record
            F: COLOUR;
            E: EDGE;
        end record;
    type LINKS is array (EDGE) of ADJACENCY;
    type FACE is
        record
            S: SURFACE;
            ATTACHMENTS: LINKS;
        end record;

    CUBE: array (COLOUR) of FACE :=      -- set all faces to centre colours
                                         -- and establish adjacencies.

        (R => ((1 .. 9 => R), ((Y, 4), (B, 4), (O, 4), (W, 2))),
         B => ((1 .. 9 => B), ((Y, 3), (G, 4), (O, 1), (R, 2))),
         G => ((1 .. 9 => G), ((Y, 2), (W, 4), (O, 2), (B, 2))),
         W => ((1 .. 9 => W), ((Y, 1), (R, 4), (O, 3), (G, 2))),
         Y => ((1 .. 9 => Y), ((W, 1), (G, 1), (B, 1), (R, 1))),
         O => ((1 .. 9 => O), ((B, 3), (G, 3), (W, 3), (R, 3))));

    procedure ROTATE(SIDE: in COLOUR; SHIFT: in ROTATION) is separate;
    procedure DISPLAY is separate;

end RUBIK;

separate (RUBIK)
procedure ROTATE (SIDE: in COLOUR; SHIFT: in ROTATION) is
    procedure ROTATE_ONCE is
        HOLD: COLOUR_SEQUENCE(1 .. 3);
    begin
            -- rotate chosen surface
        HOLD(1 .. 2) := CUBE(SIDE).S(7 .. 8);
```

```
CUBE(SIDE).S(3 .. 8) := CUBE(SIDE).S(1 .. 6);
CUBE(SIDE).S(1 .. 2) := HOLD(1 .. 2);

     -- now store edge joined to edge 4 of current face
declare
     E4: EDGE   renames CUBE(SIDE).ATTACHMENTS(4).E;
     F4: COLOUR renames CUBE(SIDE).ATTACHMENTS(4).F;
begin
     HOLD(1 .. 3) := CUBE(F4).S(2*E4-1 .. 2*E4+1);
     if E4 = 4 then HOLD(3) := CUBE(F4).S(1); endif;
end;

     -- now shuffle edges joined to edges 1 .. 3
     -- of current face
for I in EDGE range 1 .. 3 loop
     declare
          E2: EDGE renames CUBE(SIDE).ATTACHMENTS(I+1).E;
          E1: EDGE renames CUBE(SIDE).ATTACHMENTS(I).E;

          F2: COLOUR renames CUBE(SIDE).ATTACHMENTS(I+1).F;
          F1: COLOUR renames CUBE(SIDE).ATTACHMENTS(I).F;
     begin
          CUBE(F2).S(2*E2-1 .. 2*E2+1)
                       := CUBE(F1).S(2*E1-1 .. 2*E1+1);
          if E1=4 then CUBE(F2).S(2*E2+1);
                       := CUBE(F1).S(1);
          endif;
          if E2=4 then CUBE(F2).S(1) := CUBE(F2).S(9);
          endif;
     end;

     -- now restore edge joined to edge 1 of current side
     -- from HOLD
declare
     E2: EDGE   renames CUBE(SIDE).ATTACHMENTS(1).E;
     F2: COLOUR renames CUBE(SIDE).ATTACHMENTS(1).F;
begin
     CUBE(F2).S(2*E2-1 .. 2*E2+1) := HOLD(1 ..3);
     if E2=4 then CUBE(F2).S(1):= HOLD(3); endif;
```

```
        end;
    end ROTATE_ONCE;

begin
    for N in ROTATION range 1 .. SHIFT loop
        ROTATE_ONCE;
    end loop;
end ROTATE;
```

10.3
```
package IMPERIAL_MEASURE is
    type MEASURE is private;
    function YARDS(X: MEASURE)  return INTEGER;
    function FEET (X: MEASURE)  return INTEGER;
    function INCHES(X: MEASURE)  return INTEGER;
    function MAKE_IMPERIAL(Y,F,I: INCHES) return MEASURE;
private
    type MEASURE is new INTEGER;
end IMPERIAL_MEASURE;
```

The hidden structure may be a record with three fields for the yards, feet and inches. However, it would be just as satisfactory to store all lengths in INCHES as an integer. (of course fractional inches could be catered for).

The functions either compute the feet and inches, or return the fields of the record. The user cannot feel the difference.

10.4
```
package TIC_TAC_TOE is
    type SYMBOL is (NOUGHT, CROSS, BLANK);
    type INDEX is range 1 .. 3;
    type BOARD_TYPE is array (INDEX,INDEX) of SYMBOL
                          := (1 .. 3 => (1 .. 3 => BLANK));
    type MOVE is
        record
            ROW, COLUMN: INDEX;
        end record;
    type RESULT is (WIN, DRAW, UNFINISHED);
    procedure MAKE_MOVE (X: in MOVE);
    function CHECK_BOARD return RESULT;
```

```
     BOARD: BOARD_TYPE;
end TIC_TAC_TOE;

with TIC_TAC_TOE;
use  TIC_TAC_TOE;
procedure MAIN is
          -- this  uses  access types;   may be better reviewed  after
          -- reading chapter 12
     type PLAYER_NAME;
     task type PLAYER is
          entry START(FRIEND: PLAYER_NAME, SIGN: SYMBOL);
          entry YOUR_MOVE;
     end PLAYER;
     type PLAYER_NAME is access PLAYER;
     task body PLAYER is
          NEXT_MOVE: MOVE;
          OPPONENT: PLAYER_NAME;
          MY_SYMBOL: SYMBOL;
     begin
          accept START(FRIEND: PLAYER_NAME, SIGN: SYMBOL) do
               OPPONENT := FRIEND;
               MY_SYMBOL:= SIGN;
          end START;
          loop
               accept YOUR_MOVE;
               ... --choose NEXT_MOVE;
               MAKE_MOVE(NEXT_MOVE);
               case CHECK_BOARD is
                  when  WIN         =>
                        PUT(  SYMBOL'IMAGE(MY_SYMBOL)  & "WINS");
                        abort OPPONENT;
                        exit;
                  when  DRAW        =>
                        PUT( "GAME DRAWN")
                        abort OPPONENT;
                        exit;
                  when  UNFINISHED  =>
                        OPPONENT.YOUR_MOVE;
               end case;
```

```
        end loop;
    end PLAYER;
    JOHN, MARY: PLAYER_NAME;
    X,Y: SYMBOL;
begin
    JOHN:= new PLAYER;
    MARY:= new PLAYER;
        -- toss coins to choose values for X and Y to
        -- decide who gets which symbol: X is John's
    JOHN.START(FRIEND => MARY, SIGN => X);
    MARY.START(FRIEND => JOHN, SIGN => Y);
        -- ladies first
    MARY.YOUR_MOVE;
end MAIN;
```

This problem illustrates the sharing of a package of related data and operations between two tasks. However, arranged this way the tasks are not truly concurrent. Each player plays in turn, and then triggers the other, going idle itself. Tasks operatinmg like this are often called co-routines. Since they are never concurrently active, there is no conflict over access to the board.

Exercise 11

11.1 Note that generic parameters may include ordinary variables, as well as types and functions.

```
generic
MAX: INTEGER; -- parameter giving the size of the buffer
type ELEM is private;
package  BUFFERING is
    task CONTROL is
        entry WRITE(X: in ELEM);
        entry READ(X: out ELEM);
    end CONTROL;
end BUFFERING;
```

```
package body BUFFERING is
     task body CONTROL is
          type COUNTING is range 0 .. MAX;
          subtype INDEX is COUNTING range 1 .. MAX;
          STORE: array (INDEX) of ELEM;
          INPOINT, OUTPOINT: INDEX := 1;
          COUNT: COUNTING := 0;
     begin
          loop
               select
                    when COUNT < MAX =>
                         accept WRITE(X: in ELEM) do
                              STORE(INPOINT) := X:
                         end WRITE;
                         INPOINT := 1 + INPOINT mod MAX;
                         COUNT := COUNT + 1;
               or
                    when COUNT > 0 =>
                         accept READ (X: out ELEM) do
                              X := STORE(OUTPOINT);
                         end READ;
                         OUTPOINT := 1 + OUTPOINT mod MAX;
                         COUNT := COUNT - 1;
               end select;
          end loop;
     end CONTROL;
end BUFFERING;
```

Within the scope of this declaration declare:

```
package  CHANNEL_OF_UNIT_RECORDS  is new BUFFERING
                                   (MAX => 20, ELEM  => UNIT_RECORD);
use CHANNEL_OF_UNIT_RECORDS;
```

11.2
```
generic
type INDEX is (<>);
type COMPONENT is digits;  -- any fixed point type
type LIST is array (INDEX)  of COMPONENT;
with PUT_INDEX(X: in INDEX);
```

```
with PUT_COMPONENT(X: in COMPONENT);
with NEW_LINE;
procedure TABULATE (X: in LIST) is
begin
     for I in INDEX loop
          PUT(I);
          PUT(LIST(I));
          PUTLINE;
     end loop;
end TABULATE;
```

Within the scope of this declaration, that of WEATHER_DATA and of **use** TEXT_IO, TABULATE may be used as follows:

```
package RAINFALL_IO is new FIXED_IO(RAINFALL);
package MONTH_IO is new ENUMERATION_IO (MONTH);
use MONTH_IO, RAINFALL_IO;
...
procedure DISPLAY is new TABULATE
                  (INDEX         => MONTH,
                   COMPONENT     => RAINFALL,
                   LIST          => WEATHER_DATA,
                   PUT_INDEX     => MONTH_IO.PUT,
                   PUT_COMPONENT => ENUMERATION_IO.PUT,
                   NEW_LINE      => TEXT_IO.PUT_LINE);
begin
     ...
     ...
     DISPLAY(NEW_YORK_RAINFALL);
     ...etc;
```

11.3 Is somewhat similar.

Exercise 12

12.3 Functions provided for a private data type alllow implementation details to be hidden from the user, and thus protects the integrity of trees.

```
package body TREE_STRUCTURES is

   function EMPTY(T : TREE)return BOOLEAN is
   begin
      return T := null;
   end EMPTY;

   function VALUE(T : TREE)return DATUM is
   begin
      return T.ITEM;
   end VALUE;

   function RIGHT(T : TREE)return TREE is
   begin
      return T.RIGHT_TREE;
   end RIGHT;
   -- and similarly for LEFT

   function MATCH(KEY : DATUM;T : TREE)return BOOLEAN is
   begin
      return  T.ITEM = KEY;  -- assumes "=" defined for DATUM
   end MATCH;

   function BUILD_TREE(X : DATUM; L,R : TREE)return TREE is
   begin
      return new NODE(X,L,R);
   end BUILD_TREE;

end TREE_STRUCTURES;
```

12.4

```
package body EVENT_LIST is

    type EVENT_NODE;
    type EVENT_NOTICE is record
        TIME : SIM_TIME;
        E : EVENT;
        NEXT : EVENT_NODE;
    end record;
    type EVENT_NODE is access EVENT_NOTICE;
    HEAD : EVENT_NODE;

    function IS_EMPTY return BOOLEAN is
    begin
       return HEAD = null;
    end IS_EMPTY;

    procedure SCHEDULE (WHEN : SIM_TIME; WHAT : EVENT) is
       P : EVENT_NODE := HEAD;
    begin
       if P = null then
             HEAD := new EVENT_NOTICE(WHEN,WHAT,null);
       else
             while P.TIME < WHEN and P.NEXT /= null loop
                P := P.NEXT;
             end loop;
             P.NEXT := new EVENT_NOTICE(WHEN,WHAT,P.NEXT);
       end if;
    end SCHEDULE;

    function NEXT_EVENT return EVENT is
       IT : EVENT;
    begin
       CLOCK := HEAD.TIME;
       IT := HEAD.E;
       HEAD := HEAD.NEXT;
       return IT;
    end NEXT_EVENT;

end EVENT_LIST;
```

12.5 The identical server tasks are provided by declaring a task type SERVER and then creating instances of tasks of this type. Each SERVER has an entry named SERVICE which is to be called by customer tasks.

An **entry** in an Ada task provides for a queue of calling tasks waiting to be served. However, these tasks have already chosen a server and must wait passively until their requests are processed in a rendezvous. To allow for a multiserver queue a DISPATCHER task is introduced. Server tasks report to the dispatcher when they are free and customer tasks call the dispatcher to be given the name of the first free server. This organization requires that each server task knows its own name and that these names can be passed between SERVERs, the DISPATCHER and customers. The solution below uses an access type to name the SERVERs.

```
package MULTI_SERVER_QUEUE is
   -- encloses the server tasks and their dispatcher

   -- specification of SERVER and DISPATCHER tasks
   type DATA is record -- details of data passed to server
   end record;
   type NAME_SERVER;
   task type SERVER is
       entry SERVICE (INFO:in out DATA); -- service entry call
       entry WHO_AM_I (ME:in NAME_SERVER); -- initial naming
   end SERVER;
   type NAME_SERVER is access SERVER;

   task DISPATCHER is
      -- WHO is called by customers for name of first free server
      -- a single queue forms here for service
      entry WHO (HELPER : out NAME_SERVER);
      -- I_AM_FREE is called by free servers, who form a queue
      entry I_AM_FREE (ME : NAME_SERVER);
   end DISPATCHER;
 end MULTI_SERVER_QUEUE;
```

```
package body MULTI_SERVER_QUEUE is
  -- bodies of SERVER and DISPATCHER tasks

  task body SERVER is
    IDENTITY : NAME_SERVER; -- own name
    -- declarations conserning the service provided
  begin

    -- initially accepts call giving own name
    accept WHO_AM_I  (ME:in NAME_SERVER) do
          IDENTITY := ME; -- notes own name
    end WHO_AM_I;

    -- repeatedly reports to DISPATCHER and then accepts SERVICE
    loop
      DISPATCHER.I_AM_FREE(IDENTITY);
      accept SERVICE(INFO : DATA) do
      --code to provide service
      end SERVICE;
    end loop;
  end SERVER;

  task body DISPATCHER is
     NEXT : NAME_SERVER; --next free server
  begin
     --generate servers and tell them who they are
     for COUNT in 1..HOW_MANY_SERVERS loop
        NEXT:= new SERVER; -- creates a server
        NEXT.WHO_AM_I(NEXT); -- passes name to new server
     end loop;
     NEXT := null; -- no free servers
     -- accepts free servers or customer calls
     loop
        select
           when NEXT = null =>
              accept I_AM_FREE(ME : NAME_SERVER) do NEXT:=ME end;
        or
           when NEXT /= null =>
              accept WHO(HELPER : out NAME_SERVER) do HELPER:=NEXT;
```

```
                    NEXT := null;
                end WHO;
            end select;
        end loop;
    end DISPATCHER;

end MULTI_SERVER_QUEUE;


with MULTI_SERVER_QUEUE;
use MULTI_SERVER_QUEUE;
procedure MAIN_PROGRAM is
    -- contains customer tasks who use SERVERs
    ......
  -- an outline customer:
  task CUSTOMER is
     TO_CALL:NAME_SERVER;
     .....
  begin
     .....
     .....
     --now needs a server
     DISPATCHER.WHO(TO_CALL);
     TO_CALL.SERVICE(INFO);
     .....
     .....
  end CUSTOMER;

begin

--imperative part of main program

-- SERVERs, DISPATCHER and customers now execute concurrently
end MAIN PROGRAM;
```

Exercise 13

13.1 This is a modification of the task given in 9.2. The time at which a message is received is obtained from CALENDAR.CLOCK and ten minutes is added to give TIME_OUT. Selection of a READ_MESSAGE continues until TIME_OUT, or until all the tasks have seen the message.

```
task MAILBOX is
     -- messages can be put in the mailbox by task ID
     entry IN_MESSAGE(M : in MESSAGE; ID : in INTEGER);
     -- and read from the mailbox by tasks giving their ID
     entry READ_MESSAGE(M : out MESSAGE; ID : in INTEGER);
end MAIBOX;

task body MAILBOX is
     -- a boolean array is used to register tasks who have
     -- read a message:
     MESSAGE_SEEN : array (1..N) of BOOLEAN;
     LOCAL : MESSAGE;
     TIME_OUT : CALENDAR.TIME;
     MINUTES : constant DURATION := 60.0;
begin
     loop
          MESSAGE_SEEN := (others => FALSE);  -- not seen by any task
          accept IN_MESSAGE(M : in MESSAGE;
                            ID : in INTEGER) is
               LOCAL := M; -- copy message
               MESSAGE_SEEN(ID) := TRUE;
          end IN_MESSAGE;
          TIME_OUT := CALENDAR.CLOCK + 10.0*MINUTES;
          loop
             select
               accept READ_MESSAGE(M : out MESSAGE;
                                   ID : in INTEGER) do
                    M := LOCAL; -- give out message
                    MESSAGE_SEEN(ID) := TRUE;
               end READ_MESSAGE;
               exit when MESSAGE_SEEN /= (1..N => TRUE);
             or
```

```
                delay TIME_OUT - CALENDAR.CLOCK;
            end select;
        end loop;
    end loop; -- infinite loop
end MAILBOX;
```

13.2
```
package CALENDAR is

    subtype YEAR_TYPE is INTEGER range 1901 .. 2099;
    subtype MONTH_TYPEis INTEGER range    1 ..   12;
    subtype DAY_TYPE  is INTEGER range    1 ..   31;

    type TIME is private;
    function CLOCK return TIME;

    function YEAR (T: TIME) return YEAR_TYPE;
    function MONTH(T: TIME) return MONTH_TYPE;
    function DAY (T: TIME)  return DAY_TYPE;
    function SECOND(T: TIME)return DURATION;
    function MAKE_TIME
         (Y: in YEAR_TYPE;
          M: in MONTH_TYPE;
          D: in DAY_TYPE;
          S: in DURATION)    return TIME;

    -- MAKE_TIME will validate the correctness of the date
    -- ensuring that dates such as February 31 cannot occur

    -- possibly other operations
private
    type TIME is -- some suitable representation
                               -- according to the implementation
end CALENDAR;
```

Exercise 14

14.1 The visibility rules are such that the with clause is not transitive. Package B therefore sees A_TYPE, and can call B_PROC. However, though package C can see the variable B, it cannot see its type. The operations of type appropriate to B_VAR declared in B are visible in C however, so B_VAR can call the procedure B_PROC with B_VAR as a parameter.

The situation with respect to B_VAR in C is closely similar to that for a variable declared to be of a private data type. Specifically then:

package C cannot declare variables of type A_TYPE
it can make restricted use of the variable B_VAR
it cannot call A_PROC
it can call B_PROC, but only with parameters of type A_TYPE which were declared in B

INDEX

K

L

M

N

O

P

R

V

W

X